Teaching Communication Skills
to Students with Severe Disabilities

Teaching Communication Skills to Students with Severe Disabilities

by

June E. Downing, Ph.D.
Department of Special Education
California State University–Northridge

with invited contributors

·P·A·U·L·H·
BROOKES
PUBLISHING C°

Baltimore • London • Toronto • Sydney

Paul H. Brookes Publishing Co.
Post Office Box 10624
Baltimore, Maryland 21285-0624

www.brookespublishing.com

Typeset by Barton Matheson Willse & Worthington, Baltimore, Maryland.
Manufactured in the United States of America by
Hamilton Printing Company, Rensselaer, New York.

The cases described in this book are composites based on the authors' actual experiences. Individuals' names have been changed, and identifying details have been altered to protect their confidentiality.

The photographs in this book are printed with permission. The photograph on the cover is by Margo Taylor. The photograph on page ii is by Margo Yunker.

Cover design by Brushwood Graphics, Inc.

Library of Congress Cataloging-in-Publication Data

Downing, June, 1950–
    Teaching communication skills to students with severe disabilities / by June E. Downing; with invited contributors.
        p.   cm.
    Includes bibliographical references and index.
    ISBN 1-55766-385-8 (pbk.)
    1. Handicapped children—Education.   2. Language arts.   3. Communicative disorders in children.   4. Language disorders in children.   I. Title
LC4028.D69   1999
371.95'36—dc21   98-52005
                                                                                                              CIP

British Library Cataloguing-in-Publication data are available from the British Library.

Contents

About the Author

June E. Downing, Ph.D., Associate Professor, Department of Special Education, California State University–Northridge, 18111 Nordhoff Street, Northridge, California 91330

Dr. Downing is Associate Professor in the Department of Special Education at California State University–Northridge, where she assists in preparing teachers to meet the needs of students having moderate to severe and multiple disabilities. In this capacity, she teaches courses, advises students, and supervises teachers in their practicum experiences. Dr. Downing has invested considerable time in providing in-service training to teachers, administrators, parents, and support staff around the United States. She has been interested in the education of students having severe and multiple disabilities since 1974 and has served as paraprofessional, teacher, work experience coordinator, consultant, and teacher trainer. Her research areas include educating all students together, enhancing the sociocommunicative skills of students with severe disabilities, adapting classrooms for the unique needs of individual students, developing paraprofessional skills, and preparing teachers for inclusive education. She is also author of *Including Students with Severe and Multiple Disabilities in Typical Classrooms: Practical Strategies for Teachers* (Paul H. Brookes Publishing Co., 1996).

Also Contributing to This Volume

V. Mark Durand, Ph.D., Professor and Chair, Department of Psychology, University at Albany, State University of New York, 1400 Washington Avenue, Albany, New York 12222

Dr. Durand received his doctoral degree in clinical psychology from the State University of New York at Stony Brook. He is Professor and Chair of the Department of Psychology at the State University of New York at Albany, which honored him in 1991 with an Excellence in Teaching Award for his undergraduate and graduate teaching efforts. Dr. Durand conducts research on the nature and treatment of challenging behaviors, sleep problems, and communication problems. He has lectured nationally and internationally and has published in various journals, including the *Journal of Autism and Developmental Disorders,* the *Journal of Applied Behavior Analysis,* and the *Journal of The Association for Persons with Severe Handicaps.* Dr. Durand is the author of *Sleep Better! A Guide to Improving Sleep for Children with Special Needs* (Paul H. Brookes Publishing Co., 1998)—the result of a decade working with families and conducting research on sleep problems of children—and has co-authored two textbooks with Dr. David Barlow on abnormal psychology. His best-selling book, *Severe Behavior Problems: A Functional Communication Training Approach* (Guilford Press, 1990), outlines the treatments of problem behaviors using communication. Dr. Durand is also the Director of the New York Autism Network, a statewide consortium of people interested in the education of children with autism.

Eileen Mapstone, Doctoral Candidate, Psychology Resident, Department of Psychiatry and Human Behavior, University of Mississippi Medical Center, 2500 North State Street, Jackson, Mississippi 39216

Ms. Mapstone's research interests include sleep disorders in children with autism and other developmental disorders, the role of setting events in challenging behaviors, conversation-skills training, and functional communication training with students who are deaf-blind.

Pat Mirenda, Ph.D., Associate Professor, Department of Educational Psychology and Special Education, University of British Columbia, 2125 Main Mall, Vancouver, British Columbia, V6T 1Z4 Canada

Dr. Mirenda earned her doctorate in behavioral disabilities from the University of Wisconsin–Madison and specializes in the education of people with severe and profound disabilities. For 8 years, she was a faculty member in the Department of Special Education and Communication Disorders, University of Nebraska–Lincoln. From 1992 to 1996, she provided a variety of training, research, and support services to individuals with severe disabilities through CBI Consultants, Ltd., in Vancouver, British Columbia.

Through the years, Dr. Mirenda has concentrated on augmentative and alternative communication (AAC) for people with developmental disabilities. In addition, she has focused on the integration and inclusion of students who use AAC in general education classrooms. She is co-author with David Beukelman of the second edition of *Augmentative and Alternative Communication: Management of Severe Communication Disorders in Children and Adults, Second Edition* (Paul H. Brookes Publishing Co., 1998), and is the author of book chapters and extensive research publications concerning severe disabilities and augmentative communication. She is Editor of the journal *Augmentative and Alternative Communication*.

Lise Youngblade, Ph.D., Instructor, Department of Psychology, University of Colorado at Colorado Springs, 1420 Austin Bluffs Parkway, Colorado Springs, Colorado 80933

Dr. Youngblade is a developmental psychologist who is published in the areas of young children's family and peer relationships, child maltreatment, and family homelessness. She is Associate Editor of the *Journal of Family Relations*.

Foreword

I am pleased to have a part in introducing to you this new book, *Teaching Communication Skills to Students with Severe Disabilities*. Through my work in the past 20 years as a teacher, consultant, researcher, and faculty member, I have had the opportunity to work with many individuals with severe disabilities who had difficulty communicating effectively. Although it was only a little more than 10 years ago, in the mid-1980s, my ideas about enhancing communication interactions for students with severe disabilities were published when the fields of special education and augmentative communication were just beginning to consider *specialized* intervention for learners who did not use symbols to communicate. In fact, as a doctoral student I remember being advised that publishing my views might be received by some as negative and not worthwhile. I was influenced, however, by others during this same time period who focused on early communication skills and initial augmentative and alternative communication systems (e.g., Goetz & Sailor, 1988; Halle, 1982; Musselwhite & St. Louis, 1988; Reichle & Keogh, 1986; Rowland & Stremel-Campbell, 1987; Stillman & Battle, 1984; van Dijk, 1986) and by the students I was teaching.

My interest in examining communication intervention was inspired by the individuals with whom I worked—the students with severe disabilities and their families. The interventions I had learned in college and the resources available at that time did not match the needs of learners in my classrooms who were not speaking or using American Sign Language. I remember these children well. Shiloh would react to hearing the word *this* or *that* and would repeat over and over, "this way, this way" or "that way, that way." She would become increasingly agitated, which culminated in her screaming these phrases and trying to destroy items around her. At other times she rarely spoke. José often occupied himself by collecting his saliva in his cheeks and then vocalizing "eee" as the saliva dripped out of his mouth. Kalinda, when asked a question, would go through her limited signing repertoire one sign at a time (e.g., CRACKER, MORE), and if she did not receive the response she expected, she would become aggressive or self-abusive. These individuals and many others taught me that children and youth with the most severe disabling conditions do indeed communicate. As a result, I realized the importance of enhancing the interaction skills of *both* the student and his or her partners (Siegel-Causey & Guess, 1989).

I see the process of improving interventions for learners with severe disabilities as a journey. Much has been accomplished in supporting students in inclusive classrooms and refining communication interventions; yet more remains to be done. It is wonderful to have the opportunity to profit from the advances that this book offers. I know for some, though, this information will be new. Although we have come a long way on our journey to provide the best educational interventions available, I am often reminded of just how far we have to go. Today, for instance, as I was writing this foreword I received a telephone call from a mother. She introduced herself and told me that another university faculty member from the East Coast recommended that she call me to get some advice about her son's school program. One issue that troubled her was that she believed her son needed to have speech-language services within his general education classroom. She wanted him to learn to use his communication skills within activities and with partners who were part of his school community. Her son's speech-language therapist was providing him pull-out therapy and had voiced concerns about his ability to communicate because he had autism. The son's individualized education program planning meeting date was fast approaching, and this mother was worried. I did my best to provide her with ideas about how to proceed and with resources she might use to help convey her wishes about her son. I helped her prioritize her top issues. These issues were that she wanted her son to continue to be included in a general education classroom with peers of his age and to receive therapy services (physical therapy and speech-language therapy) within classroom and school activities rather than during pull-out sessions.

The conversation with this parent was troubling on many levels. She was in the position of advocating on behalf of her child for things that the field of severe disabilities has accepted as recommended practices for years. I believe that this young man's education team, given its members' training and experiences, was providing the best possible services and that they probably lacked some expertise with autism and communication intervention. Clearly we have more work to do so that families no longer need to advocate for services that should be readily available. Many of the concepts in this book are based on both language literature and intervention research in special education and are expressed with examples of interventions in general education environments: These concepts would likely help this school staff improve the services for this young man.

Professionals who have the responsibility of providing services for individuals with severe disabilities, whether they are special educators, general educators, physical or occupational therapists, speech-language pathologists, paraeducators, or others, are faced with many challenges. First and foremost, they must respond to the individual needs of those with severe disabilities. Second, they must perceive the individual, regardless of the severity of his or her disability, as someone who does communicate. Third, they should use the most up-to-date strategies available to enhance communication; and fourth, they should provide support in inclusive environments so that both the varied partners (peers, family members, school staff) and the student with a severe disability can better interact.

June E. Downing, with chapters by Pat Mirenda and V. Mark Durand with Eileen Mapstone and Lise Youngblade, has written a practical resource that can help guide you to provide state-of-the-art interventions within general education classrooms. I welcome you to this high-quality book that contains updated strategies on how to provide communication intervention for individuals with severe disabilities who have difficulty communicating. Inclusion is a complex concept, but this book provides readers with practical ideas, real-life examples, and research support. This text focuses in part on the dynamics of teaming, in which members strive toward the common goal of increasing students' communication abilities, that make inclusion feasible. Providing such intervention in inclusive environments may require a change in philosophy that may influence the reader to reevaluate and question current intervention practices. It is these sorts of shifts in thinking about past assumptions concerning communication (e.g., prerequisite skills, developmental teaching, pull-out therapy) that has allowed us to further learning and understanding. I believe you will benefit from this highly readable, practical text. I hope that you will gain new, effective intervention strategies and acquire high expectations that will give your students with severe disabilities the chance to communicate more effectively.

Ellin Siegel, Ph.D.
University of Nebraska–Lincoln

REFERENCES

Goetz, L., & Sailor, W. (1988). New directions: Communication development in persons with severe disabilities. *Topics in Language Disorders, 8*(4), 41–54.

Halle, J. (1982). Teaching functional language to the handicapped: An integrative model of natural environment teaching techniques. *Journal of The Association for the Severely Handicapped, 7*(4), 29–37.

Musselwhite, C.R., & St. Louis, K.W. (1988). *Communication programming for persons with severe handicaps: Vocal and augmentative strategies.* San Diego, CA: College-Hill Press.

Reichle, J., & Keogh, W.J. (1986). Communication instruction for learners with severe handicaps. Some unresolved issues. In R.H. Horner, L.H. Meyer, & H.D.B. Fredericks (Eds.), *Education of learners with severe handicaps: Exemplary service strategies* (pp. 189–219). Baltimore: Paul H. Brookes Publishing Co.

Rowland, C., & Stremel-Campbell, K. (1987). Share and share alike: Conventional gestures to emergent language for learners with sensory impairments. In L. Goetz, D. Guess, & K. Stremel-Campbell (Eds.), *Innovative program design for individuals with dual sensory impairments* (pp. 49–75). Baltimore: Paul H. Brookes Publishing Co.

Siegel-Causey, E., & Guess, D. (1989). *Enhancing nonsymbolic communication interactions among learners with severe disabilities.* Baltimore: Paul H. Brookes Publishing Co.

Stillman, R.D., & Battle, C.W. (1984). Developing prelanguage communication in the severely handicapped: An interpretation of the van Dijk method. *Seminars in Speech and Language, 5*(3), 159–170.

van Dijk, J. (1986). An educational curriculum for deaf-blind multi-handicapped persons. In D. Ellis (Ed.), *Sensory impairments in mentally handicapped people* (pp. 375–382). London: Croom Helm.

Preface

Expressing feelings, sharing information, teasing, joking, conveying needs—communicative interactions like these contribute to self-confidence, self-esteem, and general enjoyment of life. Communication is an essential human skill and is usually acquired rather easily. Unfortunately, for many individuals with severe disabilities, communicating can be very difficult. Even expressing very basic needs can require a significant effort for an individual who must overcome physical, sensory, and intellectual disabilities to do so.

Despite the difficulty some individuals may have with essential communication, learning how to understand others and to be understood are critical life skills. The inability to communicate effectively can lead to frustration, lack of friendship, loss of employment, isolation, and depression. Educators must help *all* individuals communicate by providing appropriate motivation, keeping expectations high, and letting those with disabilities realize that what they have to say is valued. Once this basic premise is in place, specific intervention and support can produce excellent results.

This book is one attempt to share some ideas for helping students with severe disabilities communicate as effectively as possible with teachers and classmates in general education environments. These ideas come from teachers; speech-language pathologists; parents; teaching assistants; and, of course, the students themselves. In the future, it is hoped, the ideas presented in these pages will become archaic as time, technology, and human ingenuity work toward giving everyone an equal voice. Until that time the information presented in this book may serve to enhance the communicative efforts, and hence, the quality of life, of some individuals.

Acknowledgments

Writing a book is rarely a solitary venture. I owe a lot to those friends who helped with this one. First, I would like to thank Pat Mirenda, V. Mark Durand, Eileen Mapstone, and Lise Youngblade for their valuable contributions to this text. I greatly admire their work and was thrilled when they agreed to add their knowledge and expertise to this book. Their chapters add considerably. Despite some major challenges in her life, my dear friend, Ellin Siegel, agreed to give of her time and energy to read this text and write the foreword. This has become a very special gift for me, and I will treasure it always. Thank you, Ellin.

Two of my past graduates (from the University of Arizona and California State University–Northridge) willingly gave of their time to contribute photographs of students they serve: Margo Taylor took several photographs of elementary-age students, and Margo Yunker took photographs of students in middle and high school. These photographs add a great deal to the text. I very much appreciate the efforts of both Margos and am very glad they are a part of this production. I also appreciate the excellent photographs by Diane Andres at California State University–Northridge who promptly and expertly redid the rather poor photographs that I took and had originally intended to use. Hers are much better.

I also would like to acknowledge the willingness of several parents to allow me to include pictures of their children in this book. I have had the pleasure of knowing and working with three of these families, and I am very excited that their children's pictures are included. For the sake of confidentiality their names are not mentioned, but that should not lessen their contribution. I am so very grateful to these children and their parents: They know who they are, and they make the book.

My secretary, Cecilia Flores-Adams, tackled several tables and figures when my own lack of computer expertise became a hindrance. She also patiently printed draft after draft, making changes here and there that must have seemed terribly tedious at the time. In addition, she persistently tracked down some elusive references, which saved considerable time. I am grateful for her very able support. I know she breathed a sigh of relief when the text was completed.

Several individuals at Brookes Publishing greatly facilitated the writing of this book. Lisa Benson, Acquisitions Editor, did a great job managing the course of the development of the manuscript, and I very much appreciate her understanding and support. Lisa Yurwit, her assistant, kept things moving smoothly between the two of us. Havely Taylor, Book Production Editor, did a very thorough and competent job editing the initial drafts of this book. Her hard work is well noted.

Finally, I need to acknowledge the individuals for whom this book is written. They continually teach me what I need to know. Despite the lack of formal words and the burdens imposed by special education labels, they have endeavored to tell their stories and to teach anyone who will listen. My hope is that I can continue to listen and to learn.

To all the students I have known
who have struggled so hard and for so long
to make their thoughts known:
I can only hope that they keep trying.

1

The Importance of
Teaching Communication Skills

Communication is the key to learning, for much of what we learn depends on interactions with others. Although all human beings communicate, some individuals, due to the severity of their disabilities, may have limited communication skills. Individuals with severe and multiple disabilities may not have full access to or full control of the multiple means by which most individuals communicate (e.g., speech, facial expressions, body language, print). This inability to express themselves as others would does *not* mean that these individuals have nothing to say, nor does it diminish their need and right to communicate. Teachers and other service providers must respect this desire to communicate, using their expertise, experience, and commitment to make this possible. As Brown and Gothelf (1996) contended, we must assume that individuals with profound disabilities want to control their environment, despite the difficult time they may have doing so.

WHO IS THE TARGET POPULATION?

Some individuals have acquired a few speech skills that enable them to express basic concepts (e.g., requesting a desired food or activity). Limitations in using complex language patterns, however, hamper more abstract communication (e.g., discussing dreams, concerns, future plans). Even though these individuals may have multiple means of communicating without abstract symbols, the ability to clearly express more complex thoughts and feelings is not possible without the use of some kind of system of representative symbols.

Any child who has a disability that interferes with the normal acquisition and development of language will experience difficulties in communicative exchanges (both receptively and expressively). Individuals with severe cognitive disabilities often have difficulty acquiring an abstract means of communication, such as speech or American Sign Language (ASL). Those with autism and severe developmental delays, as well as those with severe sensory impairments (vision or hearing or both) (Heller, Alberto, & Bowdin,

1

1995), may also find it difficult to communicate effectively. Certainly a severe physical disability, especially when it is in addition to an intellectual impairment, can hinder the development of speech and language. The intricate physical movements of the oral musculature required for speech are negatively affected by a severe physical disability, and a severe intellectual impairment makes it very difficult for the individual to associate symbols with their referents. According to Haring and Breen (1989), individuals with severe or profound cognitive and physical disabilities may never develop expressive language skills beyond those of a very young child.

This book addresses the needs of children and youth whose severe disabilities make even the most basic of interactions difficult. Many of these children use alternative forms of communication in their efforts to understand and be better understood by others. Because this is a large and extremely heterogeneous group of individuals, information in this book concentrates on those children and youth (ages 3–22) who receive their education in age-appropriate general education classes with the support of teachers, classmates, paraprofessionals, parents, administrators, and related services providers. With the belief that separating students from one another because of specific characteristics is not conducive to learning, general education classrooms afford both students and teachers with incredible opportunities for learning (Downing, 1996; Stainback, Stainback, & Jackson, 1992; Stremel & Schutz, 1995; Villa & Thousand, 1995). Much of the information presented in this text also has applicability to other natural environments such as the home, the workplace, and other community facilities.

WHAT IS COMMUNICATION?

Communication occurs when one individual sends a message to another and that message is received and understood (Butterfield & Arthur, 1995). Competence in a symbolic and abstract language system, with formalized rules of word representation, production, and use (e.g., spoken English or Spanish, manual ASL), is not a prerequisite for communication. In fact, one can be quite facile with a spoken language and not communicate at all if there is no one to talk to, no one present who understands the spoken language used, or no one who is attending to or hearing the message. A trip to a foreign country or an interaction with a preoccupied teenager illustrates this point.

Just as the presence of language does not necessarily mean that communication will follow, the absence of language does not always mean that communication cannot occur. In fact, those not using language can communicate quite well at times. For example, graduate students putting away their papers and pens let the professor know that class has ended; rumbling stomachs and glazed eyes let the principal know that the meeting is over (or should be); and the fidgety behavior of young children who need to go to the bathroom is easily recognized. For all of these situations and countless others, the absence of symbolic language behavior is irrelevant. In fact, as much as 90% of any message exchanged between two very verbal people can be attributed to nonverbal behavior (Evans, Hearn, Uhlemann, & Ivey, 1984). In addition, many nonverbal communicative behaviors are universal (Ekman, 1980, 1982; Izard, 1994). Recognizing the power of nonsymbolic yet highly communicative behavior (e.g., facial expressions, body movements, gestures) is critical for those interested in facilitating the communication skill development of students who are unable to master symbolic languages. Such behaviors form the foundation for enhanced communicative interactions (Siegel-Causey & Downing, 1987; Siegel-Causey & Guess, 1989) because, unlike speech, they are easier to shape and, therefore, easier to learn.

WHO NEEDS COMMUNICATION INTERVENTION?

When students demonstrate such minimal communication skills that they are not adequately expressing themselves, others tend to assume that they have nothing to communicate or simply do not care about anything. Unfortunately, such assumptions are dangerous because they dehumanize the student, casting him or her in an extremely dependent and vulnerable position (Biklen, 1993; Crossley, 1992; Kochmeister, 1997). Following the least dangerous assumption, it is always preferable to perceive *all* students, regardless of the severity of the disability, as individuals who have something to say but who have extreme difficulty making their thoughts heard and understood by others. With this latter assumption, it is the responsibility of those who communicate with greater ease to do whatever they can to help the student understand what is being said and to find a way to give him or her a "voice."

Operating on the assumption that all individuals need to communicate, the tendency to wait until certain "prerequisite skills" are demonstrated before providing helpful intervention makes little sense. Mirenda (1993) firmly stated that breathing is the *only* real prerequisite to communication. The process to determine whether students with severe disabilities qualify for communication intervention becomes extremely simple given such a prerequisite. The question, then, should be not whether students with severe disabilities will benefit from communication intervention but how best to provide that support.

Unfortunately, practitioners in many states seem to be spending valuable time and energy determining eligibility for communication intervention services. Several parents and teachers have expressed to the author their frustration at not being able to gain access to quality speech-language therapy services for a student who does not speak. When speech becomes a prerequisite for communication intervention, many students with severe disabilities will be denied important support. Several states adhere to a model of cognitive referencing to determine eligibility for intervention services (Notari, Cole, & Mills, 1992). Cognitive referencing is the practice of identifying a discrepancy between a child's cognitive and language abilities to qualify for services. For children with severe intellectual challenges who are determined to have similar speech-language and cognitive abilities, communication services can be considered irrelevant. Presumably these children would not benefit from intervention. However common this approach may be, the belief that children with equal delays in both language and cognitive development are not able to benefit from language intervention has not been substantiated (Cole & Mills, 1997; Fey, Long, & Cleave, 1994). These children can and do benefit. If anything, the assessment procedures used to determine eligibility are questionable.

CHARACTERISTICS OF COMMUNICATION

As stated previously, communication by definition requires at least two people—a sender of the message and a receiver—and these two people must understand each other for communication to occur. Having appropriate communication partners constitutes the essential social aspect of communication. Other critical components of communication include form (i.e., a way to send the message), content (i.e., something to talk about), and a reason or purpose to communicate (Gruenewald, Schroeder, & Yoder, 1982). Beyond these basic conditions, no specific skill level is needed. Given such characteristics, it is easy to see how everyone can and does communicate; however, students with severe disabilities may find themselves in situations where competent social partners are not present (e.g., a self-contained special education classroom), and the behaviors (form) they have to use for communication are not clear to others. In addition, life experiences may have been severely limited due to their disabilities, leaving little to talk about (content) and little reason to communicate (when all needs are anticipated in advance). Educational team members, therefore, must ensure that these aspects of communication are addressed.

Social Aspect

One major difficulty for students with severe disabilities who are educated in special classrooms is that they tend to have extensive interactions with adults but limited interactions with other students (Lewis, Feiring, & Brooks-Gunn, 1987). Not only can this lack of social opportunity make it difficult for students with severe disabilities to learn the skills of communication, but it also can interfere with their ability to make friends (Falvey & Rosenberg, 1995; Hendrickson, Shokoohi-Yekta, Hamre-Nietupski, & Gable, 1996). In special education classrooms composed solely of students with similar communication difficulties, the brunt of the responsibility for being a responsive communicative partner falls to the teacher or any other adult in the room. Because the adult usually must attend to a number of students, all needing considerable support, opportunities for meaningful communication with individual students are limited. When students with disabilities are full-time members of general education classrooms, the other students in the class serve as communicative partners. In fact, these students may have a better perspective given the closeness in age to their classmate with severe disabilities and may therefore be better able to understand what their classmate is trying to say. Certainly, they serve as more effective (more age-appropriate) models for communication skills (Calculator, 1994; Janney & Snell, 1996; Werts, Caldwell, & Wolery, 1996). Furthermore, they allow the student to achieve friendships via communication much more directly than learning communication skills first with a teacher and then having to transfer those skills to an interaction with a peer. As an added benefit, students without disabilities acquire a better understanding of diversity and learn ways to interact with those having disabilities.

Form of Communication

Individuals need some identifiable form of communication to effectively convey a message. Sometimes the form or forms used by the individual is very clear (e.g., spoken language, signs, universally understood gestures). Sometimes forms of communication are more difficult to discern. For individuals with the most severe and complex disabilities, the form used may be more difficult to interpret (e.g., fast breathing to indicate "no" and smooth, easy breathing to say "yes"). In addition, the forms of communication used by the individual must be understood by his or her recipient.

Professionals in the field of communication disorders generally recognize the multimodal nature of communication (Coots & Falvey, 1989; Johnson, Baumgart, Helmstetter, & Curry, 1996; National Joint Committee for the Communicative Needs of Persons with Severe Disabilities, 1992; Reichle, 1997; Reichle & Karlan, 1985). No one form of communication will suffice all needs or meet all social expectations of a given situation. With multiple ways to convey messages, more options are available for choosing a communicative alternative that "fits" each individual. For example, some students with severe disabilities may not hear or understand speech because of difficulties processing auditory information. These individuals, however, may benefit from receiving messages visually— for example, through pictures, photographs, or natural gestures (von Tetzchner & Martinsen, 1992). Conversely, students with limited or no vision may do well with simple speech and representative objects or parts of objects to feel. For students who cannot rely on speech to convey messages clearly, the use of gestures, facial expressions, objects, pictures, and vocalizations may be an effective alternative. Communication will take place with whatever "works." In other words, direct services providers should avoid relying on one mode of communication for either receptive or expressive communication because it is likely that a combination of different modes will be necessary. As Ferguson (1994) contended, it is not the form that is important but the effectiveness of the interaction.

Content

When there is nothing to say, there is no communication. The awkward pauses that develop between individuals when they have run out of conversation topics is one example of no content, no communication. Therefore, it is imperative that individuals with severe disabilities (who may have particular trouble thinking of things to talk about) have the support they need to remember how to convey something and what they intended to convey. Having access to a variety of objects, parts of objects, pictures, and photographs can help the student decide on something to say. These potential aids to communication are static (unlike speech) and can be maintained in front of a student as an obvious cue. Furthermore, they serve the same function for individuals with no disabilities and, therefore, do not necessarily draw unwanted attention to the disability. Looking through a photo album with a friend is one such example.

When individuals have remained in a routine for a while with nothing new to interrupt the routine, finding something interesting to share with another may become difficult. When individuals have engaged in interesting, novel, and stimulating activities, something to talk about emerges easily from an interaction with another. Vacations, new jobs, challenging assignments, new friends, or an exciting project at school can all provide the speaker with something interesting to say and the listener with something about which to ask. It is when day-to-day activities hold no surprises and are of little interest that thinking of something to say, other than expressing basic needs, becomes challenging. This challenge is further aggravated when the individual already has difficulty communicating basic thoughts.

The social interaction of a typical age-appropriate classroom naturally generates interesting topics for conversation. Students bring items to class to show friends, and teachers expose students to new and challenging materials. For example, Gemini, a high school student, seemed quite fascinated with the fashion sense of one of her classmates: her abundance of earrings and other body piercings and her ever-changing hair color, from green to purple and orange. Other classmates also seemed interested in bringing their creative means of self-expression to her attention, which gave her something to comment about. Using a voice-output communication aid (SpeakEasy) in addition to her own facial expressions, she was able to let classmates know how she felt (e.g., "That's rad!" "Wow!" "My mother would *never* let me do that").

Students with severe disabilities will need help sharing information with others or asking questions of another. The support they receive will have to be more creative than allowing the student to request a break, go to the bathroom, or get a drink of water. Chapter 6 focuses on augmentative communication devices. Certainly a strong consideration in designing these devices is the student's need to converse with friends and not just make requests. Conversation books provide an excellent way to stimulate this kind of communication. The work of Hunt, Alwell, and Goetz (1991) and Hunt, Farron-Davis, Wrenn, Hirose-Hatae, and Goetz (1997) confirmed how such devices aid students in forming relationships with others. The books that these researchers studied contained pictures that prompted the user to "talk" about topics of interest. Conversation partners were able to facilitate interactions using these communicative aids, and the resulting conversations appeared to have been more balanced, giving the student with severe challenges some control over the content of the discussion (Hunt et al., 1997).

Purpose

When individuals feel the need or the desire to communicate, then communication is more likely to occur. An individual will use whatever means are available to convey a message, especially one that is very important. Needing to communicate is the motivation, and having those needs met is the positive reinforcement. When there is no need or purpose to communicate, communication is unlikely to occur. Because the goal of the direct services provider is to encourage students to communicate, sometimes this requires that the provider creatively generate a purpose for the student to communicate.

One way that a direct services provider can orchestrate this scenario is by being somewhat less solicitous at times, thereby placing the student in a situation of need. For instance, giving the student only some of the items required for an art or science project encourages that student to request the additional materials. "Accidentally" blocking the door to recess or lunch requires the student to ask for help overcoming the obstacle. Asking a student to turn off the lights in order to show a film for science class requires the student to understand and respond to the request. Offering the student a book or other item that the student probably does not want gives that student a chance to reject the item and request something else. Rejecting items and protesting others' actions are a typical part of anyone's day. Catering to every need of the student with severe challenges does not help that student learn to communicate. The student needs opportunities throughout the day to say "no" to things; to be understood; and, when possible, to be allowed to do something different. For example, a student can reject using a pencil to do some work and yet accept a red marker to do the same work. A student can say "no" to one student's offer to read to him but "yes" to another student. Although expressing preferences is commonplace for many, those with severe communication challenges may need their teachers' encouragement to do so.

Students also need the opportunity to make comments. At lunch a classmate can show a student something brought from home and allow the student to respond to the item. Students should be encouraged to use different forms of communication to convey interest, dislike, fascination, appreciation, or lack of interest. Facial expressions as an unaided mode of communication say a lot, although an interpreter of those expressions may be necessary initially to keep the conversation going.

Educators need to be aware of communicative opportunities that occur naturally as well as to those that need to be created in order to give the student sufficient practice with different purposes and reasons to communicate. For example, when a student brings in a new litter of puppies to show her second-grade class, several opportunities naturally exist for a classmate with severe disabilities to make comments, request information, and ask permission to touch them. With a less exciting situation, the teacher may have to devise a reason for this student to communicate. For example, when handing out colored paper for students to make Christmas ornaments, the teacher can purposefully "forget" to give Michael, a student with severe disabilities, and the student next to him the paper. Michael's classmate says, "Hey! I need some paper," and waves his hand. The teacher gives this student the paper, then stands close to Michael and waits. In this way, the teacher has created the need for Michael to communicate, and his peer has provided a model for that communication.

THE ROLE OF COMMUNICATION IN DAILY LIFE

Communication is vital to a productive and healthy life. Unfortunately, when a student has extreme difficulty communicating, the tendency for communicative partners is often either to not spend the extra energy required to facilitate communication or to assume that the student does not need to communicate because if the need were there, then communication would follow naturally. As with anything in life, we often do not realize how vital something is until we have lost it. In the same way, having a disability that impairs communication does not mean, then, that communication is no longer important; if anything, it means that it is more important than ever. Communication gives the individual some control over the environment, a means of emotional catharsis, and a way to make friends, all of which are critical to a meaningful existence.

Communication and Control

Effective communication allows the individual control over his or her physical and social environment. Having a certain amount of control (e.g., what to wear, what to do and with whom) enhances feelings of self-worth and self-esteem (Mirenda, Iacono, & Williams, 1990; Noonan & McCormick, 1993). All individuals deserve this ability to control important aspects of their lives. Individuals with severe disabilities may need some help in asserting their control, but, like everyone else, having as much control as possible is important (Shevin & Klein, 1984) and becomes increasingly important as one ages. Parents, teachers, and other services providers striving to empower individuals with severe disabilities to play an active role in the development of their future plans must recognize the importance of these individuals' ability to express their desires. Effective communication skills allow for greater participation in person-centered planning activities, thus facilitating the individual's control over his or her life (Whitney-Thomas, Shaw, Honey, & Butterworth, 1998). Having one's sense of self-determination constantly thwarted can lead to either extreme passivity or frustration and anger, yet Kishi, Tellucksingh, Zollers, Park-Lee, and Meyer (1988) found that individuals with developmental disabilities had limited opportunities to make choices and express their preferences.

Communicating to others in order to gain control over our environment is an essential life skill; however, it is not a skill that will just emerge when needed. If adults are to be able to make choices that will affect their lives, they will need to learn how to do this during childhood. Teaching young children to learn how to make choices in order to gain greater control over their lives is essential (Brown & Cohen, 1996). Early intervention to teach this critical communication skill can lay the foundation for more and more complex decision making that will be expected as the child develops.

Communication and Learning

Learning typically occurs through the interactions of one who knows a particular skill (the teacher) with one who does not (the learner). The teacher guides the learner to an understanding of the skills through practice and, ideally, to some form of mastery of the skill. The success of these interactions between teacher and learner depends heavily on their ability to communicate effectively. Therefore, ineffective communication can seriously hinder the acquisition of new skills. Piaget (1926) and Vygotsky (1978) saw a clear relationship between communication skills and the development of cognitive skills.

Ineffective communication makes it difficult to determine what students understand receptively and what they are attempting to convey expressively. Students may or may not understand what is being taught but may not be able to respond in a manner that makes that clear. Students may appear to act as if they understand when they do not, or the teacher may think that they do not understand when, in fact, they do. When educators have difficulty gauging the effectiveness of their teaching, they may limit students' learning opportunities, claiming that the students are simply unable to benefit. An effective mode of communication, then, is critical to the learning process.

Communication and Catharsis

When a young child becomes extremely upset and resorts to kicking or slapping others out of frustration, a parent or teacher might be caught saying, "use your words," hoping that with this reminder the child will express the frustration with words rather than violence. Physical violence is not acceptable, but sharing information verbally is. Languages comprise many words and expressions that are quite colorful, forceful, and clearly meant to attract attention. Saying certain words with enough volume, appropriate tone, inflection, and facial expression can offer some emotional release.

Individuals with severe disabilities get angry, but they often do not have any socially acceptable way to deal with their anger. Judging from many interactions observed by the author, students with severe disabilities are often expected to behave even better than students without disabilities. Students without disabilities can make considerable noise in class, but when a student with severe disabilities yells, all eyes are upon him or her, and there is a fear that the disturbance will result in the student being denied access to the learning environment. Yet these students generally have much higher levels of frustration and thus, if anything, should have more leeway in expressing themselves. Not only do they have limited control over their environment and are highly controlled by others (Guess & Siegel-Causey, 1985), but they may face extreme challenges when trying to undertake even simple tasks. Also, at the same time that we try to teach these students to use words to express themselves, we must also recognize that much of their frustration comes from the effort it takes them to do just that. All of these factors clearly predispose the student with a severe disability to feel the need to express anger. In order for students with severe disabilities not to resort to physical violence, they need help in developing appropriate ways to express all of their feelings.

If students are to be able to communicate to release tension, the way they express themselves will need to have some emotional content. For students unable to effectively communicate frustration unaided, augmentative devices will have to accommodate this need. Voice output communication aids that capture at least some of the emotional content will be necessary. Certainly, facial expressions and body tone (and posturing) should be acknowledged and encouraged. In general, we must recognize that the inability to produce communicative behavior that is understood by others is the most frustrating experience imaginable and act accordingly (Reichle, Mirenda, Locke, Piché, & Johnson, 1992).

Communication and the Development of Friendships

Friendships add considerably to one's quality of life. They reduce loneliness and isolation, build self-esteem, and create a valuable support system. Researchers have identified the formation of friendships between preschool children with and without disabilities (Buysse, 1993; Diamond & Hestenes, 1996) as well as in much older students (Hendrickson et al., 1996; Schnorr, 1997; Williams & Downing, 1998). Teenagers often report that the primary reason they attend school is to be with their friends (Schnorr, 1997; Williams & Downing, 1998). If anything, the importance of forming meaningful relationships with others increases as we age.

Individuals with severe disabilities have friends. Friendships can and do develop between individuals despite a lack of truly effective communication skills (Falvey & Rosenberg, 1995; Ferguson, 1994; Strully & Strully, 1985); however, although friendships may not depend entirely on communicative interactions, they are certainly facilitated by such interactions. Communication is fundamental to participating and interacting with others, which can lead to friendships (Biklen, 1993; Calculator, 1994; Ferguson, 1994; Schnorr, 1997). According to Barnes and Lehr, "just as social relationships are the basis for learning, communication is central to the establishment and maintenance of those relationships" (1993, p. 84). Without an effective means of communication, it is difficult to maintain interactions. The communicative partner may not receive sufficient positive reinforcement for continuing to facilitate the interaction—the effort to interact may be too great. Helmstetter, Peck, & Giangreco (1994) found that high school students reported feeling uncomfortable with the lack of social skills displayed by students with severe disabilities, as well as by the unique physical and behavioral characteristics of some of these students. In addition, the individual with limited communication skills can easily become passive in interactions and then frustrated with his or her inability to participate more fully. The individual can "drop out" of the conversation by becoming nonresponsive, further reducing the enjoyment of the interaction for the other person. Because friendships by definition are relationships that are enjoyed mutually by each participant, the rewards of the relationship need to outweigh whatever costs exist in terms of effort, anxiety, and embarrassment (Kelly & Thibaut, 1978; Stainback & Stainback, 1987).

Many students with severe communication challenges are initially taught to make requests to satisfy basic needs (Gobbi, Cipani, Hudson, & Lapenta-Nendeck, 1986; McDonnell, 1996; Reichle, Sigafoos, & Remington, 1991; Sanchez-Fort, Brady, & Davis, 1995). Although these kinds of communicative functions are essential, they fail to provide the student with a satisfactory way to interact with peers. Try maintaining a conversation using only words for "want," "cracker," "milk," "music," and "swing." After responding to the initial request (if, in fact, it was a request), the conversation stops abruptly. Although students with severe communication challenges tend to learn to make requests earlier than other types of communication (Goodman & Remington, 1993; Light, 1997), they need to learn other communicative functions if they are to reap the true rewards of effective communication skills. They certainly need to be responsive to efforts made by others to engage in an interaction. For this reason some interventionists feel that one extremely important goal of special education is to develop friendships between children with and without disabilities (Haring & Breen, 1992; Strully & Strully, 1989, 1996).

Friendships do not develop overnight. Time is a critical component of friendship development as well as ongoing opportunity for interaction. At a very basic level, physically bringing students together to learn from each other and to have an opportunity to get to know each other is a necessary condition; however, several researchers have discovered that bringing students together on a part-time basis, where the student with severe disabilities is essentially a guest in the general education classroom, does not suffice (English, Goldstein, Shafer, & Kaczmarek, 1997; Haring, Haring, Breen, Romer, & White, 1995; Schnorr, 1990). Consistent and ongoing interactions on a daily basis are essential for giving students the time they need to have a chance at developing friendships. The full inclusion of students with severe disabilities in their age-appropriate general education classrooms provides this type of consistency and opportunity for interaction. In this environment individual students with severe disabilities can belong to a specific group of students, are surrounded by communicative partners who serve as role models, and can

Figure 1.1.   This photograph of two fifth graders depicts a friendship that developed when a student with disabilities was included on a full-time basis in a general education classroom. (Photographer: Margo Taylor)

learn to interact with these students on a daily basis. Figure 1.1 depicts a friendship that developed when a student with disabilities, who does not see or speak and who has significant impairments, was included on a full-time basis in her home school and general education classroom.

Time and opportunity to interact with one another certainly contribute to friendship development, although they are not the only requirements. Students do need to know how to interact with one another to some degree. Several researchers have found that specific instructional support is necessary to facilitate positive interactions between students with and without disabilities (Haring & Breen, 1992; Hunt et al., 1997; Odom, Chandler, Ostrosky, McConnell, & Reaney, 1992; Schnorr, 1997; Utley, Mortweet, & Greenwood, 1997). Although students do not have to be able to speak or be at a certain developmental level as determined by some standardized assessment in order to interact with others, certainly learning to look at a conversation partner or turn toward them, accept items from them, take turns, and express feelings about particular topics can facilitate interactions that may lead to the development of friendships.

If children can gain some experience interacting with their peers at an early age, perhaps the foundation for developing skills required of friendships would be laid. Children can develop friendships at the preschool level and can learn a great deal about getting along with others, sharing, initiating interactions, and responding to others (Buysse, 1993; Diamond & Hestenes, 1996; Hanson, Gutierrez, Morgan, Brennan, & Zercher, 1997). Children without disabilities can learn to become comfortable with their classmates who have disabilities. They can learn alternative means of interacting when speech is not the best mode. If children are not provided the opportunity to learn together at an early age, that does not mean that they will not be able to make friends later on in life; however, opportunities do exist for young children to learn together—to interact and develop socially. Educators would do well to take advantage of these opportunities.

Unfortunately, many students with severe disabilities have limited opportunities to interact with their peers without disabilities (Schwartz, Carta, & Grant, 1996; Shapiro, 1993; Stremel & Schutz, 1995). The majority of students with severe disabilities continue to be educated in special education environments where it is difficult to find responsive and interactive communication partners. When students with severe disabilities are educated in general education classrooms, however, social contacts increase, resulting in a larger social network and more durable relationships (Hendrickson et al., 1996; Jenkins, Odom, & Speltz, 1989; Kennedy, Shukla, & Fryxell, 1997). Although friendships cannot be mandated in a general education classroom, at least the opportunity exists for regular and recurring interactions that could lead to the formation of friendships. No such opportunities exist in special education classrooms where these kind of interactions are rarely seen.

THE IMPORTANCE OF EARLY INTERVENTION

The need and ability to communicate is typically present at birth. Although perhaps somewhat unrefined, most human beings do communicate their basic needs and feelings from the moment of birth. Some individuals may be very limited in *how* they do this, but the effort and need are nevertheless still present. Infants cry, grimace, tense their muscles, and/or breathe irregularly to communicate pain, irritation, frustration, anger, discomfort, or hunger. Responsive partners interpret and respond to such communicative efforts promptly to reinforce these efforts and to address the needs of the individual (Johnson et al., 1996; Kaiser et al., 1996; Reichle, 1997).

Because the first 2 years of life are considered to be the most rapid period of neurological development when the brain grows to approximately 70% of its adult size (Damasio, 1990), early communicative efforts are critical. During the first 2 years of life, children experience the bonding with their parents that lays the foundation for language development. Also, within this time period, children understand hundreds of words, engage in turn-taking, and begin to learn how to control the speech mechanism (Bleile, 1997; Ingram, 1989). Between birth and 6 years of age, children appear to rapidly acquire the rules and building blocks of their native language. Indeed, if individuals do not acquire language prior to puberty, later acquisition can be considerably more difficult and not nearly as efficient (Lenneberg, 1967).

Given this early learning window and the basic need to communicate, helping young children with disabilities learn communication skills is extremely critical. Waiting for children to demonstrate certain cognitive skills prior to any type of communication intervention holds little merit. Some children, due to the severity of their disabilities, may never spontaneously show skills once considered prerequisites for communication skill development. Despite an inability to respond to a sound, for example, or to demonstrate cause and effect or object permanence, children and adults still have a need to express thoughts and feelings, and they need the assistance of others to make this possible. They will demonstrate their "prerequisite" skills while learning to communicate. For example, when a child learns that a behavior draws another to his side, that supports the learning of cause and effect (e.g., "I did something that caused this person to come see me").

Bricker, Bailey, and Bruder (1984) and Warren and Kaiser (1988) demonstrated the efficacy of early intervention programs. One premise of early intervention is that intensive support services at an early age will lessen the need for extensive services later on. This premise, combined with the critical need of the young child to make needs known and to understand what others say, demands a focus on early communication skill development. Furthermore, children with severe intellectual challenges *can* be taught to communicate using augmentative and alternative means (Sevcik, Romski, & Wilkinson, 1991). They will not learn such skills if they are not provided with opportunities to do so, which is why early intervention is vital to their development.

THE OLDER STUDENT WITH LIMITED COMMUNICATION SKILLS

Although helping the young child develop communication skills is critical, many older children and adults may not have received any early intervention, or if they did, may not have benefited from it. These individuals are very much in need of assistance so that they can learn to communicate as effectively as possible. Lacking effective communication skills, they may have become quite frustrated in their efforts to be heard and, as a result, may resort to unconventional ways of expressing themselves (Carr et al., 1994; Durand, 1990). These unconventional means can be very disruptive, perhaps even harmful, to those around them, and possibly self-injurious. They also may be firmly ingrained as the individual's main means of communicating. Helping these individuals acquire alternative ways to express themselves will take time, patience, effort, and understanding; giving up on a person because of past history and age is the least helpful and most unproductive avenue to take.

It is never too late to begin teaching individuals to communicate more effectively and conventionally (Kenneally, Bruck, Frank, & Nalty, 1998; Romski & Sevcik, 1996). Even if the individual does not develop a comprehensive communication system that meets all needs and addresses all demands, having some means to communicate is far preferable to having fewer or no communicative means. Due to their years of experience, older individuals undoubtedly will have much to say. Sometimes parents and teachers may be a bit reluctant to listen, especially when what is said reflects negatively on past efforts; but in order to truly help these individuals, we cannot just provide them with a way to communicate and then disregard what they say.

THE PROBLEMS WITH WAITING

Waiting for individuals with disabilities to reach some predetermined level of communicative proficiency prior to intervention places these individuals in jeopardy (Kangas & Lloyd, 1988). Lacking conventional communication skills, they will resort to whatever means of communication prove to be effective, which are often unconventional as well as undesirable. Because the need to communicate does not fade as these individuals age, they need to be taught conventional ways to communicate so that they are not compelled to resort to unconventional or undesirable behavior.

Aggressive Behavior

The relationship between the lack of effective and conventional communication skills and "aberrant" behaviors has been well documented (Carr & Durand, 1985; Doss & Reichle, 1991; Durand, 1990; Reichle & Wacker, 1993). When individuals are unable to adequately communicate their needs or desires, they will often resort to displaying their anger and frustration physically. Individuals may lash out by biting, kicking, screaming, hitting, destroying materials, or engaging in self-injurious behavior. Although the behavior may at times seem quite aberrant and abnormal, the sensitive and responsive communication partner should be able to see it as the individual's most effective means of expressing frustration, anger, pain, or intense boredom. There is nothing abnormal about such emotions—they are commonplace and would seem to be quite understandable for individuals for whom communication is so challenging. When individuals without disabilities are deprived of their ability to communicate, even temporarily (e.g., severe laryngitis), their ability to interact with others is seriously impaired and the resulting frustration can be extreme. Unconventional behaviors should be seen as a cry for help—for someone to listen to the individual and help that person learn—and not as a reason to wait for "better" behavior to emerge. Certainly punishing the behavior would be inappropriate and is not recommended (Lovett, 1996; Reichle & Wacker, 1993). Instead, the educator should ask questions in order to understand what the student is attempting to communicate. Could their behavior be a reflection of their education to date? Do they wish their teachers had tried to do things another way?

Passivity

If not supported in a positive and effective manner, some individuals with severe disabilities may decide that the energy needed to communicate is not worth the effort. Over time, these individuals may feel that they cannot make themselves understood and may stop trying, a behavior known as learned helplessness. *Learned helplessness,* a term coined by Seligman (1975), occurs when a student can do something but chooses not to because he or she has concluded that the situation is beyond his or her control. This situation is troubling for all students but particularly for those with severe disabilities who are unable to counter the kind of interactions that can lead to learned helplessness.

Once students with severe disabilities have given up trying to communicate, they lose control over their physical and social environments and become extremely passive, waiting instead for the environment to act on them (Basil, 1992; Light, 1988). Because teaching students who seem disinterested and resigned is extremely difficult, avenues to learning become blocked, therefore, intervening before the onset of passivity and learned helplessness is of utmost importance. For example, one of the author's former students would stand outside the door to the lunch room while considerable amounts of snow accumulated on his head. He was physically able to enter on his own, yet he would stand there waiting for instructions or assistance. This teenager was capable of taking control of the situation, either to enter independently or request assistance, but years of being physically manipulated by adults and told what to do had created a form of learned helplessness in him, even in potentially life-threatening situations. Teachers must listen to students and teach them the power of communication in order to prevent them from perceiving the situation as hopeless and beyond their control.

DIFFICULTIES WITH ENTERING THE ADULT WORLD

Interacting effectively with others helps individuals achieve major life goals, such as employment, volunteerism, recreation, and residence sharing. For example, communicating a basic interest in a job can lead to employment. Employers like to be able to interact with those they hire; they want their directions understood and followed. Just as social relationships formed with co-workers make work more pleasant, the lack of appropriate social skills can lead to unemployment. Considerable documentation exists that supports the need for individuals with mental retardation to display appropriate social behavior in order to keep their jobs (Butterworth & Strauch, 1994; Greenspan & Schoultz, 1981; Lagomarcino, 1990).

Employment is not the only aspect of adult life that can be negatively affected by minimal communication skills. Forming relationships for recreation can depend to some degree on interaction skills. Although one can enjoy leisure time alone, much of the joy of seeing and doing things comes from sharing experiences with a friend. Unfortunately, most adults with moderate to severe disabilities tend to have a limited number of friends and few interactions with others outside of family members and experience a fair amount of loneliness (Newton & Horner, 1993). Individuals with severe disabilities typically have more people who are paid to be in their lives than those without disabilities (Forest & Lusthaus, 1989; Forest & Pearpoint, 1992; McKnight, 1994), yet they need the opportunity to experience life with people who are there simply because they want to be. Helping individuals with severe disabilities experience recreational events and acquire social skills is certainly a worthy goal of education. Furthermore, we know that such a goal is possible—adults with mental retardation do have reciprocal friendships with adults without disabilities (Jameson, 1998).

These skills, such as getting a job, finding a roommate, and enjoying leisure time, will not just emerge as viable opportunities for individuals with severe disabilities. Skills learned at an early age and developed throughout the life span can greatly enhance the individual's ability for true inclusion as an adult.

COMMUNICATION IS A LIFELONG SKILL

The communication skills that students learn in school will be needed long after they leave school and assume life in their community as contributing adults. If teachers have done their job well, graduates will be able to use their communication skills as needed in different adult environments. According to Halpern (1993), the establishment of desirable social and interpersonal networks is one of the preferred outcomes of education. Teaching students to engage in tasks without regard for the potential social aspects of the activity will only promote loneliness and isolation. For example, considerable effort goes into teaching students with severe disabilities to eat during meals, yet very little attention is paid to teaching these same students to interact socially at this time, even though one glance at a school cafeteria where students inhale their food and spend the majority of the time interacting underlies the importance of this critical social time. Obviously, individuals need relationships to battle loneliness, and these relationships are greatly enhanced with effective communication skills.

In general, communication is essential to an improved quality of life, allowing individuals to make choices, communicate desires, acquire information, and form relationships with others (Chadsey-Rusch, Drasgow, Reinoehl, & Halle, 1993). Even if physically unable to actively engage in typical activities, individuals with severe disabilities can use their social and communication skills to be a part of the action. They can express choices, solve problems, or terminate an activity and be more independent and perceived as more competent than when they are struggling to acquire the physical steps of an activity (Brown & Cohen, 1996). In fact, having to cope with a physical, sensory, or intellectual disability probably will increase the need for communicative interaction as individuals will be in a position to request assistance more frequently than if they did not have a disability; therefore, those seeking to enhance the lives of these students must make communication skills intervention a priority.

SUMMARY

Helping students at an early age develop and build on their ability to interact with others will provide them with skills that will last a lifetime. As Williams (1991) contended, communication is essential to the growth of the individual. The sooner we can give children a voice and help them to understand others, the better chance we have of helping them gain some control of their lives, reduce their frustrations, learn what they want to learn, enjoy interactions with others, and develop friendships. The ultimate goal is to enhance their quality of life so that they can live their lives to their fullest potential.

REFERENCES

Barnes, E., & Lehr, R. (1993). Including everyone: A model preschool program for typical and special needs children. In J.L. Roopnarini & J.E. Johnson (Eds.), *Approaches to early childhood education* (pp. 1–96). New York: Macmillan.

Basil, C. (1992). Social interaction and learned helplessness in severely disabled children. *Augmentative and Alternative Communication, 8,* 188–199.

Biklen, D. (1993). *Communication unbound.* New York: Teachers College Press.

Bleile, K.M. (1997). Language intervention with infants and toddlers. In L. McCormick, D.F. Loeb, & R.L. Schiefelbusch (Eds.), *Supporting children with communication difficulties in inclusive settings: School-based language intervention* (pp. 307–333). Needham Heights, MA: Allyn & Bacon.

Bricker, P., Bailey, E., & Bruder, M. (1984). The efficacy of early intervention and the handicapped infant: A wise or wasted resource? In M. Wolraich & D. Routh (Eds.), *Advances in developmental and behavioral pediatrics* (pp. 373–423). Greenwich, CT: JAI Press.

Brown, F., & Cohen, S. (1996). Self-determination and young children. *Journal of The Association for Persons with Severe Handicaps, 21,* 23–30.

Brown, F., & Gothelf, C.R. (1996). Community life for all individuals. In D.H. Lehr & F. Brown (Eds.), *People with disabilities who challenge the system* (pp. 175–188). Baltimore: Paul H. Brookes Publishing Co.

Butterfield, N., & Arthur, M. (1995). Shifting the focus: Emerging priorities in communication programming for students with a severe intellectual disability. *Education and Training in Mental Retardation and Developmental Disabilities, 30,* 41–50.

Butterworth, J.J., & Strauch, J.D. (1994). The relationship between social competence and success in the competitive work place for persons with mental retardation. *Education and Training in Mental Retardation and Developmental Disabilities, 29,* 118–133.

Buysse, V. (1993). Friendships of preschoolers with disabilities in community-based child care settings. *Journal of Early Intervention, 17,* 380–395.

Calculator, S.N. (1994). Communicative intervention as a means to successful inclusion. In S.N. Calculator & C.M. Jorgensen (Eds.), *Including students with severe disabilities in schools: Fostering communication, interaction, and participation* (pp. 183–214). San Diego, CA: Singular Publishing Group.

Carr, E.G., & Durand, V.M. (1985). Reducing behavior problems through functional communication training. *Journal of Applied Behavior Analysis, 18,* 111–126.

Carr, E.G., Levin, L., McConnachie, G., Carlson, J.I., Kemp, D.C., & Smith, C.E. (1994). *Communication-based intervention for problem behavior: A user's guide for producing positive change.* Baltimore: Paul H. Brookes Publishing Co.

Chadsey-Rusch, J., Drasgow, E., Reinoehl, B., & Halle, J. (1993). Using general-case instruction to teach spontaneous and generalized requests for assistance to learners with severe disabilities. *Journal of The Association for Persons with Severe Handicaps, 18,* 177–187.

Cole, K.N., & Mills, P.E. (1997). Agreement of language intervention triage profiles. *Topics in Early Childhood Special Education, 17*(1), 119–130.

Coots, J., & Falvey, M.A. (1989). Communication skills. In M.A. Falvey (Ed.), *Community-based curriculum: Instructional strategies for students with severe handicaps* (2nd ed., pp. 255–284). Baltimore: Paul H. Brookes Publishing Co.

Crossley, R. (1992). Getting the words out: Case studies in facilitated communication training. *Topics in Language Disorders, 12*(4), 46–59.

Damasio, A. (1990). Category-related recognition defects as a clue to neural substrates of knowledge. *Trends in Neuroscience, 13,* 95–98.

Diamond, K.E., & Hestenes, L.L. (1996). Preschool children's conceptions of disabilities: The salience of disability in children's ideas about others. *Topics in Early Childhood Special Education, 16,* 458–475.

Doss, L.S., & Reichle, J. (1991). Replacing excess behavior with an initial communicative repertoire. In J. Reichle, J. York, & J. Sigafoos (Eds.), *Implementing augmentative and alternative communication: Strategies for learners with severe disabilities* (pp. 215–237). Baltimore: Paul H. Brookes Publishing Co.

Downing, J.E. (1996). *Including students with severe and multiple disabilities in typical classrooms: Practical strategies for teachers.* Baltimore: Paul H. Brookes Publishing Co.

Durand, V.M. (1990). *Severe behavior problems: A functional communication training approach.* New York: Guilford.

Ekman, P. (1980). *The face of man: Expressions of universal emotions in a New Guinea village.* New York: Garland STPM Press.

Ekman, P. (1982). *Emotion in the human face* (2nd ed.). New York: Cambridge University Press.

English, K., Goldstein, H., Shafer, K., & Kaczmarek, L. (1997). Promoting interactions among preschoolers with and without disabilities: Effects of a buddy skills-training program. *Exceptional Children, 63,* 229–243.

Evans, D., Hearn, M., Uhlemann, M., & Ivey, A. (1984). *Essential interviewing: A programmed approach to effective communication* (2nd ed.). Pacific Grove, CA: Brooks/Cole.

Falvey, M.A., & Rosenberg, R.L. (1995). Developing and fostering friendships. In M.A. Falvey (Ed.), *Inclusive and heterogeneous schooling: Assessment, curriculum, and instruction* (pp. 267–283). Baltimore: Paul H. Brookes Publishing Co.

Ferguson, D. (1994). Is communication really the point? Some thoughts on intervention and membership. *Mental Retardation, 32*(1), 7–18.

Fey, M.E., Long, S.H., & Cleave, P.L. (1994). Reconsideration of IQ criteria in the definition of specific language impairment. In S.F. Warren & J. Reichle (Series Eds.) & R.V. Watkins & M.L. Rice (Vol. Eds.), *Communication and language intervention series: Vol. 4. Specific language impairments in children* (pp. 161–178). Baltimore: Paul H. Brookes Publishing Co.

Forest, M., & Lusthaus, E. (1989). Promoting educational equality for all students: Circles and maps. In S. Stainback, W. Stainback, & M. Forest (Eds.), *Educating all students in the mainstream of regular education* (pp. 43–57). Baltimore: Paul H. Brookes Publishing Co.

Forest, M., & Pearpoint, J. (1992). Families, friends, and circles. In J. Nisbet (Ed.), *Natural supports in school, at work, and in the community for people with severe disabilities* (pp. 65–86). Baltimore: Paul H. Brookes Publishing Co.

Gobbi, L., Cipani, E., Hudson, C., & Lapenta-Nendeck, R. (1986). Developing spontaneous requesting among children with severe mental retardation. *Mental Retardation, 24,* 357–363.

Goodman, J., & Remington, B. (1993). Acquisition of expressive signing: Comparison of reinforcement strategies. *Augmentative and Alternative Communication, 9,* 26–35.

Greenspan, S., & Schoultz, G. (1981). Why mentally retarded adults lose their jobs: Social competence as a factor in work adjustment. *Applied Research in Mental Retardation, 2,* 23–38.

Gruenewald, L., Schroeder, J., & Yoder, D. (1982). Considerations for curriculum development and implementation. In B. Campbell & V. Baldwin (Eds.), *Severely handicapped/hearing impaired students: Strengthening service delivery* (pp. 163–179). Baltimore: Paul H. Brookes Publishing Co.

Guess, D., & Siegel-Causey, E. (1985). Behavioral control and education of severely handicapped students: Who's doing what to whom? and why? In J. Filler & D. Bricker (Eds.), *Severe mental retardation: From theory to practice* (pp. 230–244). Reston, VA: The Council for Exceptional Children.

Halpern, A.S. (1993). Quality of life as a conceptual framework for evaluating transition outcomes. *Exceptional Children, 59,* 486–498.

Hanson, M.J., Gutierrez, S., Morgan, M., Brennan, E.L., & Zercher, C. (1997). Language, culture, and disability: Interacting influences on preschool inclusion. *Topics in Early Childhood Special Education, 17,* 307–336.

Haring, T.G., & Breen, C. (1989). Units of analysis of social interaction outcomes in supported education. *Journal of The Association for Persons with Severe Handicaps, 14,* 255–262.

Haring, T., & Breen, C. (1992). A peer-mediated social network intervention to enhance the social integration of persons with moderate and severe disabilities. *Journal of Applied Behavior Analysis, 25,* 319–333.

Haring, T., Haring, N.G., Breen, C., Romer, L.T., & White, J. (1995). Social relationships among students with deaf-blindness and their peers in inclusive settings. In N.G. Haring & L.T. Romer (Eds.), *Welcoming students who are deaf-blind into typical classrooms: Facilitating school participation, learning, and friendships* (pp. 231–247). Baltimore: Paul H. Brookes Publishing Co.

Heller, K.W., Alberto, P.A., & Bowdin, J. (1995). Interactions of communication partners and students who are deaf-blind: A model. *Journal of Visual Impairments and Blindness, 89,* 391–401.

Helmstetter, E., Peck, C.A., & Giangreco, M.F. (1994). Outcomes of interactions with peers with moderate or severe disabilities: A statewide survey of high school students. *Journal of The Association for Persons with Severe Handicaps, 19,* 263–276.

Hendrickson, J.M., Shokoohi-Yekta, M., Hamre-Nietupski, S., & Gable, R.A. (1996). Middle and high school students' perceptions of being friends with peers with severe disabilities. *Exceptional Children, 63,* 19–28.

Hunt, P., Alwell, M., & Goetz, L. (1991). Interacting with peers through conversation turn taking with a communication book adaptation. *Augmentative and Alternative Communication, 7,* 117–126.

Hunt, P., Farron-Davis, F., Wrenn, M., Hirose-Hatae, A., & Goetz, L. (1997). Promoting interactive partnerships in inclusive educational settings. *Journal of The Association for Persons with Severe Handicaps, 22,* 127–137.

Ingram, D. (1989). *First language acquisition: Methods, description, and explanation.* New York: Cambridge University Press.

Izard, C.E. (1994). Innate and universal facial expressions: Evidence from developmental and cross-cultural research. *Psychological Bulletin, 115,* 288–299.

Jameson, C. (1998). Promoting long-term relationships between individuals with mental retardation and people in their community: An agency self-evaluation. *Mental Retardation, 36,* 116–127.

Janney, R.E., & Snell, M.E. (1996). How teachers use peer interactions to include students with moderate and severe disabilities in elementary general education classes. *Journal of The Association for Persons with Severe Handicaps, 21,* 72–80.

Jenkins, J.R., Odom, S., & Speltz, M.L. (1989). Effects of social integration of preschool children with handicaps. *Exceptional Children, 55,* 420–428.

Johnson, J.M., Baumgart, D., Helmstetter, E., & Curry, C.A. (1996). *Augmenting basic communication in natural contexts.* Baltimore: Paul H. Brookes Publishing Co.

Kaiser, A.P., Hemmeter, M.L., Ostrosky, M.M., Fischer, R., Yoder, P., & Keefer, M. (1996). The effects of teaching parents to use responsive interaction strategies. *Topics in Early Childhood Special Education, 16,* 375–406.

Kangas, K.A., & Lloyd, L.L. (1988). Early cognitive skills as prerequisites to augmentative and alternative communication use: What are we waiting for? *Augmentative and Alternative Communication, 4,* 211–221.

Kelly, H., & Thibaut, J. (1978). *Interpersonal relations: A theory of interdependence.* New York: John Wiley & Sons.

Kenneally, S.M., Bruck, G.E., Frank, E.M., & Nalty, L. (1998). Language intervention after thirty years of isolation: A case study of a feral child. *Education and Training in Mental Retardation and Developmental Disabilities, 33,* 13–23.

Kennedy, C.H., Shukla, S., & Fryxell, D. (1997). Comparing the effects of educational placement on the social relationships of intermediate school students with severe disabilities. *Exceptional Children, 64,* 31–47.

Kishi, G., Tellucksingh, B., Zollers, N., Park-Lee, S., & Meyer, L. (1988). Daily decision making in community residences: A social comparison of adults with and without mental retardation. *American Journal on Mental Retardation, 92,* 430–435.

Kochmeister, S.J. (1997). Excerpts from "Shattering walls." *Facilitated Communication Digest, 5*(3), 3–5.

Lagomarcino, T.R. (1990). Job separation issues in supported employment. In F.R. Rusch (Ed.), *Supported employment models, methods, and issues* (pp. 301–316). Pacific Grove, CA: Brooks/Cole.

Lenneberg, E. (1967). *Biological foundations of language.* New York: John Wiley & Sons.

Lewis, M., Feiring, C., & Brooks-Gunn, J. (1987). The social networks of children with disabilities and without handicaps: A developmental perspective. In S. Landesman, P.M. Vietze, & M.J. Begab (Eds.), *Living environments and mental retardation* (pp. 377–400). Washington, DC: American Association on Mental Retardation.

Light, J. (1988). Interaction involving individuals using AAC systems: State of the art and future directions. *Augmentative and Alternative Communication, 2,* 98–107.

Light, J. (1997). Communication is the essence of human life: Reflections on communicative competence. *Augmentative and Alternative Communication, 13,* 61–70.

Lovett, H. (1996). *Learning to listen: Positive approaches and people with difficult behavior.* Baltimore: Paul H. Brookes Publishing Co.

McDonnell, A.P. (1996). The acquisition, transfer, and generalization of requests by young children with severe disabilities. *Education and Training in Mental Retardation and Developmental Disabilities, 31,* 213–234.

McKnight, J. (1994). Two tools for well-being: Health systems and communities. *American Journal of Preventive Medicine, 10,* 23–25.

Mirenda, P. (1993). AAC: Bonding the uncertain mosaic. *Augmentative and Alternative Communication, 9,* 3–9.

Mirenda, P., Iacono, T., & Williams, R. (1990). Communication options for persons with severe and profound disabilities: State of the art and future directions. *Journal of The Association for Persons with Severe Handicaps, 15,* 3–21.

National Joint Committee for the Communicative Needs of Persons with Severe Disabilities. (1992). Guidelines for meeting the communication needs of persons with severe disabilities. *Asha, 34*(Suppl. 7), 1–8.

Newton, J.S., & Horner, R.H. (1993). Using a social guide to improve social relationships of people with severe disabilities. *Journal of The Association for Persons with Severe Handicaps, 18,* 36–45.

Noonan, M.J., & McCormick, L. (1993). *Early intervention in natural environments: Methods and procedures.* Pacific Grove, CA: Brooks/Cole.

Notari, A., Cole, K.N., & Mills, P.E. (1992). Facilitating cognitive and language skills of young children with disabilities: The mediated learning process. *International Journal of Cognitive Education, 2,* 169–179.

Odom, S.L., Chandler, L.K., Ostrosky, M., McConnell, J.R., & Reaney, S. (1992). Fading teacher prompts from peer-initiation interventions with young children with disabilities. *Journal of Applied Behavior Analysis, 25,* 307–317.

Piaget, J. (1926). *Language and thought of the child.* London: Kegan & Paul.

Reichle, J. (1997). Communication intervention with persons who have severe disabilities. *Journal of Special Education, 31*(1), 110–134.

Reichle, J., & Karlan, G. (1985). The selection of an augmentative system in communication intervention: A critique of decision rules. *Journal of The Association for Persons with Severe Handicaps, 10,* 146–156.

Reichle, J., Mirenda, P., Locke, P., Piché, L., & Johnson, S. (1992). Beginning augmentative communication systems. In S.F. Warren & J. Reichle (Series & Vol. Eds.), *Communication and language series: Vol. 1. Causes and effects in communication and language intervention* (pp. 131–156). Baltimore: Paul H. Brookes Publishing Co.

Reichle, J., Sigafoos, J., & Remington, B. (1991). Beginning an augmentative communication system with individuals who have severe disabilities. In B. Remington (Ed.), *The challenge of severe mental handicap: A behavior analytic approach* (pp. 189–213). New York: John Wiley & Sons.

Reichle, J., & Wacker, D.P. (Vol. Eds.). (1993). In S.F. Warren & J. Reichle (Series Eds.) *Communication and language intervention series: Vol. 3. Communicative alternatives to challenging behavior: Integrating functional assessment and intervention strategies.* Baltimore: Paul H. Brookes Publishing Co.

Romski, M.A., & Sevcik, R.A. (1996). *Breaking the speech barrier: Language development through augmented means.* Baltimore: Paul H. Brookes Publishing Co.

Sanchez-Fort, M.R., Brady, M.P., & Davis, C.A. (1995). Using high-probability requests to increase low-probability communication behavior in young children with severe disabilities. *Education and Training in Mental Retardation and Developmental Disabilities, 30,* 151–165.

Schnorr, R.F. (1990). "Peter? He comes and goes . . .": First graders' perspectives on a part-time mainstream student. *Journal of The Association for Persons with Severe Handicaps, 15,* 231–240.

Schnorr, R.F. (1997). From enrollment to membership: "Belonging" in middle and high school classes. *Journal of The Association for Persons with Severe Handicaps, 22,* 1–15.

Schwartz, I.S., Carta, J.J., & Grant, S. (1996). Examining the use of recommended language intervention practices in early childhood special education classrooms. *Topics in Early Childhood Special Education, 6,* 251–272.

Seligman, M. (1975). *Helplessness: On depression, development and death.* San Francisco: W. H. Freeman.

Sevcik, R.A., Romski, M.A., & Wilkinson, K.M. (1991). Roles of graphic symbols in the language acquisition process for persons with severe cognitive disabilities. *Augmentative and Alternative Communication, 1,* 161–170.

Shapiro, J. (1993, December 13). Separate and unequal. *US News and World Report, 115*(3), 46–56.

Shevin, M., & Klein, N.K. (1984). The importance of choice-making skills for students with severe disabilities. *Journal of The Association for Persons with Severe Handicaps, 9,* 159–166.

Siegel-Causey, E., & Downing, J. (1987). Nonsymbolic communication development: Theoretical concepts and educational strategies. In L. Goetz, D. Guess, & K. Stremel-Campbell (Eds.), *Innovative program design for individuals with dual sensory impairments* (pp. 15–48). Baltimore: Paul H. Brookes Publishing Co.

Siegel-Causey, E., & Guess, D. (1989). *Enhancing nonsymbolic communication interactions among learners with severe disabilities.* Baltimore: Paul H. Brookes Publishing Co.

Stainback, S., Stainback, W., & Jackson, H.J. (1992). Toward inclusive classrooms. In S. Stainback & W. Stainback (Eds.), *Curriculum considerations in inclusive classrooms: Facilitating learning for all students* (pp. 3–17). Baltimore: Paul H. Brookes Publishing Co.

Stainback, W., & Stainback, S. (1987). Facilitating friendships. *Education and Training in Mental Retardation, 22,* 18–25.

Stremel, K., & Schutz, R. (1995). Functional communication in inclusive settings for students who are deaf-blind. In N.G. Haring & L.T. Romer (Eds.), *Welcoming students who are deaf-blind into typical classrooms: Facilitating school participation, learning, and friendships* (pp. 197–229). Baltimore: Paul H. Brookes Publishing Co.

Strully, J., & Strully, C. (1985). Friendship and our children. *Journal of The Association for Persons with Severe Handicaps, 10,* 224–227.

Strully, J.L., & Strully, C.F. (1989). Friendships as an educational goal. In S. Stainback, W. Stainback, & M. Forest (Eds.), *Educating all students in the mainstream of regular education* (pp. 59–68). Baltimore: Paul H. Brookes Publishing Co.

Strully, J.L., & Strully, C. (1996). Friendships as an educational goal: What we have learned and where we are headed. In S. Stainback & W. Stainback (Eds.), *Inclusion: A guide for educators* (pp. 141–154). Baltimore: Paul H. Brookes Publishing Co.

Utley, C.A., Mortweet, S.L., & Greenwood, C.R. (1997). Peer-mediated instruction and interventions. *Focus on Exceptional Children, 29*(5), 1–23.

Villa, R.A., & Thousand, J.S. (1995). The rationales for creating inclusive schools. In R.A. Villa & J.S. Thousand (Eds.), *Creating an inclusive school* (pp. 28–44). Alexandria, VA: Association for Supervision and Curriculum Development.

von Tetzchner, S., & Martinsen, H. (1992). *Introduction to symbolic and augmentative communication.* San Diego, CA: Singular Publishing Group.

Vygotsky, L.S. (1978). *Mind in society: The development of higher psychological processes.* Cambridge, MA: Harvard University Press.

Warren, S.F., & Kaiser, A.P. (1988). Research in early language intervention. In S. Odom & M. Karnes (Eds.), *Early intervention for infants and children with handicaps: An empirical base* (pp. 89–108). Baltimore: Paul H. Brookes Publishing Co.

Werts, M.G., Caldwell, N.K., & Wolery, M. (1996). Peer modeling of response chains: Observational learning by students with disabilities. *Journal of Applied Behavior Analysis, 29,* 53–66.

Whitney-Thomas, J., Shaw, D., Honey, K., & Butterworth, J. (1998). Building a future: A study of student participation in person-centered planning. *Journal of The Association for Persons with Severe Handicaps, 23,* 119–133.

Williams, L.J., & Downing, J.E. (1998). Membership and belonging in inclusive classrooms: What middle school students have to say. *Journal of The Association for Persons with Severe Handicaps, 23,* 1–13.

Williams, R. (1991). Choices, communication, and control: A call for expanding them in the lives of people with severe disabilities. In L.H. Meyer, C.A. Peck, & L. Brown (Eds.), *Critical issues in the lives of people with severe disabilities* (pp. 543–544). Baltimore: Paul H. Brookes Publishing Co.

2

Assessing Communication Skills

When communicative behavior is vague and idiosyncratic due to severe and multiple disabilities, the recipients of the communicative exchange must be particularly sensitive and responsive, not only in order to communicate but also to assess the communication skills of the individual with disabilities (Kaiser et al., 1996; Reichle, 1997; Siegel-Causey & Downing, 1987). Assessing the communication skills of students with severe and multiple disabilities is often difficult because their impairments may interfere with their ability to engage in clear, reliable, and intentional communicative behavior (Yoder & Munson, 1995). Assessment strategies, therefore, must be sufficiently sensitive to determine the communication skills and strengths of these individuals.

THE IMPORTANCE OF ASSESSMENT

Many reasons exist for assessing skills. Assessment can be used to determine whether a student needs assistance, whether a student is progressing according to a specific intervention plan, and what a student should tackle next. Assessment information can clarify a student's current skills and can help all educational team members recognize those skills. Because caregivers often base their intervention strategies and expectations of children on their perceived communication skills of those children, it is important to make sure that the assessment process is as accurate as possible (Yoder, Warren, Kim, & Gazdag, 1994).

Current Eligibility Guidelines

The purpose of assessment is not to determine eligibility for services but rather to determine the areas in which a student needs support and how that support can be provided. All students communicate, but students with severe disabilities could benefit from various support strategies to communicate more effectively. This need to communicate more effectively should automatically qualify students for support services.

Unfortunately, many think that students cannot benefit from communication services until they demonstrate certain prerequisite cognitive skills (e.g., an understanding of cause and effect or object permanence) (Casby, 1992). Others have argued that individuals need to demonstrate a discrepancy between their cognitive abilities and their language or communication skills before communication services are needed (see Notari, Cole, & Mills, 1992). The assumption behind this approach is that students who do not exhibit such a discrepancy are performing as expected and, therefore, should not need to have specific skills targeted for remediation. Such a belief, however, leaves students lacking formal communication skills with no recourse for services. Although such guidelines may be widely practiced in the United States, the American Speech-Language-Hearing Association (ASHA) recommends that a child's communication needs and intervention plan be determined by a team and not based on any such cognitive–communication discrepancy. In fact, considerable growth in communication skill development for students with severe disabilities, who show little discrepancy between cognitive and communication skills, has been documented (Hunt & Goetz, 1988; Mirenda, Iacono, & Williams, 1990; Romski, Sevcik, & Pate, 1988).

Given that children with severe disabilities can benefit from communicative intervention, assessment should then focus on what the individual might need to say, to whom, for what purposes, and in what manner. This type of assessment is most productive when it takes place in the natural environment where the communication skills are required (Cipani, 1989) because then the direction needed for intervention is clearer.

Standardized Tests

Students with severe disabilities typically do not perform well on standardized tests—tests that are based on typical expectations and/or require the student to respond to direct commands. Experts in the field of severe disabilities have thus been critical of standardized tests for these students (Biklen, 1985; Cole, Dale, & Thal, 1996; Neill & Medina, 1989). Such tests tend to be given in a manner that is not customary for the student, is out of sequence, and is not contextually based in familiar environments and/or routines. Because of this lack of context, the student will not be able to make use of routine and environmental cues (both social and physical) to prompt behavior and, as a result, may not be able to perceive any reason to perform as desired. Essentially, all of the conditions for communicative behavior as stated by Mirenda (1993) and described in Chapter 1 are not in place when administering standardized tests. Resulting test scores probably will *not* reflect what that student could do in a much different and more natural situation. They do not differentiate between what a child needed to do (as dictated by the social environment) and could not (due to physical or intellectual challenges) and between what the student was or was not motivated to say. They fail to provide the educator with practical information that can be used for intervention purposes (Beck, 1996; Downing & Perino, 1992). Because a major purpose for assessing students is to determine how best to intervene, the value of such standardized practices is questionable.

An alternative form of assessment is needed that more accurately reflects the individual's communication skills (Calculator, 1994; Falvey, 1995). An ecological-functional assessment process, which uses observational techniques to analyze skill demands of the natural environment and determine how the student performs within these environments, is recommended (Downing, 1996; Sigafoos & York, 1991). Different observational techniques allow for a more in-depth, comprehensive, and accurate estimate of a given student's abilities and areas of need. In fact, the majority of speech-language pathologists surveyed in a study by Beck (1996) reported using informal assessments (e.g., language samples) in addition to standardized tests in order to plan for their students. Cole et al. (1996) advocated a shift from standardized assessments of communication and language to assessments that are more contextual, naturalistic, and process-oriented. Although observational measures do not provide the assessor with a cognitive age, they do provide valuable information about how individual students typically perform. Given typical and familiar situations, the student is more apt to be motivated to communicate and to understand the reason to do so (Reichle, 1997). When the student is familiar with the environment, routine, and expectations of natural communication partners, a more accurate picture of that student's skills is attainable.

The obvious benefit of an ecological-functional assessment rather than a standardized one is that it leads directly to an appropriate intervention plan (Downing, 1996; Downing & Perino, 1992). The teacher does not have to extract information from a standardized form that may not reflect the immediate needs of the student and then attempt to conform those findings to a completely different environment. Instead, the assessment is completely individualized to meet the unique needs of the student as he or she performs meaningful activities. There is no guesswork involved or difficulty applying the information because the assessment occurs in the environment and activities in which the student is already engaged.

WHO SHOULD ASSESS

Assessment is a team effort. No one person is solely responsible. Instead, various individuals contribute their expertise to the assessment process to obtain the richest and most important information about a student's communication skills (Orelove & Sobsey, 1996; Siegel-Causey & Downing, 1987).

One way of obtaining practical information concerning a student's communication skills is to interview those most familiar with that student in a variety of situations and environments. Parents and other family members provide considerable information regarding how their child interacts, with whom, and in which situations. They provide information pertaining to the child's communicative behavior in the home, which can easily be different than what is observed at school. They also identify circumstances surrounding communication breakdowns and areas in which they wish the student could do more, and they can provide considerable information regarding what intervention strategies have been tried and how successful they were. Finally, they can be valuable resources for understanding what the student may do if his or her communicative efforts are not accepted. Figure 2.1 provides an example of an interview guide used to obtain this kind of information from those closest to the student.

Significant members of the student's life need to feel comfortable stating which communication skills would be most helpful or critical for the student to learn. Expressing basic needs may be a priority for some family members, while following directions and understanding what is being said could be priorities for others. Some families will value communication skills that help develop friendships, and others will prefer skills that help the student respond to direct questions. Priorities of family members typically represent a good place to start. As their children acquire essential communication skills, both receptive and expressive, family members will probably expect increased communicative competence.

Family members and significant others, such as friends, will also have preferences for the kinds of communication modes they use with the student. Some will prefer to interact with the child (or adult) without the use of augmentative communication devices, while others will want to utilize whatever is the most effective. Some will prefer advanced technological devices; others will opt for simpler modes. Some families will eagerly em-

---

COMMUNICATION STYLE ASSESSMENT

Individual's name _____   Age _____

Completed by _____   Date _____

---

1. How does the individual generally make himself or herself understood (e.g., vocalizing, gestures, graphic, object cues)?

   _____

   _____

2. How do you communicate with the individual?

   _____

   _____

3. What kinds of information does the individual communicate spontaneously?

   _____

   _____

4. How does the individual gain your attention when you are not paying attention to him or her?

   _____

   _____

5. How does the individual ask questions for information, personal needs, and directions?

   _____

   _____

6. When the individual likes something, how does he or she communicate it (gestures, smiles, takes, vocalizes)?

   _____

   _____

7. When the individual dislikes something, how does he or she communicate it (gestures, tantrums, looks away, cries)?

   _____

   _____

8. Under what circumstances does the individual interact with others (play games with others, have a conversation)?

   _____

   _____

9. How does the individual communicate choices or indicate preferences?

   _____

   _____

Figure 2.1.   Communication Style Assessment. (From Gothelf, C.R., Woolf, S.B., & Crimmins, D.B. [1995]. Reprinted by permission of the authors.)

brace the use of a visuospatial mode of communication, such as one of many different manual sign systems, while others will feel uncomfortable with such an approach. Each family is unique, and their dreams and hopes for the ways they wish to interact with their family member need to be respected. Cultural beliefs and values will also play a major role when supporting those closest to the student (Hanson, Lynch, & Wayman, 1990; Lynch & Hanson, 1998; Parette, 1995). Demonstrating sensitivity to cultural differences is of critical importance when collecting information that will lead to effective intervention (Blackstone, 1993; Soto, Huer, & Taylor, 1997).

The general educator can provide information on whether the student responds to directions, commands, questions, or social initiations at school. The general educator also can observe whether the student is following communication role models of other students. Educators and paraprofessionals working closely with a student can document specific forms of communication used by the student, whether the student is responding appropriately to peer initiations or initiating interactions him- or herself. The speech-language pathologist (SLP) can assess those skills previously mentioned as well as differentiate between receptive and expressive skills and identify problem areas (e.g., lack of opportunities to communicate, factors contributing to communication breakdowns, need for alternative modes). The questions presented in Figure 2.2 are useful for teachers, paraprofessionals, and other school faculty, although family members can contribute answers as well.

Specialists in the areas of occupational therapy, physical therapy, and visual and hearing impairments all need to contribute their knowledge to the assessment of a student's communication skills. Physical therapists can provide information on appropriate positioning and equipment and how these affect the student's movement and range of motion. The occupational therapist can assess the student's ability to produce manual signs, to select a message by pointing, to manipulate objects, or to utilize a keyboard. This person can also introduce adaptations, such as orthotic aids and adaptive keyboards, and determine how they influence the student's performance. A vision specialist can help determine how well the student sees and how a vision loss may impair communication skills.

- What mode(s) is the student using to communicate?

- Does the student have a means to initiate an interaction? How?

- Does the student have opportunities to initiate an interaction? When? With whom?

- Do others in the environment understand and respond to the student?

- Does the student have a means to engage in different functions of communication, or does he or she primarily make requests or protests?

- Does the student have different things to talk about? What are they?

- Does the student have the means to respond to others and maintain conversation? How?

- Does the student have a way and know how to end a conversation? How?

- Does the student have a way to correct a communication breakdown? How?

Figure 2.2.   Interview questions for professionals and others interested in determining a student's communication skills.

This individual can also help determine the size of symbols needed and the benefit of adding color, contrast, or specific lighting. If vision is not a viable mode for the student to acquire information, then this specialist can help devise some kind of tactual or auditory system. Along these same lines, the hearing specialist can help determine the student's ability to hear as well as the need for adaptations in the event the student has a hearing loss (e.g., hearing aids, FM system). This specialist can provide information on optimal acoustic environments for the student and can explain discrepancies in performance based on different environments.

Finally, classmates can provide anecdotal information about how they interact with students with severe disabilities. An observation and interpretation of the student's interactions with his or her classmates can be added to assessment findings. Because many students appear to be more motivated to interact with peers rather than adults, it makes a great deal of sense to ask for input from classmates regarding the student's communication skills (Light, 1997). These same-age peers can be particularly helpful identifying important topics of conversation and noting times and places that the student needs support.

WHAT TO ASSESS

Both the student's receptive and expressive communication skills need to be assessed. Do students understand what is said to them? When does understanding appear to be greatest? How are they currently expressing themselves? Can they "say" everything they need or want to "say"? Where are communication breakdowns occurring and with whom? Everything that the student is doing to convey understanding and to express thought and feeling needs to be documented.

Intentional and Nonintentional Behavior

In some cases, a student's behavior may, at first glance, appear not to be communicative. For example, a child may make a slight movement, gasp or startle, hit an object, or make an unusual sound. The initial assumption may be that the behavior is not intended to communicate thoughts or feelings; however, because these students have limited ways of making themselves understood, they *may* be engaging in these behaviors precisely for that purpose. The alert partner can respond to these behaviors, helping the student realize that such behaviors can gain someone's attention and convey a message.

Unfortunately, some research suggests that adults may find it difficult to recognize efforts by individuals with severe disabilities to interact (Houghton, Bronicki, & Guess, 1987; Walden, Blackford, & Carpenter, 1997). For instance, Walden et al. (1997) found that adults who lacked significant experience working with children with disabilities, when presented with videotaped segments of young children with developmental disabilities and Down syndrome, were less able to recognize the intent on their faces than on faces of children without disabilities. Such a finding has distinct implications for educational personnel because initial efforts by children may go unrecognized.

Once a behavior is recognized as an attempt to communicate, consistent pairing of a specific response to a particular behavior can teach the student that certain behaviors can be used to convey communicative intent. Until the student can acquire a more pronounced, clear, and obvious form of expression, his or her behaviors (as obscure as they may seem) must be attended to and supported. The least dangerous assumption to make is that students are trying to communicate. Therefore, a student's behaviors, regardless of their opaqueness, should be documented (e.g., facial expressions, movements, looks), especially when that student is having particular difficulty getting a message across. Decisions about whether the behavior is in fact intentionally communicative can be made at a later date if important.

Receptive Communication Skills

Receptive communication skills include any behaviors that indicate an understanding of what was directed to the student. For example, a student who laughs when another student makes a funny comment should be credited with some understanding. A student shows understanding of a teacher's question regarding who wants to work on the computer by raising his or her head and looking toward the computer. A student stops and turns to look at a teacher who says "hi." A student looks at a book and not manipulatives for math when asked what she would like to do. A young child grins when teased by a classmate. A student returns to his seat when asked to do so. All of these responses should be accepted as indicators of a student's ability to receive communication. When analyzing an activity, the receptive communication skills required of that activity need to be identified. How well the student performs in an activity can provide considerable information regarding a student's receptive communication skills. Depending upon the severity of the physical disability, it may be difficult to completely ascertain a student's true receptive ability. Looking for any indication of understanding is important, as well as assuming competence when in doubt. The greater number of environments and activities in which a student is observed will provide a more comprehensive picture of the student's receptive skills.

Expressive Communication Skills

Expressive communication skills include any behavior that is used to convey a thought. As stated previously, how the message is conveyed can vary from very clear and obvious to very vague and idiosyncratic. In some cases, the student's intent to communicate may be questionable. Any attempt by the student to start, maintain, or end a communicative exchange should be recognized. Expressive communication is obviously closely linked to receptive communication, because understanding what another says is required prior to responding. The student who laughs at something funny demonstrates receptive understanding and at the same time may be trying to express, "That's funny." The student who pushes work on the floor may be trying to say, "I can't do this—it's too hard." The student who stands and stares transfixed at a large garbage truck could be making the comment, "This is really amazing!" The student who grabs a teacher's hand and drags her to the window could be trying to direct her attention and to ask, "Do you see the big bird out there?"

To avoid the risk of overlooking a student's efforts to communicate, some direct services providers may want to get into the habit of putting words to the student's efforts. Instead of just seeing a behavior as potentially communicative, this practice of verbal interpretation may help them, and other individuals on the team, to respond to the student in a more conversational manner. For example, when Ariel starts to rock back and forth in her seat, her teacher responds by asking, "Oh, Ariel, are you bored?" This serves as a model for other students in the class to respond to Ariel in a similar manner. Teachers can also prompt students without disabilities to interpret their classmate's communicative efforts by asking them, for example, "What's Ariel trying to say?"

Form, Function, and Content   Carefully analyzing a student's current modes or forms of expressive communication is important in determining the need for further intervention. The *form* of communication is the way the student expresses thoughts and needs. Whenever possible, students will use multiple forms or means of expression (e.g., facial expressions, gestures, vocalizations, objects), and the effectiveness of these means will determine their continued use. Some forms of communication may be very effective for the student, but not exactly conventional for the situation. In order to make the student's expressive behavior more universally understood, whenever the behavior is particularly ambiguous, the student should be provided an alternative way to meet the same need.

Physical and/or sensory disabilities both can significantly affect the communicative forms used by a given student; therefore, team members need to know how and what the student sees and hears. Vision and hearing specialists can share important sensory information that may help to explain why a student may use certain behaviors to communicate and not others. For example, a student may hear well enough to use speech receptively but also use touch cues and objects due to a severe visual and cognitive impairment. For expressive purposes, this same student does not use speech but does vocalize certain sounds in different tones. She also uses facial expressions, objects, and touch.

A student's physical abilities also will affect what forms of communication will be most efficient. For instance, although a student may be able to relax his arm sufficiently to bring it down to his tray to activate a voice output communication aid (VOCA), the movement may be very difficult for him and may require considerable concentration. Physical and occupational therapists can assess students' physical abilities to determine the positions that will allow them to communicate most effectively, as well as any adaptations that may be needed. For example, Carl is physically able to produce some simple signs when he is in his wheelchair with head and trunk support; however, when he is prone on a wedge he is unable to produce the signs and must use facial expressions and looking at pictures as alternatives.

The *function* of communication is the reason or purpose for the exchange. Subsequent chapters use several functions of communication to describe intervention strategies. Although making requests and protesting the actions of others may be the easiest reasons to discern, each student has many other reasons for communicating. Too often, those working with students with severe disabilities misinterpret many of these students' attempts to communicate as requests, when, in fact, the students may simply be attempting to draw someone's attention to an item of interest. Assessment that documents the reasons that the student engages in communicative exchanges will identify whether the student's communication is being limited. Both the student and the conversational partner may need support to engage in different types of exchanges.

The *content* of students' communication will change and will be determined by several different variables, such as interest, age, culture, specific conversational partner(s), and situation. For example, a student with a new toy to share with friends at lunch will most likely be "talking" about the toy. Another student who has returned to school from a camping trip with his family and has brought in photographs to show the class will most likely be interested in discussing this trip. Of course, this kind of situation is not always available. Typically, the possibilities of what the student may want to discuss are limitless, and providing the needed support (in terms of symbols to use) is quite difficult; however, interactions in which the student shows the greatest interest in communicating may provide some indication that the topic of conversation is an important one. It may be that the student interacts the most when this particular subject is being "discussed"; therefore, documenting the content of communication that seems to most often engage the student is important and can be used in the creation of alternative and augmentative communication devices.

Initiations, Responses, and Turn-Taking

When assessing student communication skills, it is important to observe whether a student initiates the interaction, responds to another's comments, and maintains the conversation by taking turns. Typically, students with severe disabilities are unlikely to initiate interactions but are placed in the role of respondent (Cipani, 1990; Reichle & Sigafoos, 1991). Detailed information related to the conditions under which the student initiates communication is critical to understanding the student's skills. Rowland, Schweigert, and Stremel (1992) devised a means of closely examining interactions with children who have severe and multiple disabilities. Their assessment form provided a way of collecting data on the form, purpose, and content of the student's communication. Figure 2.3 is an adaptation of their tool and adds the number of conversation partners, number of turns taken by the student, and whether the student initiated or responded to the partner. In addition, the form enables the data collector to document the exact content of the interaction. By recording both what the peer without disabilities says and an interpretation of the student's communicative effort, a true conversation between the two (or more) students can be read down the last column. Transcribing the student's various forms of nonspeech communication into speech helps to remind the observer not to overlook the potential communicative intent of various forms of behavior. This type of interpretation may also aid in the development of augmentative communication devices for the student if needed. Figure 2.4 shows a completed observation form.

HOW TO ASSESS

Structured Observations

Communication skills do not develop in a vacuum. They are very much contextually bound. What is said, how it is said, and for what reasons are based on the setting, participants, and subject of any given interaction; therefore, a valid assessment of an individual's communication skills must occur within a typical communicative context (Calculator, 1994; Light, 1997). As has already been noted, individuals are most apt to demonstrate maximum communication skills in familiar and comfortable environments (Cipani, 1989; Reichle, 1997). Observing individuals in these environments provides a much clearer idea of how they actually communicate. Structured observations can make note of both receptive and expressive skills, as well as most frequent communication partners, frequently recurring topics, forms of communication, reasons for interaction, and activities in which communicative exchanges most often occur.

Before making observations, the team must agree on what is critical to observe. Listening to team members who spend the greatest amount of time with the student helps determine in which environments and activities the student should be observed. Family members, teachers, and paraprofessionals will express the goals they have for the student, but the student should also have a voice in expressing what motivates him or her and where he or she would appreciate some assistance in order to participate more actively. These goals are then incorporated into specific activities that occur on a regular basis. In other words, if parents, teachers, and the student make it clear that having friends is extremely important, then it is the team's responsibility to identify where students of the same age make friends, what types of activities facilitate the development of friendship, and what social skills enhance this development. Team members decide that social interactions are most prevalent during unstructured times, such as breaks between classes, nutrition breaks, and lunch, and during structured academic times when students work together (e.g., cooperative learning groups, teams or partnerships during physical education, lab partnerships in science classes). The team then needs to observe these activities to analyze the student's communicative behavior as well as other skills required for him or her to participate successfully and to meet individualized education program (IEP) goals and objectives.

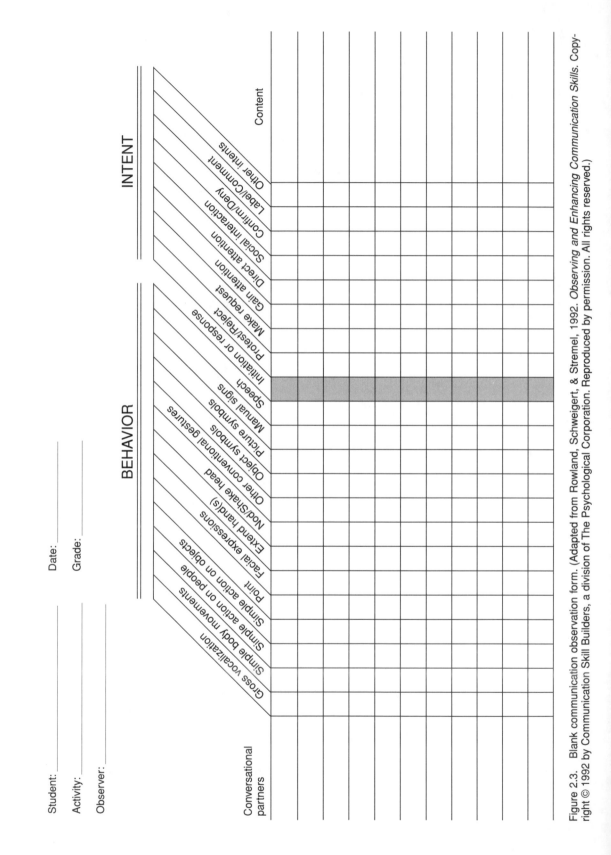

Student: _____ Date: _____

Activity: _____ Grade: _____

Observer: _____

INTENT

Content

Other intents

Label/Comment

Confirm/Deny

Social interaction

Direct attention

Gain attention

BEHAVIOR

Make request

Protest/Reject

Initiation or response

Speech

Manual signs

Picture symbols

Object symbols

Other conventional gestures

Nod/Shake head

Extend hand(s)

Facial expressions

Point

Simple action on objects

Simple action on people

Simple body movements

Gross vocalization

Conversational partners

Figure 2.3. Blank communication observation form. (Adapted from Rowland, Schweigert, & Stremel, 1992. *Observing and Enhancing Communication Skills.* Copyright © 1992 by Communication Skill Builders, a division of The Psychological Corporation. Reproduced by permission. All rights reserved.)

Student: _Megan_   Date: _3/23/98_

Activity: _Story Mapping_

Observer: _J.D._   Grade: _1_

BEHAVIOR / INTENT

Conversational partners	Gross vocalization	Simple vocalization	Simple body movements	Simple action on people	Simple action on objects	Point	Facial expressions	Extend hand(s)	Nod/Shake head	Other conventional gestures	Picture symbols	Object symbols	Manual signs	Speech	Initiation or response	Protest/Reject	Make request	Gain attention	Direct attention	Social interaction	Confirm/Deny	Label/Comment	Other intents	Content
Crystal	X													R										"Megan, want me to be your partner?"
Megan	X X					X	X							R						X				"Sure!"
Megan																								"Okay. We're going to map our story."
Megan																								_____
Teacher																								"Here are the pictures for Megan to use."
Crystal																								"Okay. Megan, look at these. Get the caterpillar."
Megan							X				X			R							X			"This one."
Crystal																								"That's not the caterpillar! Which one's the caterpillar?"
Megan											X			R							X			"Okay. This one."
Crystal																								"Yup. That's the caterpillar."
Megan	X X		X	X										I		X								"Can we do something else?"

Figure 2.4. Communication observation form for Megan. Megan is nonverbal and what is in quotation marks under *Content* is how others interpret what she is trying to say. (Adapted from Rowland, Schweigert, & Stremel, 1992. *Observing and Enhancing Communication Skills*. Copyright © 1992 by Communication Skill Builders, a division of The Psychological Corporation. Reproduced by permission. All rights reserved.)

(continued)

32

Figure 2.4. (continued)

BEHAVIOR / INTENT

Conversational Partners	BEHAVIOR														INTENT								Content
	Gross vocalization	Simple body movements	Simple action on people	Simple action on objects	Point	Facial expressions	Extend hand(s)	Nod/Shake head	Other conventional gestures	Object symbols	Picture symbols	Manual signs	Speech	Initiation or response	Protest/Reject	Make request	Gain attention	Direct attention	Social interaction	Confirm/Deny	Label/Comment	Other intents	Content
Crystal																							"What's the matter? Don't you want to do this?"
Teacher																							"Maybe you could ask Megan what pictures she wants you to use…"
Crystal					X																		"Okay, Megan, look at these. Which one do you want?"
Megan						X				X			R		X								"I want the Flower."
Crystal				X																			"Alright. Let me put it here."
Megan	X				X								I		X								"Let me glue it."
Crystal				X																			"Okay. You can glue it. Put it here."
Megan	X												I							X			"I can't do this!"
Crystal				X																			"It's all right. I'll help you. There."

Ecological Inventories   Ecological inventories hold considerable value for determining the communication expectations of the natural environment (e.g., fifth-grade classroom, high school biology class, hallway, library, playground) (Calculator, 1994; Calculator & Jorgensen, 1991; Downing, 1996). These inventories are designed to analyze the behavior of those without disabilities in specific environments. Chapter 3 takes a close look at typical environments with regard to general opportunities, expectations, and ways to obtain this information. For assessment purposes, ecological inventories can identify specific skill requirements of a given activity. An inventory of typical peers delineates the steps performed by those without disabilities to successfully engage in the activity. These steps include a variety of different skills, including communicative behavior. Figures 2.5–2.9 provide illustrations of this type of inventory for a preschool play activity, a first-grade show-and-tell activity, a fifth-grade science activity, an eighth-grade language arts activity, and a twelfth-grade American history activity. Each student assessed in these figures has unique strengths and limitations as indicated in the brief descriptors next to the student's name. The combination of these strengths and limitations along with the demands of the environment and expectations of the teacher and others for appropriate behavior will determine how best to support the student.

Ecological inventories not only provide information about what one would expect to see of normal behavior for a given activity but also provide information about the natural cues in the environment that prompted the desired behavior (Sigafoos & York, 1991). Natural cues can be anything that serves to help elicit the desired response. They can be internal (e.g., feelings of hunger, a full bladder, a desire to say something) or external (e.g., a teacher's directions to line up, the teacher's "in box," friends eating at a particular table). Therefore, sometimes they can be readily observed (e.g., a friend says "hi" and the student says "hi" in return) and sometimes they are presumed to be in operation given the resulting behavior (e.g., the natural cue for requesting a drink of water is probably a sense of thirst). Of course, motivational cues can be hidden but can strongly influence behavior. For example, in the case of requesting to get a drink of water, this could be cued naturally by thirst or by a desire to escape (if only briefly) some task that is undesirable. Using the ecological inventory format provided in Figures 2.5–2.9, the assessor or recorder of the information notes the natural cues probably responsible for the behavior expected of the students. In classrooms, the natural cues often come from the general educator who is giving a group of students directions to follow. However, many other natural cues exist in the environment. When targeting communication skills, it is important to document the many natural cues that exist that prompt both receptive and expressive communication skills. Although the teacher's directions may serve to cue receptive communication skills (understanding what is said), several other natural cues prompt expressive communication (being asked a question by another student, not knowing what to do, having a strong desire to share some information). Observing and carefully noting the natural cues that exist in various activities provide the educational team with considerable information pertaining to both expressive and receptive communication skills.

Discrepancy Analyses   Using the information obtained from the ecological inventory, the actual performance of the student with severe disabilities can be assessed. As the student performs the specific steps of any given activity, the observer records whether the student satisfactorily engages in each step. The observation is made when *no additional help* is given the student other than what exists for other students without disabilities (e.g., the natural cues). If the student performs a step successfully, one can assume that the student was able to respond to natural cues (both internal and external). The way in which the student performs may be somewhat topographically different (i.e., may look

Student: Katie, age 4 (happy, great smile, loves to be with others, stubborn, and has severe physical and intellectual challenges)
Activity: Pretending - Trains
Level: Preschool

Steps in activity	Natural cues	Student performance	Communication skills needed	Discrepancy analysis	Intervention plan
Goes to pretend play area	Teacher direction, options, preference	-	Receptive: understands teacher's directions	Cannot physically move to area	Teach her to use pictorial device to choose area, then push her to that area.
Decides on role to play	Options, preference	-	Expressive: states role Receptive: understands what others have chosen	Cannot use speech	Teach her to use pictorial ACD with voice output to state desired role.
Puts on costume; gets props	Costume/props available	-	Expressive: asks for help if needed	Cannot use speech	Teach her to look for adult and use BIGmack to request help.
Acts out role	Knowledge of role, what others say and do	-	Receptive: understands others Expressive: responds to others; plays role	Limited language, cannot use speech	Teach her to use pictorial ACD with voice output. Teach peers to interact.
Stops playing	Teacher direction	+	Receptive: understands teacher		
Puts items away	Teacher direction, knowledge of class rule	-	Receptive: understands teacher	Cannot physically handle items	Have aide support her arm while Katie works with a peer to hold and release item to peer.

Figure 2.5.   Functional ecological inventory of communication skills for Katie, a 4-year-old with severe physical and intellectual disabilities.

Student: Molly, age 6 (active, loves books, likes to laugh, and has severe autism)
Activity: Show and Tell
Level: 1st grade

Steps in activity	Natural cues	Student performance	Communication skills needed	Discrepancy analysis	Intervention plan
Goes to carpet area	Teacher direction, seeing carpet area	-	Receptive: understands teacher's directions	Not motivated and not attending	Have teacher get close to Molly and give her directions; show her picture of group on floor; allow her to carry favorite book to area; allow her to sit in chair rather than on floor.
Sits on carpet facing teacher	Teacher at front of area, empty carpet space	+			
Raises hand if desiring to share	Desire to share, teacher asks if anyone wants to share	-	Receptive: understands teacher Expressive: raises hand	May not understand teacher; not interested in sharing or does not know to raise hand	Notify parent occasionally to have her bring in an item to share; direct attention to teacher by pointing; model raising hand and physically cue at Molly's elbow.
If sharing, describes to class the item brought and responds to questions	Item, knowledge of item, knowing procedure, hands raised	-	Receptive: understands classmates' questions Expressive: talks about item and responds to questions	Does not use speech; may not understand classmates' questions	Have parents get Molly's sister to record message about item; physically assist her to stand in front of class and hold item; teach her to use switch to activate cassette recorder.
Listens to person sharing	Student talking, knowledge of class rules	-	Receptive: understands what peers say	May not understand classmates; has a hard time staying with group (too stimulating)	Sit close to Molly to help her focus on peers; let her hold item if possible or give her something to doodle with.

Figure 2.6.   Functional ecological inventory of communication skills for Molly, a 6-year-old girl with severe autism.

(continued)

Figure 2.6. (continued)

Steps in activity	Natural cues	Student performance	Communication skills needed	Discrepancy analysis	Intervention plan
Raises hand to ask questions/make comments	Having a question or comment, being called on	-	Receptive: understands what was said Expressive: asks questions or make comments	Does not use speech, may not have attended long enough to know what to ask	Give her three different colored cards with a different question on each one; teach her to choose one and raise it; have a fourth card with a smiley face and a positive comment on it.
Returns to seat	Teacher direction, activity concludes	+	Receptive: understands teacher's direction		

Student: Trent, age 10 (loves his pets, responds well to praise, tries hard, is blind, and has mental retardation requiring limited support and hemiplegia cerebral palsy)

Activity: Science - Study of the Solar System

Level: 5th grade

Steps in activity	Natural cues	Student performance	Communication skills needed	Discrepancy analysis	Intervention plan
Listens to teacher	Teacher talking	-	Receptive: understands teacher	May not understand all the words	Show him model of what is to be designed, and have him help teacher show it to class.
Gets materials	Teacher direction, others doing this	-	Receptive: understands teacher	Does not know where materials are and has a hard time carrying them	Have a classmate provide sighted guide to shelf and help him put materials in pack.
Gets into cooperative learning group	Teacher direction	+	Receptive: understands teacher		
Works on building model portion of solar system	Pictures of solar system, classmates' comments	-	Receptive: understands classmates' comments Expressive: talks to classmates about project	May not understand the comments, cannot see pictures, has very limited speech	Teach him to follow one-step directions provided by peers to give them materials, respond to Y/N questions, and to use voice output ACD to comment on project.
Puts materials away	Teacher direction	-	Receptive: understands teacher	Has a hard time finding where things go and carrying them	Have him use a fanny pack and a peer for a sighted guide to return items.

Figure 2.7. Functional ecological inventory of communication skills for Trent, a 10-year-old who is blind, has mental retardation requiring limited support, and has hemiplegia cerebral palsy.

Student: Micah, age 13 (curious, strong mechanical skills, likes gadgets, has severe autism, and is nonverbal)
Activity: Language Arts - Acrostic Poetry
Level: 8th grade

Steps in activity	Natural cues	Student performance	Communication skills needed	Discrepancy analysis	Intervention plan
Listens to teacher	Teacher talking	-	Receptive: understands teacher	Not motivated to pay attention, may not understand words	Have aide assist Micah in getting books and passing them out (math goal = 1:1 correspondence).
Participates in class discussion of poem	Teacher asking questions, others' comments, having something to say	-	Receptive: understands teacher and classmates Expressive: responds to questions and makes comments	Not motivated to attend, may not understand words, cannot speak and has no symbolic communication system	Once he is finished passing out books, show him examples of poetry with graphics so he knows the end product. Have Micah play taped poem upon the teacher's request.
Reads acrostic poetry	Teacher direction, poetry to read	-	Receptive: understands teacher and understands print	May not understand teacher, does not read	Pair Micah with peer, and have peer read poetry to him; use graphics to help him understand the topic.
Gets with peer buddy	Teacher direction	+	Receptive: understands teacher		
Writes acrostic poem as a team	Teacher direction, ideas, blank piece of paper	-	Receptive: understands classmates Expressive: stating ideas, writing ideas	Does not speak or write	Allow pair to work on computer with graphic programs and voice output; have peer type and Micah choose subject of poem and select graphic design and colors per line.
Turns into teacher or take home as homework	Knowledge of teacher expectation	+			

Figure 2.8. Functional ecological inventory of communication skills for Micah, a 13-year-old with severe autism.

Student: Nico, age 17 (likes to please others, loves art, fairly athletic, wants to make money, deaf, and has moderate intellectual challenges)
Activity: American History - Study of World War II
Level: 12th grade

Steps in activity	Natural cues	Student performance	Communication skills needed	Discrepancy analysis	Intervention plan
Listens to directions	Teacher talking	-	Receptive: understands teacher	Cannot hear	Have aide work quietly with Nico showing him a sample of the finished product and the materials to make it. Introduce some signs.
Gets materials	Teacher directions	-	Receptive: understands teacher	Cannot hear	Have teacher use gestures and show materials to get; ask peers to assist.
Gets with others in groups of three	Teacher directions, others doing this	+	Receptive: understands teacher		
Works on presentation with group members	Project not done, peers' comments	-	Receptive: understands others' talking Expressive: makes decisions, jokes, asks questions	Cannot hear, only knows a few signs	Have aide and classmates use signs, pictures, and gestures; show him a sample of one finished project; have aide teach all students a few signs to go with activity.
Cleans up area	Teacher direction, others doing this	+	Receptive: understands teacher		
Presents project to class	Teacher direction, project to present	-	Receptive: understands classmates' questions Expressive: explains project to class, answer questions	Cannot hear, only knows a few signs	Have Nico hold graphic representation of project while classmates presented and teach entire class the few signs learned; have him model signs to class and point to representative picture.
Listens to other groups' presentations	Others presenting, interest in others' work	-	Receptive: understands classmates' presentations Expressive: asks questions	Cannot hear; only knows a few signs	Ask two classmates in his group to write a question on a card; cue him to raise the card after the presentation; ask presenters to stand close to his desk so he can easily see graphics of their project.

Figure 2.9. Functional ecological inventory of communication skills for Nico, a 17-year-old who is deaf and has moderate cognitive challenges.

different), but as long as the activity continues and the student is successful, then the student is considered independent in this step. For example, when a teacher tells his class to go to the library and Jeffrey does this by using his wheelchair or walker, the end result is the same and Jeffrey is given credit for that step. With respect to receptive communication, it is clear that Jeffrey received the direction, understood it, and acted on it; therefore, that step does not need to be taught.

If the student does not perform the required step of an activity, the student is not given credit for demonstrating this skill, and a reason for the discrepancy is recorded (see Figures 2.5–2.9). Often, the reason for the discrepancy involves the student's inability to perceive the natural cue. The student didn't hear, see, or understand the cue that was available (e.g., the teacher's directions). Sometimes the student does not attend to the natural cue and, consequently, fails to respond appropriately. Sometimes the student recognizes and understands the natural cue (e.g., directions to perform work) but has no motivation to perform. The consequences for performing the step may be insufficiently reinforcing for the student, who, as a result, refuses to engage in the behavior and seeks something else to do. Sometimes the student is receiving such close personal support from a special adult (teacher or aide), that the cues that exist for others in the class are not as accessible to the student with disabilities. Often, an adult working one-to-one with a particular student will not stop instruction to direct the student's attention to the teacher who is giving a group direction. When this happens, it is unclear whether the student could have understood the cue. Giangreco, Edelman, Luiselli, and MacFarland (1997) investigated the problem of paraeducators affixing themselves so closely to the student that their assistance may actually become intrusive and interfering. Sometimes, however, the student understands the natural cue but cannot act on it due to a physical or sensory limitation. For example, a teacher tells the class to clean up the room. Sabrina, who has severe physical and intellectual impairments, hears and understands the cue but cannot physically perform the step; however, if given two pictorial choices and asked what the teacher said to do, she can indicate by looking at the correct response, therefore communicating that she understood what was said. Using an alternative form of communication (e.g., photograph, symbol), she can "ask" a peer to help her clean up.

The importance of the discrepancy analysis is to document the reason for the incongruity between the student's performance and the desired skill. Understanding the reason for the discrepancy will provide considerable clarity for determining the requisite intervention, which could be as simple as clarifying or highlighting the natural cue (e.g., a teacher talks louder or moves closer to and touches the student when giving directions) or could require considerable adaptation to allow the student to participate in the activity.

Videotaped Observations   Most teachers are so involved with the student on a daily basis that it is difficult to step back from an activity long enough to determine the steps and skills necessary to successfully perform the activity; therefore, videotaping the student performing the activity allows the teacher and other educational team members to carefully analyze the activity without the added pressure of assisting the student. Videotaping is an excellent means of determining a student's communicative skills (Burford, 1996; Siegel-Causey & Wetherby, 1993).

With a tripod, a video camera can be set up in a classroom for an entire period in middle and high schools and for a large section of the day in preschool and elementary schools. Instead of specifically trying to catch communicative exchanges, everything that takes place in the classroom will be captured. If done with sufficient regularity, students will become accustomed to its presence and, eventually, ignore it. If possible, a member of the team (e.g., parent, SLP, paraeducator) can videotape a lesson or activity. Those watching the videos will be able to see the student performing in a typical way and will invariably obtain more information regarding many skill areas than anticipated (Siegel-Causey & Wetherby, 1993). Furthermore, individual team members can analyze the same data without having to be brought together to do so. Such taped observation is less intrusive to the student's normal routine than several adults observing in a room and has the added benefit of allowing team members to examine the same interactions as many times as needed for analysis. When it is convenient, team members can meet to discuss the taped observation and to share information, referring to what was captured on tape for clarification.

HOW TO FACILITATE COMMUNICATION AMONG TEAM MEMBERS

When interacting with other team members, especially those that will be facilitating a student's transition from one grade or school to the next, clearly describing how a student communicates is essential in working effectively with that student. Successful interactions by all concerned will depend on a clear understanding of the student's ability to understand others and to express him- or herself. A brief description of the student's communication skills should be part of the student's present level of performance as required by the IEP and should include information obtained from the assessment process. The following examples illustrate two ways of sharing this important information.

> Amy (6 years old) is nonverbal with a developmental age of 2.1 years. She has receptive communication skills of approximately a 2.5-year-old and expressive communication skills of a 9-month-old.

> Amy (6 years old) does not use speech for expressive purposes but does use speech for receptive communication (three- or four-word phrases appear to be most effective). She also uses photographs, object cues, body gestures, and facial expressions to understand what others are saying. She expresses herself using vocalizations (attention-getting sounds, screaming), facial expressions, and photographs and objects. She will scream and push away from people and activities she chooses to reject.

The first description offers minimal information regarding what team members could expect of a particular child. The information still requires considerable interpretation and does not provide a clear picture of what a communicative interaction with the student would actually look like. By contrast, the second description clearly states the most effective ways to interact with the student and, as such, is much more valuable for those interested in understanding the student's communication skills. The second description also bypasses the reference to a developmental age that is not particularly helpful. We certainly would not want to be interacting with Amy, who is 6, as if she were 2 years old, by resorting to inappropriate infantile speech patterns.

OUTCOMES OF ASSESSMENT

From Assessment to Individualized Education Program Development

One very practical use for assessing skills is to aid the educational team in developing an appropriate IEP. As with assessment, this is a team effort. One person, such as the SLP, should *not* be held responsible for independently developing appropriate communication objectives for the IEP. Instead, everyone's assessment input is combined to jointly create IEP objectives that target various skills including communication. Because communication is part of a skill cluster that is required for most activities (Guess & Helmstetter, 1986), this approach has a sound basis. For example, working in small groups during a biology lab requires fine motor skills for handling various materials and recording results; cognitive skills for following directions, reading instructions, and resolving problems; and communication skills for listening to the teacher and lab partner, asking questions, seeking help if needed, interacting socially with peers, expressing thoughts, and responding to the teacher. Different members of the team combine their observations and experiences with different activities to identify all the skills required of a given activity.

Having team input into the assessment process translates into intervention that involves the whole team. Critical communication needs are less ambiguous when all members of the team have played an active part in determining them, and isolated test results do not need to be interpreted because assessment information has been obtained jointly rather than independently. Assessment and intervention are shared responsibilities of all involved (Downing & Bailey, 1990). The educational team should first identify critical activities for each student. Giangreco, Cloninger, and Iverson (1998) developed a procedure for helping parents and other team members determine these critical activities and state priorities for yearly IEP development. Determining needed communication skills are part of this process. In fact, Giangreco and colleagues (1998) found that communication skills were a high priority of the parents they surveyed. Once activities are identified that are important for the student to perform (either partially or in full), the communication skills required as part of the activity(s), both receptive and expressive, are identified using the ecological-functional assessment process previously described. IEP objectives are written to identify skills (communication and others) that the student will learn and are based on discrepancies identified during the ecological-functional process. Objectives are for the student to attain and do not belong to individual team members (e.g., the SLP). Such a model provides a much more cohesive educational approach because each professional is not writing IEP objectives in isolation of one another. As a result, it has merit for being more efficient.

The following examples illustrate the way in which assessment helps in formulating IEP objectives. The objectives relate to broader goals, and specific skills are outlined with regard to how the student will communicate, to whom, for what reason(s), and under what conditions. Criteria to measure each student's communication skills are clear and objective as needed to demonstrate attainment of the skill.

Candy

A sixth grader, Candy, was observed in a number of her class's activities, both academic and nonacademic. Candy did not use any speech in any observed interaction and only rarely responded to others by reaching toward them when asked specific questions (e.g., "Want to come with us?" "Do you want some pop?"). Diagnosed as having Rett syndrome, severe visual impairments, and intellectual challenges, Candy had not learned how to respond in a clear and consistent manner. It was difficult to maintain interactions with her due to her lack of responsiveness. The inability to respond was stated as a clear communicative need for Candy by her team members. Her parents, in particular, were quite concerned about her lack of friendships with other students in her class. As a result, the following goal and objectives were written for Candy.

GOAL: Candy will increase her interactions with classmates during the school day to at least 10 per day.

Objective 1: When asked by a peer with whom she would like to work, Candy will reach out and touch or grab the hand of one of two peers within 5 seconds of being asked for 9 of 10 consecutive opportunities.

Objective 2: During recess, Candy will respond within 10 seconds to at least three initiations by classmates to play with them by going with one or more classmates for 10 consecutive recess periods.

Manny

Manny, an eighth grader, has Down syndrome and very rapid speech that is difficult to understand. In uncomfortable or unfamiliar situations, he would put his head down and speak very quietly. Manny had a clear "yes" and "no," enjoyed being with his classmates, and would often try repeatedly to get his message across. He appeared to understand most of what was said to him and followed directions well if he knew what he was supposed to do. A portable pictorial communication device was designed for him to help support his speech and make his messages more readily understood by others. Aiding the intelligibility of his expressive communication was a key concern for team members, especially because he would become very frustrated when he could not make himself understood. The following goal and objectives target this concern.

GOAL: Manny will increase his ability to be understood by others in order to make interactions more meaningful 50% of the time.

Objective 1: When engaged in a conversation, Manny will point to pictures to support what he is trying to say so that his conversational partner can respond appropriately at least once during every conversation for 15 different interactions.

Objective 2: When told that he is not being understood, Manny will slow his speech, look at his conversational partner, and use gestures, pictures, or objects that are readily available to clarify his intent 10 consecutive times that this happens.

Gerardo

Gerardo is 5 years old, extremely active, physically agile, and loves to do things with his hands. Gerardo is diagnosed as having severe autism and developmental delays, and he does not use speech. In his kindergarten classroom, Gerardo uses objects, directed gaze, and body movements to communicate. He also runs away, screams, spits, scratches, and destroys items when trying to convey displeasure with an activity. He follows some spoken directions and is interested in pictures, especially of dogs. He dislikes large groups and any change in the typical routine. The behavior he displayed to escape undesired activities concerned his teachers and parents and occasionally upset his classmates. The team felt that Gerardo needed an alternative way to express himself as addressed in the following goal and objectives.

GOAL:	When frustrated or angry, Gerardo will express himself in ways that are not disruptive or hurtful 80% of the time for 1 month.
Objective 1:	During an activity that Gerardo wishes to leave, he will pick up his break card and either wave it or hand it to an adult to request a break from the activity. He will do this without engaging in undesired behavior for 12 of 15 opportunities.
Objective 2:	For 8 of 10 times when told that he must stop an activity or stop handling certain materials, Gerardo will shake his head "no" instead of hitting or shoving.

Writing IEP goals and, especially, objectives can make the desired skill seem artificial or somewhat out of context. The need to document progress toward IEP objectives to show accountability sometimes forces a degree of specificity that seems unnatural; however, without such specificity, it is unclear when objectives have been met and whether the program has been successful.

Assessment to Measure Progress

Assessment is an ongoing process to ensure that intervention remains on the right track and that students acquire targeted skills. Without ongoing evaluation of the teaching process, students may fail to make expected and desired progress, and teachers will become frustrated or impatient. Considerable opportunities to learn may be lost if an intervention plan is followed for long periods of time without a critical look at whether it is effective for the student. Assessment of communication skills (as with other skills) must be formative as well as summative.

Regular checks of the student's progress toward meeting communication goals help identify where the student is successful and where the student is having difficulty. These checks allow the team to build on the student's strengths and to concentrate on areas that require greater creativity. For example, it may become apparent from the data collected that a student greets a few adults but does not respond to greetings from classmates. If the goal is to have this student greet both adults and classmates, then the collection of data with regard to this goal provides the educational team with an idea of what needs to be addressed. However, the same assessment data also make it clear that the student can and *is* greeting some adults, confirming the student's ability to perform this communicative skill. Recognizing this ability can help the team teach the student to extend the skill to his or her classmates. Figures 2.10–2.12 provide examples of data collection sheets for three of the sample objectives provided in previous pages for Candy, Manny, and Gerardo. These data collection forms obtain more information than actually needed to measure the objectives. The additional information helps guide further intervention and gives a clearer picture of the student's skills.

Assessment Used to Modify Intervention

Unless data is analyzed and applied to the decision-making process, collecting them becomes a useless practice. Collecting data and failing to make use of them seems to be an unfortunate practice of some teachers, SLPs, and paraeducators. This practice is time consuming and does little else beyond stuffing a student's files. A primary reason to collect data, other than to demonstrate accountability for the student's IEP, is to determine where changes need to be made in the intervention program.

If a student does not appear to be making progress toward communication goals and objectives, the problem lies not with the student but rather with the intervention. Lack

Objective: When asked by a peer with whom she would like to work, Candy will reach out and touch or grab the hand of one of two peers within 5 seconds of being asked for 9 of 10 consecutive opportunities.

	Date: 4/16	Date: 4/16	Date: 4/17	Date:
	Activity/Class	Activity/Class	Activity	Activity
	Language Arts	*PE*	*Science*	
Peers	(Sheri)	(Pat)	Jeremy	
	Tresa	*Heather*	(Sheri)	
Delay time (in seconds)	6	5	4	
Level of prompt needed	P	VP	+	

Figure 2.10. Data collection sheet for Candy's IEP communication objectives. Names circled indicate those peers with whom Candy has chosen to work. (Key: + = independent/natural cue, VP = direct verbal prompt, P = physical prompt to elbow.)

of progress indicates a need to regroup and reconsider teaching strategies (Cipani, 1989). Prompts being given may not be clear, the communicative behavior targeted may be too difficult to perform, or the augmentative communication device may be too complex to understand and use. The team will need to decide which elements of the intervention program need to be modified.

Ongoing assessment also indicates when a student has achieved certain skills and needs to move on. Even if the IEP is not to be amended, new objectives can always be added to an existing IEP, for the student will still need to be challenged to acquire new skills. Setting specific criteria for the student to reach will help identify when the student has achieved as desired.

Assessment Used to Determine Next Steps

Determining next steps for a student when that student has mastered certain objectives can be a difficult process with no prescribed curriculum to follow. The individual nature of communication instruction and its dependence on individual situations and needs makes it impossible to standardize next steps for a given student; consequently, these next steps must be determined on an individual basis by the team.

Comparing the rich variety of available forms of communication with those used by the student may indicate a need to add to the student's communicative repertoire. For instance, if the student is using objects but little else to express him- or herself, this may indicate the need to teach the student natural gestures, vocalizations to gain someone's

Objective: When engaged in a conversation, Manny will point to pictures to support what he is trying to say so that his conversational partners can respond appropriately at least once during every conversation for 15 different interactions.

	Date: 3/20	Date: 3/20	Date: 3/21	Date: 3/22
Activity or class/time	Leadership 9:05	Break 10:00	Science 12:50	Leadership 9:05
Picture(s) selected (topics)	Computer	• sister's photo • sports car	• help me • request for bathroom	• photo of peer • "That's silly."
Successful clarification	/	//	//	//
Number of opportunities	///	////	///	//

Figure 2.11.   Data collection sheet for Manny's IEP communication objectives.

attention, and possibly the use of pictures or photographs. Again, these decisions would be based on the given situation and the student's communicative effectiveness. If assessment results indicate that the student is only responding to others' initiations and rarely, if ever, initiating interactions, teaching the student how to do so would be a valuable next step. Likewise, if the student only appears to be interacting with one adult (perhaps a paraeducator), teaching the student to interact with others would be a natural next step. If it becomes apparent from the assessment that students without disabilities are having a difficult time understanding their classmate with a disability, then the need exists to teach the student clearer forms of expression and to work with the classmates as well.

The desires of the student, family members, and friends provide perhaps the most important information in determining that student's future steps. Skills that may have seemed important at one point in time may be replaced by other skills that have greater bearing on the student's life. For example, parents and teachers may strongly emphasize the student's ability to make use of certain social conventions of politeness, such as the use of "please" and "thank you." Although signing these words may have been targeted while the student was in kindergarten, it may become apparent that the student is confused about their meaning and is using them to mean "more." The team may decide to target other communicative functions that are more recognizable to the student. Looking at the student's current situation, present strengths, and most critical needs will determine to a great extent the next steps that will help the student be as competent a communicator as possible.

SUMMARY

This chapter on assessment has provided a rationale for an ecological and natural approach to determining communicative skills and needs. Assessment is not performed for the purpose of highlighting impairments in order to exclude students from appropriate

Objective: For 8 of 10 times, when told that he must stop an activity or stop handling certain materials, Gerardo will shake his head "no" instead of hitting or shoving.

	Date: *10/21* Situation: *Sink Transition* *9.45 a.m.*	Date: *10/21* Situation: *Computer Time*	Date: *10/22* Situation: *Playing with* *Scissors*	Date: Situation:
Adult giving direction	Mrs. T: _*X*_ Miss A: _____ Other: _____	Mrs. T: _____ Miss A: _*X*_ Other: _____	Mrs. T: _____ Miss A: _*X*_ Other: _____	Mrs. T: _____ Miss A: _____ Other: _____
Gerardo's response	shakes head no _____ hits or shoves _____ screams _____ other _*ignores her*_	shakes head no _____ hits or shoves _*X*_ screams _*X*_ other _____	shakes head no _*X*_ hits or shoves _____ screams _____ other _____	shakes head no _____ hits or shoves _____ screams _____ other _____
Prompt needed	model _*X*_ verbal prompt _*X*_ touch to head _____	model _*X*_ verbal prompt _*X*_ touch to head _*X*_	model _*X*_ verbal prompt _*X*_ touch to head _____	model _____ verbal prompt _____ touch to head _____

Figure 2.12.   Data collection sheet for Gerardo's IEP communication objectives.

services. Rather, the assessment of communication skills needs to be sensitive to the unique abilities of the student, the characteristics of the social and physical environment, and the communicative opportunities as well as expectations of the student. The intent of the assessment process is to identify current skills and build on those skills to help the student be as effective a communicator as possible. Assessment is also used to identify areas of need, not based on some standardized assumptions of communication but on each individual student's need to communicate in different environments and with different people.

Because teachers and other team members typically have limited time to perform all of the necessary tasks required for teaching, assessment should not be a tedious exercise that is unrelated to helping the student. Instead, it needs to be an efficient and shared responsibility, and it needs to have a distinct relationship to intervention. When assessment is tied to intervention and to IEP goals and objectives, the need to engage in assessment activities is clearer and perhaps more readily adopted.

REFERENCES

Beck, A.R. (1996). Language assessment methods for three age groups of children. *Journal of Children's Communication Development, 17*(2), 31–66.

Biklen, D. (1985). *Achieving the complete school: Strategies for effective mainstreaming.* New York: Teachers College Press.

Blackstone, S. (1993). Clinical news: Cultural sensitivity and AAC services. *Augmentative Communication News, 6*(2), 3–10.

Burford, B. (1996). A way of assisting carers of children with profound learning disabilities to share what they know about communication. *Network, 5*(1), 31–37.

Calculator, S.N. (1994). Designing and implementing communicative assessments in inclusive settings. In S.N. Calculator & C.M. Jorgensen (Eds.), *Including students with severe disabilities in schools: Fostering communication, interaction, and participation* (pp. 113–182). San Diego, CA: Singular Publishing Group.

Calculator, S.N., & Jorgensen, C. (1991). Integrating AAC instruction into regular education settings: Expounding on best practices. *Augmentative and Alternative Communication, 7,* 204–214.

Casby, M. (1992). The cognitive hypothesis and its influence on speech-language services in schools. *Language, Speech and Hearing Services in Schools, 23,* 198–202.

Cipani, E. (1989). Providing language consultation in the natural context: A model for delivery of services. *Mental Retardation, 27,* 317–324.

Cipani, E. (1990). "Excuse me: I'll have . . .": Teaching appropriate attention-getting behaviors to young children with severe handicaps. *Mental Retardation, 28,* 29–33.

Cole, K.N., Dale, P.S., & Thal, D.J. (Vol. Eds.). (1996). In S.F. Warren & J. Reichle (Series Eds.), *Communication and language intervention series: Vol. 6. Assessment of communication and language.* Baltimore: Paul H. Brookes Publishing Co.

Downing, J.E. (1996). *Assessing the school-age student with dual sensory and multiple impairments (age 6–15).* Columbus, OH: Great Lakes Area Regional Center on Deaf-Blindness.

Downing, J., & Bailey, B.R. (1990). Sharing the responsibility: Using a transdisciplinary team approach to enhance the learning of students with severe disabilities. *Journal of Educational and Psychological Consultation, 1,* 259–278.

Downing, J., & Perino, D.M. (1992). Functional versus standardized assessment procedures: Implications for educational programming. *Mental Retardation, 30,* 289–295.

Falvey, M.A. (1995). Communication skills. In M.A. Falvey (Ed.), *Inclusive and heterogeneous schooling: Assessment, curriculum, and instruction* (pp. 229–266). Baltimore: Paul H. Brookes Publishing Co.

Giangreco, M.F., Cloninger, C.J., & Iverson, V.S. (1998). *Choosing outcomes and accommodations for children (COACH): A guide to educational planning for students with disabilities* (2nd ed.). Baltimore: Paul H. Brookes Publishing Co.

Giangreco, M.F., Edelman, S.W., Luiselli, T.E., & MacFarland, S.Z.C. (1997). Helping or hovering? Effects of instructional assistant proximity on students with disabilities. *Exceptional Children, 64,* 7–17.

Gothelf, C.R., Woolf, S.B., & Crimmins, D.B. (1995). Transition to adult life: The transition process. In K.M. Huebner, E. Joffee, J.G. Prickett, & T.R. Welch (Eds.), *Hand in hand: Vol. 1. Essentials of communication and orientation and mobility for your students who are deaf-blind* (pp. 446–463). New York: American Foundation for the Blind Press.

Guess, D., & Helmstetter, E. (1986). Skill cluster instruction and the individualized curriculum sequencing model. In R.H. Horner, L.H. Meyer, & H.D.B. Fredericks (Eds.), *Education of learners with severe handicaps: Exemplary service strategies* (pp. 221–248). Baltimore: Paul H. Brookes Publishing Co.

Hanson, M.J., Lynch, E.W., & Wayman, K.I. (1990). Honoring the cultural diversity of families when gathering data. *Topics in Early Childhood Special Education, 10,* 112–131.

Houghton, J., Bronicki, G.J., & Guess, D. (1987). Opportunities to express preferences and make choices among students with severe disabilities in classroom settings. *Journal of The Association for Persons with Severe Handicaps, 12,* 18–27.

Hunt, P., & Goetz, L. (1988). Teaching spontaneous communication in national settings through interrupted behavior chains. *Topics in Language Disorders, 9*(1), 58–71.

Kaiser, A.P., Hemmeter, M.L., Ostrosky, M.M., Fischer, R., Yoder, P., & Keefer, M. (1996). The effects of teaching parents to use responsive interaction strategies. *Topics in Early Childhood Special Education, 16,* 375–406.

Light, J. (1997). "Let's go fishing." Reflections on the contexts of language learning for children who use aided AAC. *Augmentative and Alternative Communication, 13,* 158–171.

Lynch, E.W., & Hanson, M.J. (1998). *Developing cross-cultural competence: A guide for working with children and their families.* Baltimore: Paul H. Brookes Publishing Co.

Mirenda, P. (1993). AAC: Bonding the uncertain mosaic. *Augmentative and Alternative Communication, 9,* 3–9.

Mirenda, P., Iacono, T., & Williams, R. (1990). Communication options for persons with severe and profound disabilities: State of the art and future directions. *Journal of The Association for Persons with Severe Handicaps, 15,* 3–21.

Neill, M., & Medina, N. (1989). Standardized testing: Harmful to educational health. *Phi Delta Kappan, 70,* 688–697.

Notari, A., Cole, K.N., & Mills, P.E. (1992). Facilitating cognitive and language skills of young children with disabilities: The mediated learning process. *International Journal of Cognitive Education, 2,* 169–179.

Orelove, F.P., & Sobsey, D. (1996). Designing transdisciplinary services. In F.P. Orelove & D. Sobsey (Eds.), *Educating children with multiple disabilities: A transdisciplinary approach* (3rd ed., pp. 1–33). Baltimore: Paul H. Brookes Publishing Co.

Parette, H.P. (1995). Augmentative and alternative communication (AAC) assessment and prescriptive practices for young children with disabilities: Preliminary examination of state practices. *Technology and Disability, 4,* 215–231.

Reichle, J. (1997). Communication intervention with persons who have severe disabilities. *The Journal of Special Education, 31*(1), 110–134.

Reichle, J., & Sigafoos, J. (1991). Establishing spontaneity and generalization. In J. Reichle, J. York, & J. Sigafoos (Eds.), *Implementing augmentative and alternative communication: Strategies for learners with severe disabilities* (pp. 157–171). Baltimore: Paul H. Brookes Publishing Co.

Romski, M., Sevcik, R., & Pate, J. (1988). Establishment of symbolic communication in persons with severe retardation. *Journal of Speech and Hearing Disorders, 53,* 94–107.

Rowland, C., Schweigert, P., & Stremel, K. (1992). *Observing and enhancing communication skills.* Tucson, AZ: Communication Skill Builders.

Siegel-Causey, E., & Downing, J. (1987). Nonsymbolic communication development: Theoretical concepts and educational strategies. In L. Goetz, D. Guess, & K. Stremel-Campbell (Eds.), *Innovative program design for individuals with dual sensory impairments* (pp. 15–48). Baltimore: Paul H. Brookes Publishing Co.

Siegel-Causey, E., & Wetherby, A. (1993). Nonsymbolic communication. In M.E. Snell (Ed.), *Instruction of students with severe disabilities* (4th ed., pp. 290–318). New York: Merrill Publishing.

Sigafoos, J., & York, J. (1991). Using ecological inventories to promote functional communication. In J. Reichle, J. York, & J. Sigafoos (Eds.), *Implementing augmentative and alternative communication: Strategies for learners with severe disabilities* (pp. 61–70). Baltimore: Paul H. Brookes Publishing Co.

Soto, G., Huer, M.B., & Taylor, O. (1997). Multicultural issues. In L. Lloyd, D. Fuller, & H. Arvidson (Eds.), *Augmentative and alternative communication: A handbook of principles and practices* (pp. 406–413). Needham Heights, MA: Allyn & Bacon.

Walden, T.A., Blackford, J.U., & Carpenter, K.L. (1997). Differences in social signals produced by children with developmental disabilities of differing etiologies. *American Journal of Mental Retardation, 102,* 292–305.

Yoder, D., & Munson, L. (1995). The social correlates of co-ordinated attention to adult and objects in mother-infant interaction. *First Language, 15,* 219–230.

Yoder, D., Warren, S., Kim, K., & Gazdag, G. (1994). Facilitating prelinguistic communication skills in young children with developmental delay. II: Replication and extension. *Journal of Speech and Hearing Research, 37,* 841–851.

3

Analyzing the
Communicative Environment

Experts in communication intervention stress the value of teaching communication skills in general education classrooms where students with severe disabilities have the support of their peer role models (Calculator, 1988; Calculator & Jorgensen, 1994; Janney & Snell, 1996; Lamorey & Bricker, 1993; Mirenda, 1993). These students are generally facile at communicating and interacting socially, so opportunities for the student with disabilities to practice such skills should be plentiful.

Because communication requires at least two people, it is just as important to assess the social environment of the student as it is to assess the communication skills of the student. Although the importance of the environment on a student's communication skills is stated in Chapter 2, this chapter takes a closer look at different environments in which students with severe disabilities who are full-time members of general education classrooms will likely find themselves. Social-communicative expectations and opportunities in these environments will determine, to a large extent, what skills the student will need to acquire. Recognizing the complexities of these environments will facilitate our efforts to help students with severe disabilities become actively involved in many different social situations at school.

WHAT'S HAPPENING IN SCHOOL ENVIRONMENTS?

Students engage in several different social and learning activities throughout each school day. Because the variables controlling interactions change continually, it is difficult to target communication skills. Teachers, speech-language pathologists (SLPs), and paraeducators have little control over who will say what to whom and at what time and speed. Somehow students with disabilities must learn to communicate spontaneously without being overly dependent on stable environmental cues. To do this, they must generalize information acquired from one social situation to the next.

Some interactions are relatively stable over time and provide greater opportunities for practicing communication skills given similar cues. For instance, at lunchtime Sharon, an elementary school student, goes through the lunch line and will be asked by a cafeteria worker what kind of milk she wants—white or chocolate. The time of day, environment, cafeteria worker, and phrasing of the question may remain relatively constant from day to day. Sharon can use familiar environmental cues to help anticipate what will be asked of her and what response will be expected. Similarly, the football coach always greets John, who is ball manager, with a nudge to the shoulder and the verbal cue, "How's it going?" The consistency of initiation by a given individual at a certain time and place helps John remember to respond by turning toward the coach and touching him in return.

The majority of interactions, however, will be much less consistent. Students will ask different questions at different times (e.g., "What did you do last night?" "Where do you want to eat lunch?" "Wanna play ball?"). They will greet each other with different comments (e.g., "Hey, did you watch *Friends* last night?" "Got any food? I'm starving!" "You coming to my house tonight?"). Topics of conversation will change constantly throughout the day and with amazing rapidity. Cues from consistent interaction patterns as mentioned in the previous paragraph are not possible, and this lack of predictable cues can be quite challenging for students with severe disabilities. To help students interact successfully, teachers must first recognize the challenge and then intervene accordingly.

To help determine what vocabulary and general communication skills are needed by students with moderate or severe disabilities, teachers need to pay particular attention to typical interactions by the student's peers. Children talk about different things in different ways at different ages. Those responsible for helping a student acquire appropriate communication skills must be familiar with how typical students converse, taking into consideration cultural, gender, and age influences. Without this information, alternative communication modes may appear more artificial than they need to be. Haring, Haring, Breen, Romer, and White (1995) warned against teaching predetermined social skills without consideration of students' interests and preferences, typical student activities, and opportunities for students to interact. Information obtained from the natural communicative environment will help teachers and other team members to focus on the skills that are most relevant and important for helping the student become a true member of the class.

GATHERING INFORMATION

Gathering information on the communication opportunities that exist across different school environments needs to be simple and efficient. Most teachers have extremely limited time to document student progress, let alone the students' learning opportunities. At the most basic level, just becoming aware of when interactions occur could be very helpful. All members of the educational team could do this, incidentally, throughout the day and then share the information. Interactions occur between students, students and teachers (including support staff), students and the principal, students and cafeteria workers, students and playground monitors, and many others. All will vary somewhat in content, tone, duration, complexity, and purpose, which need to be considered. Some interactions will make use of a student's nonsymbolic communication (e.g., when children look and smile to convey a greeting), whereas other interactions will necessitate the use of more symbolic modes (e.g., sharing information about what happened over the weekend with a friend). Recognizing what forms of communication are used by students without disabilities in different situations will help determine how a particular student will need assistance. In addition, this kind of information gathering will help alleviate over-adapting for the student (e.g., not using pictorial symbols for YES and NO when the student consistently uses a head shake and nod). Certain tools are specifically designed to capture the communication potential of a given environment. For example, Rowland and Schweigert (1993) developed an assessment procedure called ACE (Analyzing the Communication Environment). ACE is designed to identify communication opportunities for students with severe disabilities across typical environments and activities. This tool has 52 statements divided into six parts that look at 1) the activity itself, 2) the student's present form of communication, 3) adult interactions, 4) group dynamics, 5) type of materials being used, and 6) specific opportunities for communication. The last section of this inventory, which is designed to record specific opportunities for communication, is based on the different functions of communication, such as requesting, commenting, and protesting.

The Educational Assessment of Social Interaction (EASI) Scale is a tool that can be used to measure the interactions between students with and without severe disabilities (Haring, Anderson, & Goetz, 1983). Interaction data provide information on initiations made by those with severe disabilities to others without disabilities, initiations by others to the individual with disabilities, interactions that involve both initiations and a response, and the type of interaction (whether social or task related). This tool also collects information on the number of interactions and the availability of communication partners in a particular environment. When this tool is used to collect information on interactions between individuals without disabilities, the information can be compared with information on interactions between individuals with and without disabilities. Such a comparison can highlight discrepancies for students with severe disabilities that should be addressed to help support interactions. Although originally used in school settings, this tool has been adapted to accommodate different social situations, such as interactions between co-workers with and without severe disabilities (Lee, Storey, Anderson, Goetz, & Zivolich, 1997).

The Social Contact Assessment Form (SCAF), developed by Kennedy and Itkonen (1994), is an activity-based measurement tool that gathers information concerning a student's social contacts at school. The number of social contacts a student has, where and when they occur, with whom, and the perceived quality of the interactions are all recorded using direct observation. Kennedy and Itkonen used this form to determine social networks of high school students with severe disabilities and their peers without disabilities.

Although formal tools can be used, information collected informally via observation can be just as helpful. Anecdotal information gleaned from conversations by others (e.g., what captured the interest of preschoolers, topics that occurred at lunch in the high school cafeteria) also contribute significantly to the understanding of the social climate and environment of the student with disabilities. Identifying when and where students are likely to interact is also the result of such informal observation.

Typical Language Samples

Language samples of interactions between students without severe communication disabilities can serve as a basis for the vocabulary needs of students with these types of disabilities. Samples need to be obtained across different situations per age group because what students talk about and how they talk will vary by situation. Actual ecological investigations of student conversation are necessary because it appears that professionals are not able to accurately predict conversational topics (Balandin & Iacono, 1998a). Situations that need to be sampled include all academic subjects or classes, recess or breaks, lunch, time in the hall between classes, and special activities (e.g., art, music, band, physical education).

The importance of obtaining a language sample of typical same-age peers as part of the assessment process cannot be overstated. Knowing what peers without disabilities say and how they say it will be of great assistance when developing augmentative communicative devices, if needed (see Chapter 6), and encouraging the student with severe disabilities to use specific spoken words. It is imperative that students with severe disabilities be given the option to "sound" like their peers and not like the adults who serve them. Although peers' input can be extremely helpful in the decision-making process of what symbols to use and what they should say, obtaining actual language samples can provide even more information.

Language samples of peers clearly indicate the vocabulary used by different-age students in different situations. The greater the diversity of samples obtained, the more useful the information. How students express themselves and relate to each other is very important information as it strongly affects what printed or spoken words will be incorporated into the augmentative communication device (Balandin & Iacono, 1998b; Beukelman & Mirenda, 1998). Language samples provide specific examples of how students gain each others' attention, introduce different topics, tease, and, in general, socially interact. For example, young children may greet each other with "Hey," or "Hi," or just by exchanging eye contact, while older students may use "Yo—What's happening?" or a topic introducer, such as, "Hey, saw ya with Elaine last night." Not only the specific vocabulary but also the phraseology is important, so that the student being supported via augmentative communication can sound as much like the peer group as possible.

Although adults may wish students to use proper English grammar and speak in complete sentences, students often do not do this; therefore, to devise an augmentative communication device that gives print or voice output in complete sentences can appear very stilted and unnatural. For example, students without disabilities are not likely to say, "Do you want to come to my house after school today?" Instead, an abbreviated version of this question may be "Comin' to my house today?" Obviously, individual style, age, geographic region, and peer group will play a major role in how students use language.

Cultural differences, which may go unnoticed using traditional assessment procedures, can also be noted with language samples. Family members, especially siblings who are close in age to the student having severe disabilities, can be particularly helpful in making sure that alternative means of communication do not violate cultural mores or preferences. Certain words have very different meanings than what an adult may have assigned them. Although the use of an interpreter is critical, direct translations are not always possible or semantically equivalent (Fradd & Wilen, 1990). Particular care must be taken, therefore, to ensure that what was said and how it was said in one language is accurately understood in another. Obtaining language samples of non–English speakers will require the observer to be fluent not only with the language spoken but also with the culture of the speakers in order to analyze how the individuals interact (using dialects, culturally bound gestures, idioms) (Blackstone, 1993).

Obtaining Language Samples

Various individuals on the student's educational team can assist in obtaining language samples of peers. In fact, sharing this assignment is critical because the same adults are not always present in the various social environments. One adult may gather information on the unique discussions that occur between teenage girls talking in the restroom, while another may pick up quite different information from a science lab group. Both sources are important if we wish to help students with severe disabilities belong to different social groups in different situations.

Language samples do not need to be long to be helpful; short conversations between students can be very informative. The difficulty is in obtaining the information in a discreet manner that does not disrupt or influence the interaction. This kind of discretion is particularly difficult when the presence of an adult is not typical for the interaction (e.g., recess for fifth graders, walking in the halls or changing clothes for physical education in locker rooms for secondary students).

No teacher has the time to follow students around writing down every word they say. It might be possible to record conversations if students and their parents were willing, but this type of intrusion probably would affect what was said and how (especially for older students). Teachers and other team members, however, can be alert for conversations they do overhear. Just being aware of the importance of gearing augmentative communication intervention to reflect typical interactions between peers would be supportive of students' with disabilities right to belong. All educators have a responsibility to de-emphasize the differences experienced by these students, not accentuate them. In order to help students with severe disabilities fit in by developing augmentative communication devices and styles of interacting nonsymbolically that are age appropriate, it is important to be aware of how their peers interact. Tables 3.1–3.3 provide examples of information obtained from observing interactions between students without disabilities at different ages.

The kind of information that teachers and other team members are able to gather by observing the interactions of students without disabilities can be supplemented by direct input from the students themselves. The problem with this approach, however, is that students may not always be cognizant of their communicative behavior. A student, when asked how he or she greets another person, for example, may answer, "I just say, 'Hi,'" but

Table 3.1. Language sample of typical first graders

Activity: Snack and recess
Setting: Outside the classroom
Forms of communication: speech, facial expressions, eye contact, pointing, handling objects, physical proximity, natural gestures

Content	Functions/purposes
Talking about the snack	Requesting "Wanna trade?" "Can I have some?" Direct attention "Look what I've got!" Protesting "Hey! Someone took my lid!"
Requesting help	Requesting "Will you push me?" "Can you open this?"
Talking about clothes	Direct attention "Look at my new shoes!" Requesting information "Where'd you get them?" Commenting "I have shoes like that."

Table 3.2.   Language sample of typical sixth graders

Activity: Decorating the room
Setting: Leadership class
Forms of communication: speech, facial expressions, gestures/body
  language, eye contact, physical proximity

Content	Functions/purposes

About the dance	Social
	  "This is going to be fun!"
	
	Requesting information
	  "When's the next dance?"
	  "Can you hold the ladder?"

About school	Commenting
	  "This assignment is so hard!"
	
	Requesting information
	  "Do you have your math homework
	  done yet?"
	
	Confirming/denying
	  "Nah."

About other students	Making comments "Jeff really got in trouble in PE."

watching this same student greet may reveal something altogether different. For some interactions that are frequently and matter-of-factly done, as in the aforementioned example, individuals may be unaware of the actual topography of their behavior; consequently, observations in natural environments can be used to either support or supplement other information. Students without disabilities can provide information on what is important to be able to discuss across a variety of different situations. The closer the alternative means of communication matches the way that the student's peers communicate, the easier it is for students using these alternative means to feel a sense of belonging.

Table 3.3.   Language sample of typical ninth-grade girls

Activity: Interacting after lunch
Setting: Cafeteria
Forms of communication: speech, natural gestures, facial expressions,
  slapping shoulders, grabbing, handling objects

Content	Functions/purposes

Other students	Direct attention
	  "Hey, look at her!"
	
	Making comments
	  "I hate her, she's a _____ !"
	  "Oh my God, you should have seen
	  him!"

Food	Protesting "Stop it! You're getting it all over me!"

Make-up	Offer to share
	  "Here, try this color."
	
	Social
	  "That looks great on you!"

Family	Making comments "My mom was so pissed!"

IDENTIFYING NATURAL OPPORTUNITIES TO COMMUNICATE

Although communication is probably occurring almost continually throughout most school days, identifying natural opportunities to teach communication skills to students with severe disabilities may not always be obvious (Haring, Neetz, Lovinger, Peck, & Semmel, 1987; Schwartz, Anderson, & Halle, 1989; Sigafoos, Kerr, Roberts, & Conzens, 1994). Perhaps the difference in skill level among students with and without disabilities and the ordinarily fast pace of the general education environment make it difficult for teachers to recognize how to include basic communication skills training. Sigafoos and York (1991) suggested that a large number of communication opportunities may go unnoticed because learners with severe disabilities are given assistance before they have a chance to express themselves. Communication partners must be aware of how they interact so that they can modify their behavior if necessary. The questions offered in Table 3.4 provide some guidelines for the adult working with the student to consider.

Certainly, using the natural environment for intervention purposes will differ significantly from discrete trial work in highly specialized settings. Intervention will look more natural and will occur throughout each day as opportunities to address skills naturally emerge (Guess & Helmstetter, 1986). Rather than planning to work repetitively on isolated skills in a massed trial format (e.g., repeatedly asking a student to press the BIG-mack switch in order to get 30 seconds of toy play), the teacher must make use of naturally occurring opportunities as they present themselves throughout the day. It is imperative, then, that teachers be astute and flexible enough to recognize and take advantage of these opportunities.

Perhaps just as important as knowing when to teach communication is knowing when instruction is *not* appropriate. When the teacher expects students to listen to him or her during lectures or directions or to another student giving an oral report, working on communicative exchanges would probably be disruptive. Instead, the teacher could facilitate the students' listening skills (if the verbal information can be understood) or help the student learn to amuse him- or herself quietly by looking through a book or magazine; "doodling" quietly with a writing instrument; or fiddling with a rubber band,

Table 3.4.   Spontaneous problem solving or at-the-moment decision making

For every activity occurring in the classroom, the support provider can ask the following questions:

1. Can the student with disabilities interact with other students? with the teacher?
2. What can the student "say" about the activity? to whom?
    Request help, more information, materials, or a particular partner?
    Reject the activity or a part of it, or certain materials?
    Respond to simple yes/no questions?
    Respond to simple questions using graphic or tactile representations?
    Ask questions?
    Comment on whether the activity is fun or not?
3. Can the activity be modified slightly to allow for more communicative interactions?
    Partner learning?
    Cooperative learning?
    Small groups?
    Teams?
4. Can different students request material from the student with disabilities instead of getting it themselves?

Table 3.5.   Identifying communication opportunities

Potential communicative opportunities	Activities lacking communicative opportunities
Lunch	Sustained silent reading
Recess	Lecture
Time in the hall	Teacher giving directions
Cooperative learning groups	Test taking
Transitioning to activities/classes	Listening to announcements
Nutrition break	Student giving a report
Small group discussion	Watching student perform a skit
Grooming in the girls' restroom	Walking quietly in line
Working with a partner	Independent seat work

twisties, paperclips, or an age-appropriate squeezable item. Table 3.5 provides a list of potential opportunities for teaching communication skills as well as a list of activities that are not optimal for teaching communication skills.

The difficulty of shifting gears from a traditional approach of discrete trial training to teaching in the natural milieu of the general education classroom has been a focus of several researchers (Billingsley & Kelley, 1994; Cosden & Haring, 1992). The change in approach will necessitate that teachers and SLPs be trained in a different manner. They will need to feel comfortable sacrificing the kind of control they experience using a pull-out service delivery model for the advantage of teaching students in natural environments in which the problem of skill generalization is less of an issue. In general, teachers and support personnel may have to be taught how to "go with the flow."

The following examples assist in identifying teachable moments for communication for preschool through college students. Obviously, each situation will be different; however, highlighting a few examples for students at different ages may help others to identify similar opportunities in their respective environments. A condensed version of these examples can be found in Table 3.6. The matrix presented in this table provides a quick reference to the communicative opportunities that are possible across subject matter.

COMMUNICATION SKILLS ACROSS CLASSES AND SUBJECTS

Greetings and Farewells

Teaching students how to greet others and how to say goodbye provides them with basic social-communication skills that are fundamental for future interactions and for developing friendships. Students with disabilities may not initiate or respond to others' greetings or farewells. This lack of appropriate behavior fails to reinforce the interactions of others, who, as a result, may stop making the effort. Students with disabilities may need to learn to either initiate or respond to greetings or, perhaps, to do both.

Before instruction begins, teachers must know *how* students perform these kinds of communication skills. Students at different ages meet and leave friends in different ways. Teaching these skills in a certain way could end up violating subtle rules of social interaction between individuals. For example, teaching preschoolers to offer their hand to a peer, say hello, and then state their name would be most inappropriate. Preschoolers tend to greet each other by looking; approaching; and perhaps smiling or touching, or both. High school students, by contrast, nod their heads or exchange eye contact, give each other a unique handshake, or say, "Hey, man!" "Yo!" "What's happening?" "What's

Table 3.6.   Communication skills matrix for third-grade student

Communicative skills	Subjects			
	Daily oral language	Social studies	Math	Spelling
Rejecting	Says "no" to the activity Rejects certain pictures to illustrate sentence	Rejects one topic for another Rejects the offer of help from a peer	Rejects certain manipulatives for others Rejects the offer of help from a peer	Rejects one picture for another Rejects the offer of help from a peer
Confirming/ denying	Confirms or denies whether picture selected is the right one	Confirms or denies correct picture or photo to accompany peer's written sentence Confirms or denies that statements made by group are okay	Responds with "yes" or "no" if peer's answers are correct/incorrect States "yes" or "no" that manipulatives are needed	Responds "yes" or "no" to whether use of spelling word in sentence is good
Social interaction skills	Exchanges visual glances Smiles in response to a comment Teases others between activities Asks others to come talk	Exchanges visual glances Smiles in response to a comment Teases others between activities Asks others to come talk	Exchanges visual glances Smiles in response to a comment Teases others between activities Asks others to come talk	Exchanges visual glances Smiles in response to a comment Teases others between activities Asks others to come talk
Making comments	Decides on what picture goes best with the DOL sentence States whether the sentence is funny	Makes comments about topic of study Responds to direct questions from teachers/peers	States whether it is fun to do math or not	Decides which picture/item goes with each spelling word States whether sentence using word and written by poor is okay or not
Greetings/ departures	Beginning and end of school Beginning and end of each class (secondary) As new people enter a room Errands to the office	Beginning and end of school Beginning and end of each class (secondary) As new people enter a room Errands to the office	Beginning and end of school Beginning and end of each class (secondary) As new people enter a room Errands to the office	Beginning and end of school Beginning and end of each class (secondary) As new people enter a room Errands to the office
Sharing	Brings in sentence or topics using words/pictures or items for subject for DOL	Brings items or pictures related to unit of study and offers to others	Brings manipulatives to use in math with peers in cooperative group	Brings items or pictures related to spelling words to share
Requesting activity/items/ information	Asks for help during activity Asks for certain paper, pen, or pictures to do assignment	Chooses to do 1 activity over another Requests different writing materials Asks for help or more information	Asks for help to solve problems Asks for manipulatives to do math Asks whether problems are correct Asks for calculator	Requests that spelling end or continue Asks for another spelling word Asks for specific partner to work with

up?" "Hi" or "How's it shakin'?" Elementary students may greet by looking, waving, saying "Hi!" "Hey!" "What's up, dude?" giving high or low fives, or smiling and looking at one another. Clearly, how students greet one another will depend on personal style, distance from each other, and current accepted greeting by a particular membership group (e.g., clique).

Asking for Attention/Help

Students have different ways of asking for help, and it is typically not, "I want some help, please." Rather, teachers hear the following kinds of "requests:" "I can't do this!" "This is too hard!" "I don't get it." "Is this right?" Students may also raise their hands, scribble on their work, erase excessively, pout, sigh deeply, slump in their chairs, put their heads down on their work, or simply avoid the task. Although teachers may not want to teach their students with severe disabilities how to request help in some of the ways stated above, they need to be careful that they are not teaching these students to request help in a way that looks or sounds strange in comparison. The class as a whole, with the teacher's guidance, may agree on a preferred way to request help, and then all members of the class can engage in that behavior, not just the student with the disability. Often teachers prefer students to quietly raise their hands to request attention. This may be appropriate for all students as long as the motor requirements of the skill are within each student's capability. If not, the teacher (and class) should discuss exceptions to this general rule (e.g., everyone raises his or her hand except Brian who can use a BIGmack).

Comments of Approval and Rejection

Every age group or clique has unique and multiple ways of expressing both approval and interest and rejection, disgust, and dislike. Not only are there many different ways to express these sentiments but they also are very dynamic, changing according to situation and to the student's age; therefore, the student with severe disabilities will need to have multiple and age-appropriate ways to express the same meanings. Usually, students with severe disabilities do have at least one effective means of stating approval or disapproval of an activity, person, or item. As long as such communication falls within the range of acceptable behavior for the group, then the student will not need an alternative mode. For example, students without disabilities may frown, wrinkle up their noses in disgust, or shake their heads "no" to express rejection, so a student with a severe disability should be allowed to reject something in the same way and, therefore, would not need intervention for this particular function if the action is within his or her capabilities.

Social Closeness

A primary purpose of communication is to achieve social closeness with others (Light, 1997). How students accomplish this depends on age, gender, culture, and characteristics of those with whom they are communicating. Careful observation of what typical students do to achieve this kind of intimacy will assist teachers in helping students with severe disabilities in their efforts to attain social closeness. Admiring a classmate's new clothes or hairstyle can promote social closeness, as can sharing feelings about a teacher or event. Asking how someone is dealing with a difficult situation at home or school is another example of how students gain emotional closeness. Even when interventions cannot currently help a student to express some of these feelings or information, that student can still be on the receiving end and can thus provide emotional support to another in this way. The author knows several students who were told important secrets by their peers, implying that their peers found them trustworthy, perhaps because of their inability to relay the secret. The student with disabilities was not excluded from participating in an exchange considered important to other students, and such communication helped the student achieve a kind of closeness with her peers.

COMMUNICATIVE SKILLS SPECIFIC TO A CLASS OR AN ACTIVITY

Students will engage in some general communication skills across different environments and activities but will use more unique and situation-specific skills in particular circumstances. Students in a high school science class will use different vocabulary as compared with those in a middle school language arts class or a fifth-grade history lesson. How the teacher is conducting the lesson will also determine what kinds of communicative skills will be expected by each student, and communicative opportunities will depend on strategies, lesson content, expectations of the teacher, and seating arrangements. In general, students need to ask questions, respond to questions and directions by the teachers, share information, and request assistance. Words and phrases (as well as facial expressions and body gestures) used to meet such needs should be documented so that they can be taught to the student with severe disabilities and incorporated into the augmentative communication device if one is needed. Do students interrupt each other and shift rapidly, and is that okay with the group? How the teacher incorporates this information is important and will affect intervention strategies. The following examples are provided to highlight communication opportunities across different age groups.

Preschool Activities

Play is the work of preschoolers and offers wonderful opportunities to practice communication skills (Lifter & Bloom, 1998; Patterson & Westby, 1994; Rescorla & Goossens', 1992). During play, children interact socially to share toys, adopt pretend roles, test boundaries, experiment with words, and achieve social closeness. Pretend or dramatic play appears to be an important aspect of young children's development of language (Johnson, Christie, & Yawkey, 1987; Linder, 1999; Marvin & Hunt-Berg, 1995). Including students with severe disabilities in typical play activities has considerable merit; however, in order for the student to truly benefit, he or she must be actively involved in the play rather than merely sitting on the sideline. If a child with severe disabilities does not have the necessary skills to participate, he or she will need instructional support from teachers (Kontos, Moore, & Giorgetti, 1998). In order to provide that support, the teachers will need to analyze the play environment to determine how children interact and what the child with severe disabilities will need to participate in these interactions.

For example, when preschoolers play "train," they assume different roles (engineer, ticket collector, passenger), wear different outfits befitting their roles, ride in different cars (large boxes of different colors), make appropriate sounds ("choo choo"), and determine the train's itinerary. Sometimes children will use additional props, such as dolls to represent their "children," tool bags for repairs, or flashlights for headlamps. Students discuss and sometimes argue about what roles they will play, so the student with severe disabilities who may not communicate using speech will need an alternative system to aid in these interactions.

Playing with blocks is another common preschool activity in which children engage during free play or as a center activity. During block play, children decide what they will build (e.g., house, fort, castle, cave, zoo), where they intend to build, and what shape and color blocks they plan to use. They make ongoing decisions throughout the course of play regarding where certain blocks will go and what they will represent, and after completing the structure, they often select other toy items, such as small toy people, toy animals, or toy soldiers, to add to their building. At the onset of the play, opportunities exist for students to communicate a preference for building a certain structure, and during the course of pretend play, many opportunities exist for students to draw attention to what is being built, make comments, respond to peers, make requests, and reject what others are saying.

During water play, students stand around a water table and engage in both solitary and interactive play. Students pretend to water plants, sail boats, put out fires, pilot submarines, and participate in an entire range of imaginative play. Opportunities exist for students to gain each other's attention, direct that attention to a specific referent, request items from each other, reject a request from another, ask and respond to questions concerning the role, give directions about the play, make choices, and tease or joke.

Preschool children typically have a snack or lunch or both during the course of their school day. Eating is a highly pleasurable activity for several reasons, and certainly one of these reasons is the social interactions that usually accompany eating. This is an unstructured time in which children talk about their families and favorite toys or comment on each other's food items. Depending on the students' age and verbal skills, these interactions can be highly complex.

Students with severe disabilities can also engage in these same or similar communicative behaviors, but they will need to be taught how. They can make use of objects, facial expressions, gestures, and vocalizations. What they need as support will depend on the expectations of the activity and the abilities of the child to meet those social expectations.

Elementary Activities

During the elementary years, learning basic academics and general knowledge takes the place of play; however, communicative opportunities are still plentiful throughout the school day. In addition to the typically social periods of lunch and recess, students interact before and after school and to varying degrees during class time depending on how the teacher orchestrates the class.

Classrooms that encourage student interaction usually utilize different instructional groupings, such as cooperative learning, small-group instruction, buddy systems, and centers (Johnson & Johnson, 1991; Jubala, Bishop, & Falvey, 1995; Putnam, 1998). With these instructional arrangements, noise level is typically higher, interactions among students are expected, and greater flexibility is evidenced. Students are expected to help each other in completing assignments, which offers more opportunities for the student with severe disabilities to at least partially participate in the same activities. Making choices, expressing opinions and understanding comments made by others are just some of the skills that these students will be able to practice in these kinds of instructional settings.

For example, during a fifth-grade science class, students spend time discussing a chapter that was assigned on DNA. They respond to questions asked by the teacher, and then they work in pairs to replicate a DNA chain using building materials. Numerous opportunities exist for students to request assistance or information, make comments, share information, confirm or deny others' comments, and socially interact for fun. The student with severe disabilities has the same opportunities but will need certain accommodations to fully participate, such as access to different materials for object cues that the student can look at, point to, or reach for, and which can be used for both receptive and expressive purposes.

In a second-grade class, students work on their unit on Mexico. They have been learning about Mexican culture by reading stories of Mexican children. Some of the parents of children in the class have taught the students some Spanish and have shared information on Mexican customs, and several children have brought in items they have purchased from Mexico to share with their classmates. This lesson prompts students to label objects in Spanish, ask questions about the language and culture, share information, draw attention to various items that have been brought to class, confirm or deny information, and request assistance when learning Spanish words. In other words, the opportunities for both expressive and receptive communication among students and teachers are plentiful.

Middle School Activities

During the middle school years, students usually take a set of prescribed courses (often as a block with the same group of students) as well as one or more electives. The typically unstructured and highly social time formerly associated with recess may now be found during nutrition breaks, passing in halls, time spent changing clothes for physical education in locker rooms, and extracurricular activities. Both academic courses and the freer periods of the day allow for a variety of different interactions. Again, the manner in which teachers conduct their classes and their expectations for student interactions will determine to a great extent the amount and type of communicative interactions that are possible.

For a sixth-grade unit on saving the rainforest, students discuss what they have learned from the Internet, compose questions to ask each other, develop reports on different aspects of the rainforest, and make presentations to the classroom. As a field trip, they visit a restaurant whose interior simulates that of a rainforest. Communicative opportunities exist for students to request information, gain each other's attention, make comments, share information, and confirm or deny information obtained from others.

In a seventh-grade social studies class, the students work with partners to drill each other on different bits of information they have acquired and compiled as a group. The class is then divided into two teams to play a variation of the game Jeopardy, based on what they have learned. This game can be a bit noisy with teammates cheering for each other and keeping an eye on the score. Obviously, opportunities for both receptive and expressive communication skill development abound.

In an eighth-grade physical science class, students are learning about the Periodic Table and about molecules and molecular formulas. They are learning the names and formulas of simple compounds such as H_2O, CO_2, and HCl. Students work in groups to develop different parts of the Periodic Table. They share information, ask questions of each other, confirm or deny statements, request help from their teacher when needed, and make comments related to their interest in the task. Their interactions throughout the activity provide numerous opportunities for communication.

High School Activities

During high school, students typically spend different periods of each school day with different groups of students as their academic needs become more highly individualized. As in middle school, the less structured times of the day (e.g., lunch, passing in the halls, nutrition break, extracurricular activities) offer considerable opportunities to interact solely for social purposes. Of course, social interaction also takes place within classes, albeit for briefer periods of time.

In a twelfth-grade English class, for instance, students are expected to sit down at their desks, listen to roll being taken, and respond appropriately when their names are called. Often they are expected to read silently in their texts for the first 20 minutes of class, which means no interactions should occur. A class discussion frequently ensues regarding what was read, followed by an assignment. During the discussion, students are expected to contribute, respond to questions, and listen to their classmates as well as the teacher. If the assignment involves working as a part of a small group or with a partner, then peer interactions are expected. This interaction provides opportunities to request help, clarify information, make comments, and confirm or deny what is said. If students are asked to research a topic for a writing assignment individually, then interactions are kept at a minimum level, although there may be some interaction with a librarian.

In a driver's education class, students start the period by discussing the chapter assigned as homework the night before. Students respond individually to direct teacher questioning. The teacher then explains what is expected for the remainder of the period, which necessitates students to be quiet and listen. Students are allowed to work individually or in small groups of two or three to learn street signs for an upcoming test. If students decide to work in groups, communicative opportunities exist for students to ask questions, share information, confirm or deny information, and make jokes. Although the social skill of telling jokes is not the focus of the class, students do engage in such interactions. This class provides considerable opportunities to interact and work on communication skills.

Postsecondary Activities

Students with disabilities between the ages of 18 and 22 are still entitled to a free, appropriate public education by law; however, this does not mean that they need to remain at a high school campus. Teachers providing services to this group of students are best placed in the community at colleges, adult learning centers, places of employment, homes, or facilities that cater to volunteerism (McDonald, MacPherson-Court, Frank, Uditsky, & Symons, 1997; Thousand, Rosenberg, Bishop, & Villa, 1997). In all likelihood, the needs of students in this age range will call for continued learning in all of the community environments mentioned previously, and as such, opportunities for instruction in communication skills will be plentiful. The following examples should clarify this point.

At the city community college where some students with severe disabilities (ages 18–22) attend classes, the student union offers several opportunities to practice communication skills. An analysis of this environment reveals that students discuss classes, instructors, assignments, general news, movies, weather, sports, and special events. Interactions can be fleeting as students pass each other with a greeting on their way to class, or they can last for a substantial period of time as they discuss various topics. Within this social context, students share information, comment on topics, ask questions for clarification, request assistance finding a certain location, accept and reject invitations from others, and engage in conversation purely for social reasons. In addition, purchasing food or drink at the student union requires students to request items and respond to the cashier's request for money.

In this postsecondary program supported by the public school district, four students work in a local hospital, but in different departments to avoid a clustered approach. Students work in the laundry room, the cafeteria, the kitchen, and the gift shop. Employees typically greet each other at the beginning of their shifts and say goodbye at the end. Requests for some basic information are also common (e.g., "Did you run the dishwasher?" "Did you shelve those items?" "Can I get some more coffee, please?") and usually require a short response (yes or no) or a brief explanation (e.g., "Al told me to wait until I had more dishes"). Opportunities exist for brief social exchanges such as asking how a coworker is doing or whether he or she had a good weekend, but in general, employees do not engage in conversation for long periods of time as that would undoubtedly interfere with completing tasks. Employees may request assistance of each other or their supervisor, or ask what is expected once tasks are completed. When employees take breaks, especially lunch breaks, then they will participate in longer social exchanges, which greatly resemble those found at the student union. Employees may talk about movies, sports, upcoming events, the news, TV shows, their families, and items they plan to purchase. Opportunities exist for employees to ask questions, make comments, tell jokes, confirm or deny statements made by others, direct attention to a specific referent, and make requests, and skills needed to initiate and respond to conversational exchanges are apparent.

CREATING OPPORTUNITIES TO ENHANCE COMMUNICATIVE SKILLS DEVELOPMENT

When the typical school day fails to provide the requisite opportunities for a given student to practice skills, certain accommodations and modifications may be needed to make the environment more supportive of interactions for the student. For example, large-group instruction and independent seat work may be modified so that students spend more time in small-group instruction or in pairs. Rather than students engaging in silent sustained reading, for example, one student can read to another student, stopping to ask questions about the story or to confirm that the student still wants to be read to. In this way, opportunities to interact are possible during a time that would not otherwise have allowed these kinds of exchanges. More engaged time was noted for students with moderate, severe, and profound disabilities when they were instructed in more cooperative arrangements versus whole-group or independent instruction (Logan, Bakeman, & Keefe, 1997). In order for these interactions to be successful, potential communicative partners may need assistance in learning how to be more responsive to their classmate with severe disabilities. Many researchers have documented the importance of training peers without disabilities in order to facilitate the interactions of their classmates of varying ability levels (Hunt, Alwell, Farron-Davis, & Goetz, 1996; Janney & Snell, 1996; Romer, White, & Haring, 1996).

Environments that encourage individuals to interact frequently throughout the day offer greater opportunities to practice socio-communicative skills. Classrooms set up for independent seatwork for most of the day or class period (at any level) emphasize quiet performance by individual students at separate desks or study carrels and, as a result, prevent interactions between students. When students without disabilities, however, are encouraged to talk with their classmates with severe disabilities; ask questions of them; show them different items or finished products; and, in general, socialize with them, students with disabilities gain the opportunity to learn receptive and expressive communication skills. In general, when students without disabilities are encouraged to interact throughout the day with their peers with disabilities, they create small but frequent opportunities for their peers to practice critical communication skills.

Finally, analyzing teachers' communicative exchanges can often identify certain opportunities for students with severe disabilities to practice communication skills. Frequently, a teacher can assign a student to give instructions to the class as a whole, which allows all of the students, including the student with severe disabilities, to practice certain leadership skills. For example, a third-grade teacher always has her students line up to go to recess, lunch, physical education, music, and the library. Although she usually gives the direction to line up, this task can be given to a student with disabilities. The teacher asks the student to have the class line up, at which point the other students must wait patiently and listen attentively for the student to give the instruction, which she does using her BIGmack. The student enjoys this responsibility because she likes the control it gives her and she likes the teasing from her classmates when she keeps them waiting a bit. Of course, the teacher alternates and gives other students this role, so that the student with disabilities is not made to appear different.

SUMMARY

This chapter has focused on analyzing the natural environment for potential opportunities for students with severe disabilities to develop their communication skills. Different activities and environments have a profound influence on the types of communication expected, the frequency of communicative exchanges, and the availability of communication partners. Determining what is naturally available can help the educational team identify the most effective ways of providing support. Once a thorough analysis of the communicative environment has been made, including unique language and social behavior of different age groups, the educational team can then design specific strategies to help students acquire and apply different communication skills. Information provided in the following chapters addresses issues of intervention.

REFERENCES

Balandin, S., & Iacono, T. (1998a). A few well-chosen words. *Augmentative and Alternative Communication, 14*, 147–161.

Balandin, S., & Iacono, T. (1998b). Topics of meal-break conversation. *Augmentative and Alternative Communication, 14*, 131–146.

Beukelman, D.R., & Mirenda, P. (1998). *Augmentative and alternative communication: Management of severe communication disorders in children and adults* (2nd ed.). Baltimore: Paul H. Brookes Publishing Co.

Billingsley, F.F., & Kelley, B. (1994). An examination of the acceptability of instructional practices for students with severe disabilities in general educational settings. *Journal of The Association for Persons with Severe Handicaps, 19*, 75–83.

Blackstone, S. (1993). Clinical news: Cultural sensitivity and AAC services. *Augmentative Communication News, 6*(2), 3–10.

Calculator, S.N. (1988). Promoting the acquisition and generalization of conversational skills by individuals with severe disabilities. *Augmentative and Alternative Communication, 4*, 94–103.

Calculator, S.N., & Jorgensen, C.M. (1994). *Including students with severe disabilities in schools: Fostering communication, interaction, and participation.* San Diego, CA: Singular Publishing Group.

Cosden, M.A., & Haring, T.G. (1992). Cooperative learning in the classroom: Contingencies, group interactions, and students with special needs. *Journal of Behavioral Education, 2*, 53–71.

Fradd, S., & Wilen, D. (1990). *Using interpreters and translators to meet the needs of handicapped language minority students and their families.* Reston, VA: National Clearinghouse for Bilingual Education.

Guess, D., & Helmstetter, E. (1986). Skill cluster instruction and the individualized curriculum sequencing model. In R.H. Horner, L.H. Meyer, & H.D.B. Fredericks (Eds.), *Education of learners with severe handicaps: Exemplary service strategies* (pp. 221–248). Baltimore: Paul H. Brookes Publishing Co.

Haring, T., Anderson, J., & Goetz, L. (1983). *Educational assessment of social interactions (EASI): An observational checklist for measuring social interactions between nondisabled and severely disabled students in integrated settings.* San Francisco: San Francisco State University, San Francisco Unified School District. (ERIC Document Reproduction Service No. ED 242 184)

Haring, T., Haring, N.G., Breen, C., Romer, L.T., & White, J. (1995). Social relationships among students with deaf-blindness and their peers in inclusive settings. In N.G. Haring & L.T. Romer (Eds.), *Welcoming students who are deaf-blind into typical classrooms: Facilitating school participation, learning, and friendships* (pp. 231–247). Baltimore: Paul H. Brookes Publishing Co.

Haring, T.G., Neetz, J.A., Lovinger, L., Peck, C., & Semmel, M.I. (1987). Effects of four modified incidental teaching procedures to create opportunities for communication. *Journal of The Association for Persons with Severe Handicaps, 12*, 218–226.

Hunt, P., Alwell, M., Farron-Davis, F., & Goetz, L. (1996). Creating socially supportive environments for fully included students who experience multiple disabilities. *Journal of The Association for Persons with Severe Handicaps, 21,* 53–71.

Janney, R.E., & Snell, M.E. (1996). How teachers use peer interactions to include students with moderate and severe disabilities in elementary general education classes. *Journal of The Association for Persons with Severe Handicaps, 21,* 72–80.

Johnson, J., Christie, J., & Yawkey, T. (1987). *Play and early childhood development.* Glenview, IL: Scott, Foresman.

Johnson, D.W., & Johnson, R.T. (1991). *Cooperative learning lesson structures.* Edina, MN: Interaction Book Company.

Jubala, K.A., Bishop, K.D., & Falvey, M.A. (1995). Creating a supportive classroom environment. In M. Falvey (Ed.), *Inclusive and heterogeneous schooling: Assessment, curriculum, and instruction* (pp. 111–129). Baltimore: Paul H. Brookes Publishing Co.

Kennedy, C.H., & Itkonen, T. (1994). Some effects of regular class participation on the social contacts and social networks of high school students with severe disabilities. *Journal of The Association for Persons with Severe Handicaps, 19,* 1–10.

Kontos, S., Moore, D., & Giorgetti, K. (1998). The ecology of inclusion. *Topics in Early Childhood Special Education, 18,* 38–48.

Lamorey, S., & Bricker, D.D. (1993). Integrated programs: Effects on young children and their parents. In C.A. Peck, S.L. Odom, & D.D. Bricker (Eds.), *Integrating young children with disabilities into community programs* (pp. 249–270). Baltimore: Paul H. Brookes Publishing Co.

Lee, M., Storey, K., Anderson, J.L., Goetz, L., & Zivolich, S. (1997). The effect of mentoring versus job coach instruction on integration in supported employment settings. *Journal of The Association for Persons with Severe Handicaps, 22,* 151–158.

Litter, K., & Bloom, L. (1998). Intentionality and the role of play in the transition to language. In S.F. Warren & J. Reichle (Series Eds.) & A.M. Wetherby, S.F. Warren, & J. Reichle (Vol. Eds.), *Communication and language intervention series: Vol. 7. Transitions in prelinguistic communication* (pp. 161–195). Baltimore: Paul H. Brookes Publishing Co.

Light, J. (1997). "Communication is the essence of human life": Reflections on communicative competence. *Augmentative and Alternative Communication, 13,* 61–70.

Linder, T.W. (1999). *Read, Play, and Learn!: Storybook activities for young children. Teacher's guide.* Baltimore: Paul H. Brookes Publishing Co.

Logan, K.R., Bakeman, R., & Keefe, E.B. (1997). Effects of instructional variables on engaged behavior of students with disabilities in general education classrooms. *Exceptional Children, 63,* 481–498.

Marvin, C., & Hunt Berg, M. (1995). Let's pretend: A semantic analysis of preschool children's play. *Journal of Children's Communication Development, 17*(2), 1–10.

McDonald, L., MacPherson-Court, L., Frank, S., Uditsky, B., & Symons, F. (1997). An inclusive university program for students with moderate to severe developmental disabilities: Student, parent, and faculty perspectives. *Developmental Disabilities Bulletin, 25*(1), 43–67.

Mirenda, P. (1993). AAC: Bonding the uncertain mosaic. *Augmentative and Alternative Communication, 9,* 3–9.

Patterson, J., & Westby, C. (1994). The development of play. In W. Haynes & B. Shulman (Eds.), *Communication development: Foundations, processes and clinical applications* (pp. 94–133). Englewood Cliffs, NJ: Prentice-Hall.

Putnam, J.W. (1998). *Cooperative learning and strategies for inclusion: Celebrating diversity in the classroom* (2nd ed.). Baltimore: Paul H. Brookes Publishing Co.

Rescorla, L., & Goossens', M. (1992). Symbolic play development in toddlers with expressive language impairment. *Journal of Speech and Hearing Research, 35,* 1290–1302.

Romer, L.T., White, J., & Haring, N.G. (1996). The effect of peer mediated social competency training on the type and frequency of social contacts with students with deaf-blindness. *Education and Training in Mental Retardation and Developmental Disabilities, 31,* 324–338.

Rowland, C., & Schweigert, P. (1993). *Analyzing the communication environment: An inventory of ways to encourage communication in functional activities.* Tucson, AZ: Communication Skill Builders.

Schwartz, I.S., Anderson, S.R., & Halle, J.W. (1989). Training teachers to use naturalistic time delay: Effects on teacher behavior and on the language use of students. *Journal of The Association for Persons with Severe Handicaps, 14,* 48–57.

Sigafoos, J., Kerr, M., Roberts, D., & Conzens, D. (1994). Increasing opportunities for requesting in classrooms serving children with developmental disabilities. *Journal of Autism and Developmental Disabilities, 24,* 631–645.

Sigafoos, J., & York, J. (1991). Using ecological inventories to promote functional communication. In J. Reichle, J. York, & J. Sigafoos (Eds.), *Implementing augmentative and alternative communication: Strategies for learners with severe disabilities* (pp. 61–70). Baltimore: Paul H. Brookes Publishing Co.

Thousand, J., Rosenberg, R.L., Bishop, K.D., & Villa, R.A. (1997). The evolution of secondary inclusion. *Remedial and Special Education, 18,* 270–284.

4

Teaching Communication Skills

First Steps

Building on the previous three chapters, this chapter describes ways of assisting students with severe disabilities to understand others and to communicate their thoughts. Initial steps focus on understanding the role of the communication partner, utilizing natural contexts, creating the need to communicate, and motivating the student to communicate. Suggestions for shaping new communicative behaviors as they are needed within general education classroom activities are also described. Examples highlight ways for teachers to address communication skills during general education activities for all age groups.

STARTING OUT

Assessing a student's communication skills and needs is the first step in any communication intervention. A functional-ecological process of assessment that minimizes the possibility of misinterpreting results and helps to clarify educational goals and objectives is described in Chapter 2. An effective intervention builds on the skills a student already has. Determining which communication skills to teach will depend on the demands of the environment and the needs of the student within that environment (see Chapter 3). Motivating the student to learn to communicate effectively is less problematic when intervention addresses the specific needs and desires of a student within a given setting and situation.

ELICITING COMMUNICATIVE BEHAVIOR: GENERAL CONSIDERATIONS

Given the limited means by which many students with severe disabilities are able to communicate, much of the responsibility for an effective interaction falls on the communication partner (Bedrosian, 1997; Sevcik, Romski, Watkins, & Deffebach, 1995). The communication partner (whether adult or child) must, therefore, be fairly astute at recognizing potential communication interactions and supporting their development (Downing, 1993; Downing & Siegel-Causey, 1988; Sienkiewics-Mercer & Kaplan, 1989). In general, responsive communication partners must be aware of and engage in ways to facilitate the communicative efforts of their partner. In order to facilitate communication, the responsive communication partner increases proximity to the student, positions him- or herself at eye level, looks expectantly to encourage participation, accepts the student's current communicative modes, waits for the student to initiate or respond, is less directive, and confirms that the student has a way to express him- or herself. Because students with moderate or severe disabilities often do not possess such skills, it is necessary for peers without disabilities to serve in this capacity.

Gaining Proximity

Increasing proximity is a typical way to gain another's attention and to nonverbally communicate the intent to interact. This strategy is particularly important for students with severe disabilities who may not respond to more subtle attention-getting devices; furthermore, students who have sensory impairments, especially a severe visual impairment, will need close proximity to perceive that communication is expected and intended. Students whose disabilities physically prevent them from moving closer to a potential communication partner will need others to assume responsibility for decreasing the distance (see Figure 4.1). For example, after lunch at Taft High School, students mingle socially until the bell rings and then they go to their next classes. James has severe physi-

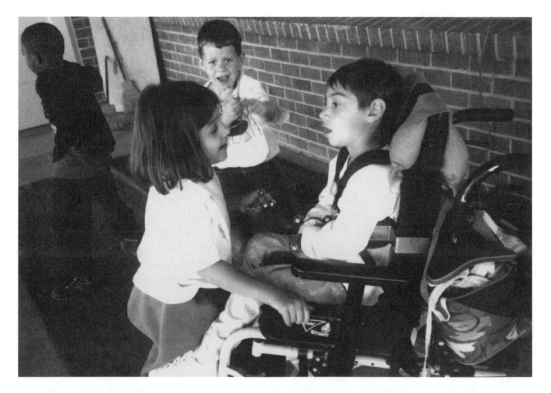

Figure 4.1.   A peer increases proximity to her classmate with disabilities to facilitate an interaction. (Photographer: Margo Taylor)

cal disabilities, which require him to use a wheelchair, and in order to move, he needs assistance from another person. The adult supporting him—teacher, paraeducator, or speech-language pathologist (SLP)—lets other students know that he is finished eating and that they can help him move to another location if he would like. These adults encourage the students to sit near James rather than stand over him, they explain his means of communication if the students are unfamiliar with them, and then they fade by moving out of close proximity. At the high school level, an adult remaining in close proximity to a student with disabilities may actually decrease the student's interactions with others (Giangreco, Edelman, Luiselli, & MacFarland, 1997). It is imperative that the adult interested in facilitating a student's communication be aware of this unwanted side effect.

Establishing Eye Contact

Because eye contact is a critical way to both obtain and maintain conversation, increasing the probability for eye contact is essential. Conversation partners of students using wheelchairs will need to sit down near the student to achieve and maintain eye contact. Adults trying to communicate with young children will need to squat, kneel, or sit on a low chair or on the floor to be at eye level. If an activity requires students to sit on the floor, students who use wheelchairs will need an adapted chair that allows them to sit at the level of other students. Students with very limited or no useable vision may need a touch on the arm or shoulder to take the place of eye contact, and some individuals who have no vision or hearing may prefer to maintain some physical contact during an entire interaction, not just during the initiation stage. Tactile signing provides such contact. For those who do not understand tactile signs, some form of mutual physical contact, such as touching hands or arms, can give them the same sense of connection that eye contact gives, thereby encouraging them to maintain the interaction.

Although eye contact helps facilitate communication, teachers should not require a student to establish eye contact without a meaningful reason for doing so (e.g., if information is being given, if conversation is to occur). Because looking directly into someone's eyes for several seconds without any reason to do so can be extremely uncomfortable, there is little sense to such instruction. The object of communication is not to force compliance (Guess & Siegel-Causey, 1985, Lovett, 1996) but to gain and maintain attention during a conversation. Depending on the purpose of the interaction, the topic of conversation, and the cultural mores of the participants, eye contact is attained quickly in an attempt to initiate communication, and conversants do not spend a lengthy amount of time gazing into each other's eyes. In fact, in some cultures, sustained eye contact can be interpreted negatively and is not desired.

Looking Expectant

If a student has useable vision, the most natural cue for the student to communicate is a facial expression from the conversation partner that communicates a sense of expectation, that says, "I'm waiting for you to say something." Looking as if we expect the student to respond to a query or to initiate a topic can be a powerful cue to the student to do something (MacDonald & Gillette, 1986). The student's response may need to be shaped into some communicative interaction that is more conventional, but any effort on the part of the student to engage in a communicative exchange should be encouraged.

If the student has no vision, maintaining a close proximity to the student without anticipating every communicative interaction can serve the same function as looking expectant. The feeling that something should be happening and isn't cues the student to break the silence and start the interaction. For example, Kasey, a 12-year-old, will push on the arm of her sighted guide when she knows that person is present but is not initiating an interaction.

Accepting and Respecting Current Modes of Communication

One very important role of the communication partner is to recognize, accept, and respect the student's present way of communicating. Ignoring how the student is communicating, especially if the communicative behavior is aggressive, will not help the student. If a student has succeeded in communicating his or her desires, even if the form of communication does not meet with social conventions, to suddenly ignore or prevent such behavior places the student in a very difficult situation. If anything, the student will probably try harder to get his or her needs met, which usually increases undesirable behavior (Carr & Durand, 1985; Durand & Carr, 1991).

Although a student's intent to communicate, however unconventional or undesirable, needs to be acknowledged, the student still needs an appropriate way to communicate. The teacher can try to teach appropriate forms of communication prior to the expression of undesirable ones or can consistently pair an appropriate form of communication with the unconventional one until the student learns that the new behavior is just as effective as the old. Researchers claim that the new behavior must be as efficient as the former one, requiring the same amount or less effort to meet the same needs (Carr, 1988; Horner & Billingsley, 1988; Horner, Sprague, O'Brien, & Heathfield, 1990; Reichle, Feeley, & Johnston, 1993). If it is more difficult to engage in the desired behavior, then the student will probably revert to the former mode of expression. For example, if a student with disabilities, Joey, effectively gains the attention he needs by biting his arm, he will probably not exert the effort to pull out a pictorial communication book and flip through some pages to find a graphically designed symbol for "come see me." Instead, he must have ready access to this symbol without much thought on his part. A bright yellow symbol attached to a wrist sweatband that he wears might be effective, especially if it is worn where he tends to bite himself. He just needs to touch it or lift it off the band if velcroed, and that action signifies that he wants to gain someone's attention. Of course, in order for the shift in communicative modes to succeed, someone must come immediately and offer the attention he needs.

Teachers must also pay close attention to the communicative efforts of students who exhibit vague or minimal potential communicative behavior for ignoring these efforts to communicate could extinguish them. Unfortunately, Houghton, Bronicki, and Guess (1987) found that direct services providers often failed to recognize students' attempts to communicate. Obviously, students with very limited means to communicate need their attempts recognized and supported so that they may be encouraged to continue to communicate. For example, Danny, a preschooler, makes a slight movement during a circle-time activity involving students moving to music. The SLP supporting him says, "Oh, you'd like to move to the music? Okay," and helps him move his body in as close an approximation to what other students are doing as possible. She'll do this for a minute or two and then wait for him to signal his interest in participating again. In this way, she strikes a good balance between recognizing his attempts to communicate and providing a need for him to continue communicating, both of which are extremely reinforcing.

De-emphasizing Symbolic Communication

When students with severe disabilities do not or cannot use speech, teachers (and parents) may feel pressured to supply these students with a replacement symbolic system, yet these students may have a fairly efficient system of nonsymbolic communication modes that merits attention. With literature suggesting that 65% or more of the message of any communication interaction occurs nonsymbolically (Birdwhistell, 1955; Evans, Hearn, Uhlemann, & Ivey, 1984), teachers should value what the student's present forms of communication are (albeit, nonsymbolic) and build on this communicative foundation. For example, Alberto, a third grader, grabs people and pulls them to different objects that represent activities in which he wants to participate. This behavior clearly communicates his desires to others; however, this method works only when the desired object is present. In addition, this communicative behavior can be quite disruptive to others and to the communicative partner; consequently, Alberto was taught to tap others on the shoulder and lead them rather than grabbing them and dragging them after him. In addition, he is given several representative objects that he keeps in a small box in his desk that he can use to indicate what he wants.

An excessive focus on getting the student to communicate using abstract symbols without an equal (or even greater) focus on the student's use of objects, gestures, facial expressions, and vocalizations could frustrate the student and make progress difficult. Because nonsymbolic communication may be easier to shape, overlooking this manner of communicating would not be effective. In fact, even highly skilled augmentative communication users rely on and often prefer nonsymbolic communication means such as facial expressions and gestures (Murphy, Markova, Moodie, Scott, & Bon, 1995). Furthermore, Beukelman (1991) advised that the focus of communicative interventions should be on helping people communicate effectively, not on teaching them to use technology per se.

Providing Wait Time

Waiting for a student to respond can be one of the most effective strategies to elicit a desired response (Glennen & Calculator, 1985; Halle, Marshall, & Spradlin, 1979; Schwartz, Anderson, & Halle, 1989). Of course, the response must already be within the student's behavioral repertoire, otherwise, waiting for an unknown behavior to occur would be pointless. Most of us, however, intervene before students have had sufficient time within which to formulate responses. In a culture for which such a lapse in time between interactions is unusual, providing sufficient time for a student with severe disabilities to respond can be quite challenging. Typically, delays between conversants are less than 3 seconds (Reichle, 1991), yet speeding up the conversation by inserting a direct question, stating a command, or giving the desired response will prohibit the student's ability to respond to natural cues (e.g., communicating based on a real need or desire rather than in response to a direct question).

Several researchers have demonstrated the effectiveness of waiting for a student to respond or initiate an interaction (Glennen & Calculator, 1985; Halle et al., 1979; McDonnell, 1987). Usually this technique is paired with other strategies, such as a mand-model or indirect verbal prompts to help the student learn the expected behavior. The actual delay will depend on the situation as well as the student's physical, sensory, and intellectual abilities. For each student the length of the pause should be based on the student's average delay between a given stimulus and response. Of course, when students are motivated, the delay time for their responses is much shorter. For instance, Patrick will often not respond regardless of the partner's proximity, expectant looks, or wait time if he is staring at the class aquarium, which he enjoys very much; however, if his view of the aquarium is blocked by an adult who stands in his view of the aquarium, Patrick will initiate an interaction by pushing the adult, which is interpreted to mean, "Get out of my way!" Obviously, Patrick needs very little wait time to respond in this particular situation. At the same time, this example makes it clear that Patrick needs an alternative way to make this request other than pushing.

When motivation to respond is not as great as in the example above, then providing sufficient wait time becomes a critical component of teaching communication skills. The following dialogue between a fourth grader and his teacher illustrates the problems that result for the student when the teacher fails to provide appropriate wait time.

Teacher: Who do you want to work with? Anthony? If you want to work with Anthony, look at him. Okay. Look at Anthony.

Roger: [Starts to lift his head up to look at Anthony]

Teacher: Anthony, push Roger over to your group. Good. Now ask Roger what materials he wants to use. Do it like this. [Holds up some crepe paper, cotton, and bits of fabric] What do you want, Roger? Look at what you want. [Turns to Anthony] Anthony, if he doesn't look right away, ask again.

Roger: [Starts to raise his head]

Teacher: Okay, I'm going to check on some other kids. Got everything you need? [Looks at Roger] Okay, then get to work.

In this example, not only does the teacher fail to give Roger, who has significant physical and intellectual challenges, sufficient time to respond to her or initiate a topic but she also completely directs the interaction. Her use of a classmate to work with Roger is good, but she fails to give either student the support they may need to be effective co-workers. These types of interactions tend to occur because the teacher feels rushed throughout the day to cover all that was planned. Teachers who feel compelled to rush students through activities may miss valuable opportunities for instruction that are just as important as other planned activities, and recognizing this may help teachers to slow down and more closely follow the student's lead.

Being Less Directive

As indicated in the previous example, teacher direction needs to be addressed if students with severe disabilities are to acquire the skills they need for successful interactions with others. In a study of eight students with significant challenges, Peck (1985) found that modifying teacher behavior by making it less directive substantially improved the students' social/communicative behavior. In addition, Marcovitch, Chiasson, Ushycky, Goldberg, and MacGregor (1996) found that young children with Down syndrome and other developmental disabilities were more verbal and vocal during play situations in which mothers talked less and were much less directive. Being less directive complements previous suggestions of following the student's lead and allowing for more wait time.

Students with severe disabilities may have experienced overly directive influences at an early age and may have become accustomed to that style of interaction. Research on maternal interaction style has found that mothers of children with mental retardation use more directives with their children than mothers of children without disabilities (Mahoney, 1988; Mahoney, Finger, & Powell, 1985). As a result, students with severe disabilities not only may expect to be directed by an adult but may in fact have become dependent on an adult to cue them to interact. To be suddenly confronted with adults who are nondirective may be confusing to the student, especially if it occurs when the student reaches middle or high school, after years of heavily directed interaction. If the student does not respond to or initiate an interaction, teachers tend to jump in and cue the desired behavior, which only succeeds in creating a pattern of greater dependency by the student on the conversation partner. MacDonald and Gillette (1986) recommended that adults avoid using direct questions all the time to elicit responses from students. These types of cues need to be faded so that the student learns to respond to more natural cues. The following example of an interaction between a paraeducator and tenth grader in an art class illustrates a highly directed approach.

Paraeducator:	Jake, go get your art materials.
Jake:	[No response for 1½ seconds]
Paraeducator:	What do you need to get, Jake?
Jake:	[No response for 2 seconds]
Paraeducator:	Go get your art materials. [Points to the cupboard and gives Jake a slight tactile cue on his shoulder]
Jake:	[Starts to head to the cupboard, but gets distracted by a classmate who is organizing his art material]
Paraeducator:	No, wrong. Where do you need to go? [Steps in between Jake and his classmate and points to the cupboard] Go on.
Jake:	[Walks to the cupboard and puts his hand on it, but does not open it]
Paraeducator:	Open the door.
Jake:	[Looks at the paraeducator]
Paraeducator:	Get your art materials, Jake. [Taps the cupboard] Open the cupboard.

In this brief interaction, the paraeducator gives six direct commands and two questions. Jake is placed exclusively in the role of the respondent. He is given little time to initiate or respond; furthermore, he does not need to respond communicatively as long as he does as directed. The one opportunity to follow Jake's lead and facilitate an interaction with a classmate (when he is distracted) is ignored.

The same scenario can be altered to be substantially less directed and more dependent on communicative exchanges as seen in the following example.

Art Teacher:	[To the entire class, while moving close to Jake] Allright, now that you know what to do, go get your materials and get to work.
Jake:	[Doesn't move, but seems to notice classmates moving around]
Paraeducator:	[After waiting 3 seconds, moves over to Jake and asks] Where is everyone going? [She points to the peers]
Jake:	[Watches his classmates, but makes no motion to follow their example]

Paraeducator:	[Asks a classmate to remind Jake of what needs to happen]
Peer:	Hey, Jake. You'd better get your stuff, man, or Mrs. B. will be on your case. [Shows Jake the materials he has gotten and points to another classmate] See where Mike is? Go over there and ask him to help you.
Jake:	[Grins. Slowly starts to go toward the cupboard and Mike; gets way-layed and stops by another student who is already working with her materials]
Peer:	[Sees that Jake has stopped, picks up a visual cue from the paraeducator, and reminds Jake that he needs to get his own materials. Noticing his interest, she says] Know what I'm making? I'll tell you after you get the stuff you need. It's over in that cupboard. [She points]
Jake:	[Starts to grab for her materials, but she blocks him with her body]
Peer:	Hey! That's mine. I need that. Go get your own. [She is laughing]
Paraeducator:	[Moving closer] Jake, let's get your materials so you can get to work like everyone else. [Points to the cupboard]
Jake:	[Heads to the cupboard and waits there]
Paraeducator:	[Says to a student standing near the cupboard] Jake needs to get some things for the project. I'm not sure what he needs, can you help? [She backs away]
Peer:	Sure. Here, this is what you need. [Gets the materials that Jake needs and waits for Jake to hold out his hands for them]

This situation was modified to show how the paraeducator refrained from using too many directions herself, elicited the aid of other students in the class, and faded back as often as possible to allow student-to-student interactions to occur. The students then know that they are expected to talk directly to Jake and not to him through the paraeducator. If the student makes a "mistake" (e.g., tries to grab materials from someone else), then this becomes an initiation on the student's part and offers an opportunity for peers to respond in an appropriate manner.

Ensuring that the Student Has a Means of Communication

As has been mentioned previously, everybody can and does communicate as long as they have the means to do so. The teacher must ensure that the student's means to communicate are appropriate for the given situation and readily available. The student will invariably be using many different modes of communication to meet the particular needs of different activities and settings (Calculator, 1988; Dowden, 1997; Romski & Sevcik, 1988). Some modes will involve specifically designed augmentative and alternative communication devices (see Chapter 6 for more information on developing different devices), while others will involve natural gestures, facial expressions, and vocalizations. Often, showing pictures or actual objects in class can serve to enhance both receptive and expressive skills. The important factor to consider is that the student does need a means of understanding (receptive communication) and will be expected to interact with others (expressive communication). Making use of available materials in the immediate situation and encouraging unaided (as well as aided) communicative behavior can be very helpful to the student. For example, in a high school government class, a student gains the attention of his classmate with severe disabilities (Maurice) and points to an unusual poster to draw his attention to it. He asks Maurice if he likes the poster and waits for him to use his augmentative communication device (ACD)—a Touch Talker—to state that he thinks it's weird. In another situation, a third grader asks her classmate with disabilities, Trenessa, what her favorite color is. Trenessa does not have access to a color palette, so her classmate points to colors on a bulletin, thereby giving Trenessa the means to communicate her preference. Because ACDs (especially those that are technologically light) cannot meet the infinite variety of communication needs for every situation, communication partners will inevitably need to utilize material in a given environment to supplement the ACD. Clearly, environments that contain pictures, printed words, and a great variety of objects will help support interactions.

If a student has a specific communication device, then it is self-evident that he or she must have access to the device in order to use it. Too often a student's device is left in the classroom when he or she goes to lunch, recess, or an assembly. A student who is separated from his or her ACD will lose opportunities to practice skills (especially use of the device) and will experience a further impediment to communicate. If an ACD does not meet the student's needs during such times, then the student should have access to devices that do meet his or her needs. ACDs should not be perceived as superfluous. If they provide a means for the student to communicate, then they are essential.

Students with severe disabilities will probably need to be supported to communicate during any given activity. Occasionally, teachers make the mistake of perceiving a student's communication device as a hindrance to engaging in particular activities; however, taking away a student's access to a communication device during an activity is equivalent to requiring complete silence from students without disabilities. For instance, Terri is a fifth grader who uses an ACD; however, her teacher decided that during art activities, the device should be left in Terri's desk so she can have room to work on her projects. To support Terri's communication needs and skills, her device needs to be available to her during art as well as all other possible times. If the device does not allow her to say what she needs to say during art activities, then another device needs to be designed for this purpose, as well as for other more specific activities. If the ACD is bulky and space-consuming, a light-technology device that is smaller and more portable may be needed to allow participation.

Teaching in Natural Contexts

There are as many different ways to teach students to communicate as there are students. Home environment, past experiences, cultural values, learning styles, and perceived importance of communicating with someone will all influence the learning process. Obviously, the manner in which students process information and interact with their environments will play a major role in determining the best (most efficient and effective) way to intervene.

In general, learning to communicate should be in and of itself motivating for the student. Communication intervention should not create a stressful or inordinately demanding situation for the student but rather one in which the student clearly sees the benefit (e.g., social, tangible). A basic premise of this text is that communication intervention occurs in natural environments and at naturally occurring times (Calculator, 1988; Kaiser, Ostrosky, & Alpert, 1993; Romski, Sevcik, & Adamson, 1997; Rowland & Schweigert, 1993). Because there is no special time or place for communication intervention, there is no need to fabricate artificial times and situations in which to address communication skills; opportunities abound in natural situations and throughout the course of any given day.

In general education classrooms, multiple opportunities exist naturally to support the development of communication skills. The educational team, however, needs to be alert to these opportunities (see Chapter 3) and able to use them to the greatest benefit for the student. Although communication intervention can occur at home, after school, and in community and work settings, Chapter 3 targets communication intervention during the typical school day. Intervention strategies can be taken from examples offered in this book, however, and applied to situations when the child is not at school.

Creating the Need to Practice Skills

Although numerous opportunities to practice communication skills exist in everyday occurrences, at times it may be necessary to create additional opportunities. One major strategy for creating these opportunities is to refrain from giving students the materials that they need for an activity until they actually request them. In home economics, for example, Marcella watches the other students get their bowls to sample foods they have been making in their small groups. In order to get Marcella to practice her communication skills, no one automatically gets her a bowl. Instead, she is expected to ask for one. If she tries to simply take the food directly from the serving bowl or tray, her classmates will prevent her from doing so and will ask her what she needs. If she can't remember the sign for bowl, students will draw her attention to their bowls and to the cupboard where the bowls are kept. Once she reaches toward or points to a bowl, her classmates will help her so that she can sample the food with them. Not only was her attempt to reach into the serving bowl (her way of asking for food) not punished but it was used as a way to engage her in an interaction that solicited yet another initiation from her.

Other ways of creating a need to communicate include giving too little of something so that the student must ask for more, giving a different item than what was requested so that the student must correct the partner, and giving most of the items that are needed but leaving out an item in order to prompt the student to request the missing item (Kaiser, 1993; Schwartz, Carta, & Grant, 1996). For example, during snack time for preschool, a teacher can pour a very small amount of juice into a child's cup in hopes of prompting the student to request more. Similarly, the teacher could pour some water and not juice into the child's cup, producing a need for the child to tell her teacher, "No!" and to request juice instead. Another example of this technique, which results in the creation of a need to communicate, can be seen during a fifth-grade art class when the teacher gives the student the wrong color paint (green) when the student had requested red. This student must now correct the teacher and restate the desired color. An example of the final technique (giving the student most of what is needed/requested but not everything) can be seen in a seventh-grade science class when the teacher gives a student with disabilities everything he or she will need to perform an experiment on the conduction of electrical current except for the student's switch, which the student needs to participate. Because the student likes this switch and uses it for many different experiments, he clearly notices its absence and is prompted to ask for it by vocalizing.

In general, the examples mentioned previously describe communication partners performing "poorly" in order to create a need for the student with disabilities to communicate, however, one word of caution is in order. These strategies are effective when the student has demonstrated significant communicative success. When the student is just learning to produce a communicative behavior, responding poorly to that student (not as expected or desired) could serve to confuse the student rather than to reinforce his or her efforts. In other words, if a student is just beginning to experiment with a vocalization to gain someone's attention, not attending to this student would be ill advised. The student needs to be reassured that unique behaviors are being understood before teachers become less attentive and responsive in hopes of creating additional communicative opportunities.

At certain times during the school day, creating opportunities to practice communication skills may be particularly challenging. When students are taking an exam, for example, targeting communication skills (based on need) does not, at first appraisal, seem possible. In fact, students with severe disabilities often engage in different activities during this time period; however, there are alternatives to excluding students with severe disabilities from highly academic activities. The following case study addresses this seemingly difficult type of situation.

> Kaya, a fifth grader, is learning to respond to others, follow through with requests, and gain greater control of her environment, both physically and socially. Although she may not be able to take a spelling test with her class because of her severe intellectual, physical, and hearing impairments, she can still be an active participant in this activity by helping the teacher administer the test, with an aide providing additional support as needed. The spelling words have been written on individual pieces of paper, each containing a paper clip. Kaya uses a magnetic wand with a built-up handle for ease in grasping. The teacher asks for a word by looking at Kaya, showing her one finger (1 in American Sign Language, ASL), pointing to the spelling words on Kaya's wheelchair tray, and holding out her hand to receive a word. If Kaya does not begin to respond within 3 seconds, the teacher repeats the request as described, while the paraeducator touches Kaya's elbow with a slight push toward the wand. The paraeducator also offers physical support to help Kaya maintain her grasp if needed. Kaya grasps the wand, moves it over the words, and picks one up (the magnetic wand attracting the paper clip). Kaya looks at the teacher and moves her arm and the wand to the teacher. Her teacher thanks her and takes the word, reads it to the class, and repeats the process with Kaya until all the words for the test have been read out loud. To speed up the process, the teacher immediately asks Kaya for another word, while she repeats the first word to the class, puts it into a sentence, and waits for the students to write the spelling word. Depending on Kaya's performance, the paraeducator may not need to physically prompt Kaya and can either give the test instead of the teacher, while the teacher plans for another activity, or can help the teacher in another capacity while the teacher and Kaya give the test. The critical aspect of the situation is that Kaya has been given a reason to interact with her teacher when normally this would not have occurred.

Motivating the Student to Communicate

As has been noted, the sheer ability to interact and be understood is usually sufficiently motivating enough in and of itself to prompt communication. Being able to communicate effectively allows the student to have some control over various situations, and this kind of control (i.e., obtaining desired objects, engaging in desired activities, having some say over who else will be involved) is powerfully reinforcing (Mirenda, Iacono, & Williams, 1990), particularly for a student who has lacked this type of control in the past. When the student can easily see how powerful communication can be in meeting various physical, social, and emotional needs, the motivation is naturally part of the learning process.

Some students, due to the severity of their multiple impairments, may fail to see the connection between their communicative efforts and having their needs met. In these cases, the educational team must be very careful to make this connection clear. Being extremely sensitive to any potential communicative behavior of the student is essential so that the student can begin to see the relationship between what he or she does and what happens as a result. When the student is just beginning to understand this cause-and-effect relationship, those around the student need to be very accepting of whatever form the student's communicative efforts take. This could mean recognizing and accepting a slight head turn, hand movement, or startle as communicative in nature instead of requiring the student to engage in more formal and conventional communicative behaviors. For example, Crystal, an eighth grader, hears a loud bang and responds with a startle that could mean, "What was *that?*" Another classmate sees this and leans over to Crystal, touches her arm, and responds to her startle as if she had asked a question: "Don't worry, that's just Stephanie's book. It fell off her desk. Made me jump, too." If attention from another person is desired by this student, she should be positively reinforced for any behavior that results in a social interaction.

Establishing a Student-Centered Approach

Following the student's lead is a recommended practice when helping students engage in new behavior (Drasgow, Halle, Ostrosky, & Harbers, 1996; Kaiser, 1993). When a student demonstrates interest in a specific activity or material, the possibility of eliciting communicative behavior about the activity is probably higher than if the student had little or no interest. Being student-centered requires the teacher to be flexible enough to recognize ways of helping the student acquire important skills that may be different from the way that the teacher originally intended. Recognizing the communicative opportunities in any activity makes this less frustrating for the teacher and possibly more motivating for the student. For example, an SLP working with a small group of students in an eleventh-grade drama class instructs students to work out their part of a skit. Jorge is supposed to listen for his cue and then activate his head switch to turn on a recording of his line in the script. His classmates have arranged the script so that he keeps saying the same thing at different times during the skit for a humorous effect. The SLP, however, notices that Jorge seems more interested in a prop worn by another member of his group than in his role (he is not responding well to her cues). Rather than requiring him to work on "saying" his line, she picks up on his lead and asks him questions about the prop. She lets him know that he is communicating interest in the item and has directed her attention to it by saying, "Jorge, what are you looking at?" When he grins at her and looks back at the prop, she continues the conversation, "What a weird hat! I bet that would look good on you." Jorge grins more, which cues a classmate to join the conversation. Some teasing interactions follow with the student stating that it is his hat and Jorge will have to get his own. In a few minutes, the intrigue with the hat is lessened and the SLP redirects the entire group back to the task of practicing the skit. Although a few minutes of work on the skit may have been lost, the end result is that Jorge had the opportunity to engage in a social interaction of his choosing and, inevitably, benefited from the practice of the skills involved in the exchange.

Offering Choices

Another strategy for motivating students is to offer them choices instead of making decisions for them. Encouraging choice making as a strategy to increase communicative behavior in students with severe and multiple disabilities has been well documented

(Brown, Belz, Corsi, & Wenig, 1993; Duker & Moonen, 1985). By simply refraining from giving the student materials or deciding what activity to do next, teachers can create opportunities for students to practice making choices. For example, when it is time for math, rather than telling Danny, a first grader, that he must do math, the teacher gives him a choice between playing Uno, which teaches number recognition and number matching, or playing dominoes, which teaches counting and pattern recognition. In order to help Danny make this decision, the teacher shows him the actual items. Examples of possible choices that are appropriate for students of different ages are listed in Table 4.1 (the lists, of course, are not exhaustive).

Choices should be quite easy so that the student does not need to deliberate too much. Initial choices would involve deciding between a preferred activity (e.g., going out for recess with a classmate) and a nonpreferred activity (e.g., staying inside to do math problems with manipulatives). Choices that are very clear for the student are easier to make, and the connection between choice and reward is easier for the student to understand. As students begin to make choices more quickly and clearly, they can be given options that are not so dramatically different and are, therefore, more difficult to make. The goal is to increase the number of available choices so that students truly have a choice. Engaging in a chosen activity is the positive reinforcement for communicating a preference. In Figure 4.2, a high school student offers a fellow student a choice between listening to music or going outside for a break.

Table 4.1.   Potential choice opportunities throughout the school day

Preschool
- Choice of snacks (food and drink)
- Choice of music to listen to
- Choice of centers
- Choice of playground equipment
- Choice of classmates to sit next to in a circle activity
- Choice of color or materials in art
- Choice of toys/materials for free play or centers
- Choice of story

Elementary school
- Choice of book to read or have read
- Choice of instrument with which to do work (e.g., marker, squiggle pen, crayon)
- Choice of classmate to push wheelchair or serve as a peer helper
- Choice of math or science materials
- Choice of graphics for a report or letter
- Choice of chocolate or white milk at lunch
- Choice of musical instrument in music
- Choice of position in which to do activity
- Choice of listening to book read by a classmate or on tape
- Choice of using a computer or a writing instrument to do an assignment
- Choice of software program

- Choice of switch to use to activate a device
- Choice to play game in physical education or sit out
- Choice of order of warm-up activities in physical education

Middle and high school
- Choice of classes to take
- Choice of tools to use in woodshop
- Choice of fabric in home economics
- Choice of where to sit in class (if an option)
- Choice of role to play in drama or task to work on
- Choice of software program for computer keyboarding
- Choice of task to tackle in leadership class
- Choice of what to eat or drink for lunch
- Choice of project to work on in media class

Postsecondary
- Choice of jobs to do and in what order
- Choice of location to eat lunch
- Choice of weights to lift in a community college class
- Choice of recreational activities
- Choice of type of soap to use for doing laundry
- Choice of classes to take at a community college
- Choice of where to sit in class

Many choices overlap the various school ages and should not be considered solely for one age group or another.

Figure 4.2.   A ninth grader indicates to his classmate which activity he would prefer to do. (Photographer: Margo Yunker)

If a student does not make a choice, it may be that the choices provided are of little interest to the student. Finding out what motivates the student to demonstrate preferences is an important first step (Johnson, Baumgart, Helmstetter, & Curry, 1996). Family members and classmates can help provide this valuable information. Offering the right number of options may also be a critical decision. For example, two options may be insufficient, but five may be excessive. The number of choices for any given situation will depend on the number of real options that exist as well as the student's ability to perceive and understand the choices being offered. The goal, of course, is to offer students as many choices as possible without overwhelming them. Obviously, all choices must be within the student's visual field, or if the student has very limited functional vision and limited movements, then choices must be presented tactually and within the physical range of motion available to the student (see Figure 4.3). Whatever the mode for representing choices (whether speech, objects, pictures, photos, textures), it must be clearly understood by the student.

Another difficulty facing students is that, even if they do have preferences, they may not know how to communicate them. In these situations, teachers will have to teach the desired choice-making behaviors. To ensure that students are actually aware of available choices, each option should be brought to their attention. Conversation partners can gain students' attention by pointing to or moving each item representing a choice and stating what the choice is. The partner should pause after each choice to give students some time to process the information, recognize the choice, and make a decision. Any movement or indication made by students should be interpreted as expressing a preference (whether accidental or not). If they are unhappy with what was "chosen," they can

Figure 4.3. Without vision, a fifth grader uses objects and textures to make a request. (Photographer: Margo Taylor)

protest or deny the "choice" and be given another opportunity to express their preference more clearly, and the conversation partner can apologize for misinterpreting them (e.g., "Whoops, I thought you wanted to get into your stander for math. I'm sorry. Let's try that again").

Enhancing the Social Environment

General education environments tend to be highly social environments. There are numerous opportunities for students with disabilities to interact with other students; furthermore, the majority of students in a general education classroom will be competent and responsive communication partners (or, at least will have the potential to be). These students not only provide communicative role models for their classmates with severe disabilities but they also serve as excellent conversation partners (Carr & Darcy, 1990; Goldstein & Kaczmarek, 1992; Odom, McConnell, & McEvoy, 1992; Werts, Caldwell, & Wolery, 1996).

The general education classroom has the potential for providing more and higher-level social interactions, and teachers and other team members need to help develop this potential (Butterfield & Arthur, 1995). If teachers resort to lecture and independent seat work for a majority of class time, then opportunities to interact socially and to work on communication skills are necessarily limited. Teachers can greatly facilitate interactions among all students by using cooperative learning, small groups, and partner learning (Hunt, Alwell, Farron-Davis, & Goetz, 1996; Logan, Bakeman, & Keefe, 1997). By participating in peer interactive techniques, students have opportunities to practice communication skills throughout most of the school day.

For example, in one ninth-grade history class, the teacher had students read excerpts from their texts out loud in a round-robin format. By the end of the 55-minute period, so many students were shuffling paper, tapping pens, passing notes, or generally fidgeting from boredom that it was difficult to hear the student reading. The students' attention to the task was greatly diminished, and Clayton, a student with severe disabilities, appeared to have joined a few other students in falling asleep. Although students interacted silently with facial expressions, gestures, body language, and written notes, the interactions were not encouraged by the teacher.

Realizing that this teaching method was not especially successful, the ninth-grade history teacher and special educator combined efforts to significantly change the learning environment. For example, to teach westward exploration and, specifically, the Lewis and Clark trail, the teachers divided students into groups of five or six to plan different western routes. They had to consider how much it would cost (using prices of the time period), what to take, and how long it would take estimating a certain number of miles per day. They also had to consider possible dangers and determine ways to circumvent them. Clayton, who had fallen asleep during the oral reading of the chapter in the previous example, was much more alert as a member of a team. His classmates showed him graphics of items that could be needed on the trip and asked him to choose what they should take. They planned different routes, printed them out, showed them to Clayton, and asked him to decide which one he thought they should select.

This alternative method of studying about the Lewis and Clark trail provided many opportunities to teach communication skills. Not only was Clayton more engaged by this lesson, but his classmates were as well. When teachers modify the structure of a lesson to actively include a student with severe disabilities, the change usually ends up benefiting all of the students (Udvari-Solner, 1994).

Making Communicating Fun

Learning any new skill should be fun or at least there should be some fun element to it. Teaching students ways to interact with classmates strictly for social purposes helps them achieve a level of closeness that can be very rewarding to the student, as evident in Figure 4.4. Students need to be able to see the immediate payoff of their communicative efforts, and certainly, when the interaction has a degree of fun and playfulness, the effort is even more strongly reinforced.

Teachers and communicative partners in general should avoid the tendency to make communication seem like work. When students with severe disabilities perceive communication as yet another task, they will be much less encouraged to make the needed effort. Practice scenarios in which students work one-to-one performing repetitions of a particular behavior are typically not much fun and not terribly communicative. For instance, asking the student to point repeatedly to the appropriate picture or object on command closely resembles compliance training, not communication. The student does not really have to point to anything if there is no reason to do so. Savage-Rumbaugh, Sevcik, Brakke, Rumbaugh, and Greenfield (1990) suggested that natural experiences may be more beneficial for symbol development and use rather than direct drill and practice. Furthermore, Koegel (1996) suggested that early attempts at teaching language that emphasized practice, controlled instruction, consistent and artificial reinforcers, and highly structured environments actually may have delayed the generalization of communication skills.

One creative way to teach communication skills at the preschool level is highlighted in the following example. Consuela, a preschooler from a Spanish-speaking home, really likes carrying purses. Her teachers recognized this and decided to fashion her ACD to

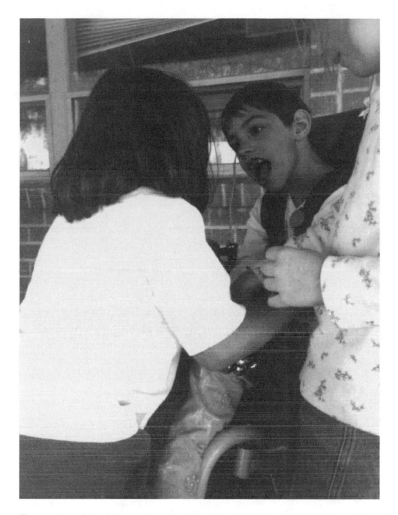

Figure 4.4. Interacting with a friend can be quite fun. (Photographer: Margo Taylor)

resemble a purse. They took a videocassette cover that looked a little like a purse and put strips of Velcro on the inside and one on the outside to which she could attach her black-and-white Mayer-Johnson Picture Communication Symbols (Johnson, 1994) that were written in Spanish (see Figure 4.5). They then attached a patterned shoestring to the contraption, turning it into a "shoulder bag" for her. The device fit well into the context of play, which perhaps increased her motivation to use it.

Not only should teachers and other team members make learning fun but they should also allow and encourage the student with severe communication difficulties to engage in playful communication. All students and adults need this opportunity, and most of us do this quite naturally without any effort; however, team members will need considerable creativity and flexibility to develop ways for students with severe disabilities to interact in this manner. Sometimes the original intent of a communication device can take on different meanings depending on the situation and the reinforcement for the student. For instance, once Sasha, a second grader with a profound intellectual disability and multiple impairments, had learned to use her BIGmack to indicate to her classmate

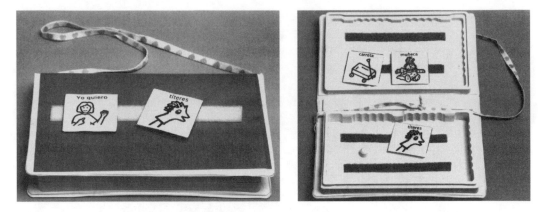

Figure 4.5.   An adapted videocassette cover becomes an augmented communication "purse" for a pre-schooler during her center time. (Photographer: Diane Andres; Designer: Roxana Daly)

to read the next page, she changed the original purpose on her own and turned it into a playful exchange. By hitting the BIGmack before the classmate was able to finish reading the page, Sasha "forced" her peer to respond with a remark such as, "Well, wait a minute—I'm not done yet." Sasha would grin and hit the switch again. This produced giggles and laughter and an ensuing tug of war over the BIGmack, which was perhaps more important to Sasha than the actual reading of the next page. She was able to initiate on her own a way to interact with a peer in a playful manner, which made it clear to the adults providing her with support that the ACDs she used and the messages she had been given were not meeting all of her needs.

SHAPING THE DESIRED COMMUNICATIVE BEHAVIOR

The learning environment of the general classroom is stimulating, somewhat unpredictable, and invariably fast-paced. When students with severe disabilities are educated in these classrooms, it may appear at first glance to be very difficult to work on specific communication skills. The pace of learning and the variety of uncontrolled variables (e.g., changed lesson plans, absentees of critical students, different reactions from other students) make it difficult to teach in ways that traditionally have been followed for students with severe disabilities (Wolery & Schuster, 1997); however, effective strategies for shaping communicative behavior can be used in typical classrooms with a bit of forethought and planning.

Strategies for shaping the desired behavior should be carefully thought out by all involved in supporting the student. Given the many different options for shaping behavior, those responsible for implementation need to be knowledgeable of the exact steps to follow when supporting a student. The specific procedure for shaping a given student's communicative behavior will need to be documented so that team members can achieve some consistency in implementation. The following pages describe some shaping strategies for consideration.

Modeling the Behavior

We all learn by watching others model behavior. Children learn by watching their parents, siblings, and others in their immediate environment. Learning through observation is a critical strategy for all children to use when trying to acquire a new skill (Bandura,

1976); furthermore, seeing the skill modeled once will probably not be sufficient for students to master it. Most students need repeated observation of the same behavior, and this is even more true for students with severe disabilities (Miller, 1993). Students who have difficulty receiving and processing information need considerable exposure to the desired model.

When the student has failed to demonstrate the desired behavior over time through simple exposure to the model, then they may need assistance in focusing their attention. The student with severe disabilities may not be attending to the appropriate elements of the modeled behavior and may not be seeing the relationship between the model (appropriate communicative behavior) and the consequence (how the student benefits from engaging in the behavior). Those involved in providing direct support to the student with severe disabilities will need to ensure that the student sees the model repeatedly over time and understands its purpose for a given situation. In the general education classroom, students without disabilities may serve as appropriate models as long as they are in close enough proximity to the student and the student is made aware of their behavior.

For the students with significant communication challenges who are also blind, the modeling will have to be tactual. A student's hands (if physically possible) can be placed over the hands of the person who is modeling the behavior. Responding to this student will also have to be done tactually these students will have to feel a gesture (e.g., a shrug or nodding of the head), a facial expression that indicates a particular mood, a sign for a word, or a message through an ACD. Because the incidental learning that is available to most students through the visual sense is unavailable to this student, more time and effort must be spent giving this student information through other modes of learning.

Prompting

Appropriate prompts for shaping communicative behavior will depend on the student, the targeted modes for communication, the purpose of the behavior, and the situation. Prompting should be as informative as necessary for the student to understand what is expected. This does not mean that prompts need to be (or should be) overly intrusive. Prompts need to clarify intent, and the most intrusive prompts (e.g., physical manipulations) may or may not provide the information needed (Riley, 1995). In a study of six children with severe developmental delays, Biederman, Fairhall, Raven, and Davey (1998) found that passive (and silent) observation of a task was more effective than verbal prompting or hand-over-hand instruction in teaching several different tasks (e.g., working puzzles, washing hands, zipping a coat). Having one's body manipulated may actually take the student's focus off the task and shift it to the person doing the manipulation. Resorting to extensive physical prompting, therefore, may not be the most direct or efficient teaching procedure. In a review of the literature on functional communication training for individuals with challenging behavior, Mirenda (1997) reported that a systematic prompting procedure of least-to-most intrusive was used to teach most communication skills. Of course, the prompting strategy chosen for a given student (whether most-to-least or least-to-most intrusive prompts) will depend on the student and the situation. No one sequence of prompts will be successful for all students in all different situations. For example, Ryland, an eighth grader, usually receives a least-to-most prompting hierarchy to help him communicate using a pictorial device; however, when a student says, "See you later," on his way to class, there is no time to use this procedure. In this case, a most-to-least prompting strategy is used to ensure that Ryland returns the interaction in a timely fashion.

Prompting should be systematic, facilitative of the behavior to be shaped, and respectful of the student's best learning modes. The goal is to fade prompts as soon as possible yet still ensure successfully completed responses from the student. Prompts that force the student to engage in a behavior against that student's preference should be avoided. For example, Tara, a sixth grader, has visual impairments, physical impairments, and severe intellectual challenges. Previous intervention called for adult services providers to physically move her head to make her look at pictorial/object communicative choices. Such a physical prompt caused Tara to throw her head back, resist, and look anywhere but where desired. Although well-intentioned, this type of prompting had the opposite effect of what was needed. Instead, a high-intensity light or laser beam could be used to shine on the paired picture/object choices to gain her attention. Because light naturally attracts one's visual attention, it achieves the desired behavior without being intrusive (Downing & Bailey, 1990; Goossens' & Crain, 1992).

To help a student select a message by pointing to a picture or reaching for an object, the educator could touch the student's elbow (a slight push forward) to cue the student that a response is expected. Another way to prompt the student that a message is being represented (e.g., pictures, objects, photographs) is by moving the object closer to the student. Not only is the communication partner drawing the student's attention to the object but he or she is also modeling a communication technique. Educators can provide the same kind of prompt for a student who is blind by touching him or her with the object. For some students, adding an auditory cue (e.g., a tap on the symbol) may also draw attention to the device. Reminding the student of possible options (e.g., things to say) while pointing to the symbol or tapping it or both directs a student's attention to the task and may lead to the desired response. Indirect verbal cues ("Do you want to say anything?") in combination with highlighting (increasing proximity of) the ACD may be sufficient for some students to use the device so that resorting to a direct verbal cue ("Touch your switch") may not be needed. Obviously, the type of prompts and the sequence in which they are used will vary for each student. The team's knowledge of the student and the situation should determine the most effective procedure to use.

Fading Communicative Prompts

To keep students from becoming dependent on adult intervention in order to communicate, educators must make sure that fading strategies are an integral part of every plan (Sigafoos, Mustonen, DePaepe, Reichle, & York, 1991). The level of prompting will need to be lessened until students recognize and respond to natural cues on their own. When adults facilitate interactions between students, they need to fade their presence over time. If they fail to do this, the student with a severe communication disorder could easily become dependent on the adult to cue the interaction with the other student.

A critical consideration for fading is to use prompting strategies that are not overly intrusive or interfering from the onset. The less intrusive or intensive the prompts, the less dependent on them students are apt to become; therefore, educators need to provide the student with the least amount of assistance necessary to demonstrate the targeted skill. Fading procedures need to be clearly stated and followed by all involved in the direct teaching of the student. Remembering that the goal of intervention is independent communication may help services providers be more aware of the need to fade. Romero, for example, needs to learn to raise his hand in many of his high school classes when the teacher calls roll. He is also learning to raise his hand to gain the attention he needs instead of jumping up and down and screaming. Romero sees his classmates raising their hands, which provides a critical model for him; however, he is not currently per-

Table 4.2.   Fading procedure for teaching appropriate attention-getting behavior

Teaching situation: When the teacher calls Romero's name or when it is apparent that Romero needs assistance (e.g., beginning of agitation)

1. Remind him to raise his hand and model that for him while physically tapping the bottom of his elbow to help raise his hand. Make sure that the teacher recognizes this effort and either acknowledges him or comes to offer assistance.
2. As Romero starts to perform this behavior on his own, stop providing the verbal reminder and tactual cue, and resort to the gesture and model of raising one's hand.
3. As Romero successfully performs this behavior with the gestural reminder, begin to fade more.
4. Wait 2 seconds before cueing at all.
5. If no response, gesture to others raising their hands or ask him whether he remembers what to do (an indirect verbal prompt) or both.
6. If he maintains the desired behavior, increase the wait time before cueing to 5 seconds.
7. Make sure that someone else acknowledges his behavior and helps him immediately if that is what he is requesting.
8. Document progress.

forming this skill. His educational support team plans a procedure that will facilitate his learning the skill, and a fading procedure is included as part of the plan. They agree to provide the most intense prompts initially to ensure successful demonstration of the desired skill and to fade the prompts as he increases his mastery. Table 4.2 outlines the intervention procedure for teaching Romero how to raise his hand, and, as is indicated, the wait time between prompts is lengthened as Romero demonstrates mastery until it is faded altogether.

Reinforcing Desired Behavior

The control that communication gives students over their environment as well as the social closeness that it allows are sometimes sufficiently reinforcing in and of themselves. When reinforcement is necessary, however, educators need to consider the way in which the communicative behavior is being taught, the environment or activity in which it is taught, and the student's need to recognize the advantage of his or her effort. When communication provides positive reinforcement for the student, increased communication should be the result (Koegel, O'Dell, & Dunlap, 1988).

Time is a critical element of positive reinforcement. When a student attempts a communicative behavior, those around him or her must respond quickly. If the student is trying to say something and no one responds, then the behavior is not reinforced and the student may have to say it "louder" (e.g., say it in such a way that it is guaranteed to get someone to respond). In such circumstances, failing to respond in a timely manner does not reinforce the desired communicative behavior but, in fact, succeeds in actually reinforcing inappropriate behavior.

When the demonstration of a behavior is not naturally reinforced, prompting the student to repeat the behavior when needed, external and additional reinforcement procedures may be necessary. For some students, interacting purely for social reasons may be particularly difficult, at least initially. They may tend to leave social situations and remain apart from others. In these instances, they may need a reason other than social closeness in order to interact. For example, a teacher can stipulate that the student be allowed to engage in a desired activity only when there are others around who are also participating. For instance, Charles, a student with severe disabilities, really enjoys a particular computer program and would gladly operate this program for a considerable length of time.

The teacher uses this activity as a way to develop his social skills by giving him access to the program when he agrees to share it and take turns with a classmate. He must respond to questions from his peer in order to gain access to the mouse (e.g., "Do you want to take a turn?"). In addition, the peer draws attention to the screen and makes comments to elicit increased excitement and enjoyment from Charles. In this way, Charles not only becomes accustomed to being in close proximity to another student but he can also learn that sharing an activity with another person can make it even more enjoyable.

Introducing New Symbols

One efficient way of introducing symbols is to pair the new symbol with the actual item, person, or activity at all possible opportunities. The most appropriate symbol to use must be decided beforehand (see Chapter 6) and should represent something the student wants to talk about and has frequent opportunities to utilize. Because the symbol must be important to the student and not necessarily the teacher, using preference assessments to determine what students respond to is one way to create meaningful symbols (Kennedy & Haring, 1993). The symbol should be within easy access to the student (consider the student's range of motion and ability to point or grasp) and within visual range (consider visual acuity and field).

When the student attempts to communicate using a previous method (e.g., reaching for an object, looking at an object), the new symbol should be placed so that it is in front of or next to the object. The student becomes used to seeing or feeling the symbolic representation of the message when it is most relevant. For example, when Jason, a third grader, is asked to choose the next song to which the class will do their aerobic exercises, Jason will go through a small stack of CDs to find the one with his favorite song. Because the team thinks that Jason can start using pictorial information instead of the actual objects to convey his thoughts, colored pictures of a few CD covers are placed right on top of each of three different CDs. To get to the CD of his choice, Jason must remove the picture (symbol). When he starts to move the picture on top of his favorite CD, the teacher quickly puts her hand out to receive it, and he hands it to her. She thanks him, shows him the picture of his CD, lets the class know which one he has selected, and then plays the CD for the class. Over time, the pictures of the CD covers are placed in a convenient place for Jason to go through, while the CDs themselves are slowly moved farther and farther away from the pictures (e.g., faded). Because handing the teacher the picture of the CD of his choice is just as effective as handing her the CD itself, Jason learns that the picture represents the CD and that he does not need the actual CD to respond to her question.

In this example, the teacher did several things that proved to be successful for Jason. She consistently asked him to select a song for the class during their aerobic exercises so that he could begin to anticipate that this would happen. She introduced the symbol for a situation that she knew was highly motivating for Jason (listening to his favorite song). She limited the number of pictorial choices to three so that he would not need to scan a large number, and she immediately and consistently responded to his initial grasp of the picture as if he had intended to convey his message using the picture and not the CD. She also used other "choices" for Jason that she knew he really did not like, therefore making the selection process easier.

For the student who uses a directed gaze to indicate a message, the same procedure of pairing the symbol with the object can be used until the object can be faded and the symbol begins to represent what the student desires. Obviously, the more opportunities the student has to use the new symbol within natural environments and activities, the faster he or she will acquire the new skill.

SUMMARY

This chapter has focused on the initial strategies to consider when teaching communication skills to students with severe disabilities within general education classrooms. The general education classroom is ideal because it affords numerous opportunities to communicate throughout each school day as well as a relatively large number of potentially responsive communicative partners.

Despite ample opportunities to practice communication skills and to see them modeled by others, students having severe disabilities will need specific and systematic instruction to acquire desired skills. Communication skill development cannot be left to chance. Educational team members will need to carefully develop teaching strategies and implement them consistently. As students acquire beginning skills, they can use these skills to acquire increasingly efficient ways to communicate.

REFERENCES

Bandura, A. (1976). Effecting change through participant modeling. In J. Krumboltz & C.E. Thorenson (Eds.), *Counseling methods* (pp. 248–265). Austin, TX: Holt, Rinehart & Winston.

Bedrosian, J. (1997). Language acquisition in young AAC system users: Issues and directions for future research. *Augmentative and Alternative Communication, 13,* 179–185.

Beukelman, D. (1991). Magic and cost of communication competence. *Augmentative and Alternative Communication, 7,* 7–20.

Biederman, G.B., Fairhall, J.L., Raven, K.A., & Davey, V.A. (1998). Verbal prompting, hand-over-hand instruction, and passive observation in teaching children with developmental disabilities. *Exceptional Children, 64,* 503–512.

Birdwhistell, R.L. (1955). Background to kinesics. *ETC: A Review of General Semantics, 13,* 10–18.

Brown, F., Belz, P., Corsi, L., & Wenig, B. (1993). Choice diversity for people with severe disabilities. *Education and Training in Mental Retardation, 28,* 318–326.

Butterfield, N., & Arthur, M. (1995). Shifting the focus: Emerging priorities in communication programming for students with severe intellectual disabilities. *Education and Training in Mental Retardation and Developmental Disabilities, 36,* 41–50.

Calculator, S.N. (1988). Promoting acquisition and generalization of conversational skills by individuals with severe disabilities. *Augmentative and Alternative Communication, 4,* 94–103.

Carr, E., & Durand, V. (1985). Reducing behavior problems through functional communication training. *Journal of Applied Behavior Analysis, 18,* 111–126.

Carr, E.G. (1988). Functional equivalence as a mechanism of response generalization. In R.H. Horner, G. Dunlap, & R.L. Koegel (Eds.), *Generalization and maintenance: Life-style changes in applied settings* (pp. 221–241). Baltimore: Paul H. Brookes Publishing Co.

Carr, E.G., & Darcy, M. (1990). Setting generality of peer modeling in children with autism. *Journal of Autism and Developmental Disorders, 20,* 45–59.

Dowden, P.A. (1997). Augmentative and alternative communication decision making for children with severely unintelligible speech. *Augmentative and Alternative Communication, 13,* 48–58.

Downing, J., & Bailey, B. (1990). Developing vision use within functional daily activities for students with visual and multiple disabilities. *RE:view, 21,* 209–220.

Downing, J., & Siegel-Causey, E. (1988). Enhancing the nonsymbolic communicative behavior of children with multiple handicaps. *Language, Speech and Hearing Services in Schools, 19,* 338–348.

Downing, J.E. (1993). Communication intervention for individuals with dual sensory and intellectual impairments. *Clinics in Communication Disorders, 3*(2), 31–42.

Drasgow, E., Halle, J.W., Ostrosky, M.M., & Harbers, H.M. (1996). Using behavioral indication and functional communication training to establish an initial sign repertoire with a young child with severe disabilities. *Topics in Early Childhood Special Education, 16,* 500–521.

Duker, P.C., & Moonen, X.M. (1985). A program to increase manual signs with severely/profoundly mentally retarded students in natural environments. *Applied Research in Mental Retardation, 6,* 147–158.

Durand, V.M., & Carr, E.G. (1991). Functional communication training to reduce challenging behavior: Maintenance and application in new settings. *Journal of Applied Behavior Analysis, 24,* 251–264.

Evans, D., Hearn, M., Uhlemann, M., & Ivey, A. (1984). *Essential interviewing: A programmed approach to effective communication* (2nd ed.). Pacific Grove, CA: Brooks/Cole.

Giangreco, M.F., Edelman, S.W., Luiselli, T.E., & MacFarland, S.Z.C. (1997). Helping or hovering? Effects of instructional assistant proximity on students with disabilities. *Exceptional Children, 64,* 7–18.

Glennen, S., & Calculator, S. (1985). Training functional communication board use: A pragmatic approach. *Augmentative and Alternative Communication, 1,* 134–142.

Goldstein, H., & Kaczmarek, L. (1992). Promoting communicative interaction among children in integrated intervention settings. In S.F. Warren & J. Reichle (Series & Vol. Eds.), *Communication and Language Intervention Series: Vol. 1. Causes and effects in communication and language intervention* (pp. 81–111). Baltimore: Paul H. Brookes Publishing Co.

Goossens', C., & Crain, S.S. (1992). *Utilizing switch interfaces with children who are severely physically challenged.* Austin, TX: PRO-ED.

Guess, D., & Siegel-Causey, E. (1985). Behavioral control and education of severely handicapped students: Who's doing what to whom? and why? In D. Bricker & J. Filler (Eds.), *Severe mental retardation: From theory to practice* (pp. 230–244). Reston, VA: Council for Exceptional Children.

Halle, J., Marshall, A., & Spradlin, J. (1979). Time delay: A technique to increase language use and facilitate generalization in retarded children. *Journal of Applied Behavior Analysis, 12,* 431–439.

Horner, R.H., & Billingsley, F.F. (1988). The effect of competing behavior on the generalization and maintenance of adaptive behavior in applied settings. In R.H. Horner, G. Dunlap, & R.L. Koegel (Eds.), *Generalization and maintenance: Life-style changes in applied settings* (pp. 197–220). Baltimore: Paul H. Brookes Publishing Co.

Horner, R.H., Sprague, J.R., O'Brien, M., & Heathfield, L.T. (1990). The role of response efficiency in the reduction of problem behaviors through functional equivalence training: A case study. *Journal of The Association for Persons with Severe Handicaps, 15,* 91–97.

Houghton, J., Bronicki, G., & Guess, D. (1987). Opportunities to express preferences and make choices among students with severe disabilities in classroom settings. *Journal of The Association for Persons with Severe Handicaps, 12,* 18–27.

Hunt, P., Alwell, M., Farron-Davis, F., & Goetz, L. (1996). Creating socially supportive environments for fully included students who experience multiple disabilities. *Journal of The Association for Persons with Severe Handicaps, 21,* 53–71.

Johnson, J.M., Baumgart, D., Helmstetter, E., & Curry, C.A. (1996). *Augmenting basic communication in natural contexts.* Baltimore: Paul H. Brookes Publishing Co.

Johnson, R. (1994). *The Picture Communication Symbols combination book.* Solana Beach, CA: Mayer-Johnson.

Kaiser, A.P. (1993). Functional language. In M.E. Snell (Ed.). *Instruction of students with severe disabilities* (4th ed., pp. 347–379). New York: Merrill Education.

Kaiser, A.P., Ostrosky, M.M., & Alpert, C.L. (1993). Training teachers to use environmental arrangement and milieu teaching with nonvocal preschool children. *Journal of The Association for Persons with Severe Handicaps, 18,* 188–199.

Kennedy, C.H., & Haring, T.G. (1993) Teaching choice making during social interactions to students with profound multiple disabilities. *Journal of Applied Behavior Analysis, 26,* 63–76.

Koegel, L.K. (1996). Communication and language intervention. In R.L. Koegel & L.K. Koegel (Eds.), *Teaching children with autism: Strategies for initiating positive interactions and improving learning opportunities* (pp. 17–32). Baltimore: Paul H. Brookes Publishing Co.

Koegel, R.L., O'Dell, M.C., & Dunlap, G. (1988). Producing speech use in nonverbal autistic children by reinforcing attempts. *Journal of Autism and Developmental Disabilities, 18,* 525–538.

Logan, K.R., Bakeman, R., & Keefe, E.B. (1997). Effects of instructional variables on engaged behavior of students with disabilities in general education classrooms. *Exceptional Children, 63,* 481–498.

Lovett, H. (1996). *Learning to listen: Positive approaches and people with difficult behavior.* Baltimore: Paul H. Brookes Publishing Co.

MacDonald, J., & Gillette, Y. (1986). Communicating with persons with severe handicaps: Roles of parents and professionals. *Journal of The Association for Persons with Severe Handicaps, 11,* 255–265.

Mahoney, G.J. (1988). Communication patterns between mothers and developmentally delayed infants. *First Language, 8,* 157–172.

Mahoney, G.J., Finger, L., & Powell, A. (1985). Relationship of maternal behavior style to the development of organically impaired mentally retarded infants. *American Journal on Mental Deficiency, 90,* 296–302.

Marcovitch, S., Chiasson, L., Ushycky, I., Goldberg, S., & MacGregor, D. (1996). Maternal communication style with developmentally delayed preschoolers. *Journal of Children's Communication Development, 17*(2), 23–30.

McDonnell, J. (1987). The effects of time delay and increasing prompt hierarchy strategies on the acquisition of purchasing skills by students with severe handicaps. *Journal of The Association for Persons with Severe Handicaps, 12,* 227–236.

Miller, J. (1993). Augmentative and alternative communication. In M.E. Snell (Ed.), *Instruction of students with severe disabilities* (4th ed., pp. 319–346). New York: Macmillan.

Mirenda, P. (1997). Supporting individuals with challenging behavior through functional communication training and AAC: Research review. *Augmentative and Alternative Communication, 13,* 207–225.

Mirenda, P., Iacono, T., & Williams, R. (1990). Communication options for persons with severe and profound disabilities: State of the art and future directions. *Journal of The Association for Persons with Severe Handicaps, 15,* 3–21.

Murphy, J., Markova, I., Moodie, E., Scott, J., & Bon, S. (1995). Augmentative and alternative communication systems used by people with cerebral palsy in Scotland: Demographic survey. *Augmentative and Alternative Communication, 11*(1), 26–36.

Odom, S.L., McConnell, S.R., & McEvoy, M.A. (Eds.). (1992). *Social competence of young children with disabilities: Issues and strategies for intervention.* Baltimore: Paul H. Brookes Publishing Co.

Peck, C.A. (1985). Increasing opportunities for social control by children with autism and severe handicaps: Effects on student behavior and perceived classroom climate. *Journal of The Association for Persons with Severe Handicaps, 10,* 183–193.

Reichle, J. (1991). Developing communicative exchanges. In J. Reichle, J. York, & J. Sigafoos (Eds.), *Implementing augmentative and alternative communication: Strategies for learners with severe disabilities* (pp. 133–156). Baltimore: Paul H. Brookes Publishing Co.

Reichle, J., Feeley, K., & Johnston, S. (1993). Communication intervention for persons with severe and profound disabilities. *Clinics in Communication Disorders, 3*(2), 7–30.

Riley, G.A. (1995). Guidelines for devising a hierarchy when fading response prompts. *Education and Training in Mental Retardation and Developmental Disabilities, 30,* 231–242.

Romski, M.A., & Sevcik, R.A. (1988). Augmentative and alternative communication systems: Considerations for individuals with severe intellectual disabilities. *Augmentative and Alternative Communication, 4,* 83–93.

Romski, M.A., Sevcik, R.A., & Adamson, L.B. (1997). Framework for studying how children with developmental disabilities develop language through augmented means. *Augmentative and Alternative Communication, 13,* 172–178.

Rowland, C., & Schweigert, P. (1993). Analyzing the communication environment to increase functional communication. *Journal of The Association for Persons with Severe Handicaps, 18,* 161–176.

Savage-Rumbaugh, E.S., Sevcik, R.A., Brakke, K., Rumbaugh, D., & Greenfield, P. (1990). Symbols: Their communicative use, combination, and comprehension by bonobos (Pan paniscus). In L. Lipsett & C. Rovee-Collier (Eds.), *Advances in infancy research* (Vol. 6, pp. 221–278). Norwood, NJ: Ablex.

Schwartz, I.S., Anderson, S.R., & Halle, J.W. (1989). Training teachers to use naturalistic time delay: Effects on teacher behavior and on the language use of students. *Journal of The Association for Persons with Severe Handicaps, 14,* 48–57.

Schwartz, I.S., Carta, J.J., & Grant, S. (1996). Examining the use of recommended language intervention practices in early childhood special education classrooms. *Topics in Early Childhood Special Education, 6,* 251–272.

Sevcik, R.A., Romski, M.A., Watkins, R., & Deffebach, K.P. (1995). Adult partner-augmented communication input to youth with mental retardation using the System for Augmenting Language (SAL). *Journal of Speech and Hearing Research, 38,* 902–912.

Sienkiewics-Mercer, R., & Kaplan, S.B. (1989). *I raise my eyes to say yes.* Boston: Houghton Mifflen.

Sigafoos, J., Mustonen, T., DePaepe, P., Reichle, J., & York, J. (1991). Defining the array of instructional prompts for teaching communication skills. In J. Reichle, J. York, & J. Sigafoos (Eds.), *Implementing augmentative and alternative communication: Strategies for learners with severe disabilities* (pp. 173–192). Baltimore: Paul H. Brookes Publishing Co.

Udvari-Solner, A. (1994). A decision-making model for curricular adaptations in cooperative groups. In J.S. Thousand, R.A. Villa, & A.I. Nevin (Eds.), *Creativity and collaborative learning: A practical guide to empowering students and teachers* (pp. 59–77). Baltimore: Paul H. Brookes Publishing Co.

Werts, M.G., Caldwell, N.K., & Wolery, M. (1996). Peer modeling of response chains: Observational learning by students with disabilities. *Journal of Applied Behavior Analysis, 29,* 53–66.

Wolery, M., & Schuster, J.W. (1997). Instructional methods with students who have significant disabilities. *Journal of Special Education, 31*(1), 61–79.

5

Interactions for Different Purposes, Conversations, and Generalization of Skills

For students with severe disabilities, as well as for all students, efforts to acquire, maintain, utilize, and increase communication skills will continue throughout their school life and into adulthood. Teachers and other direct services providers cannot afford to be content with a student's ability to merely express "yes" or "no" and make basic requests. The value of such limited communication training is questionable (Reichle, 1991). Acknowledging the limitations of science to date, educators must continue to improve their knowledge and techniques and, above all, to keep their expectations for all students, including those with disabilities, high. Maintaining high expectations challenges professionals to develop more efficient and effective means to serve those with the greatest need.

TEACHING STUDENTS SPECIFIC FUNCTIONS OF COMMUNICATION

Although reasons for communicating are limitless, those working with students with significant challenges tend to concentrate on teaching them how to make requests, probably because these students already have some ability to express desire, which means that those working with them experience positive results with relative ease (Goodman & Remington, 1993; Light, 1988). Students with significant challenges may also communicate in order to protest or reject and, again, seem to do so rather easily. Of course, the manner in which the protest or rejection occurs may be less conventional than desired (e.g., kicking, screaming, biting, holding one's breath) but is probably easily interpreted by the responsive partner.

Students with limited communication skills need to broaden their abilities to interact with others by engaging in a wide array of communicative functions. The following paragraphs provide suggestions for targeting several different functions of communication for different activities and grade levels.

Requesting

As mentioned previously, teaching students with severe disabilities to make requests appears to be a relatively easy task (Light, 1988). The student's motivation to make requests, as well as the reinforcement that occurs whenever the student's request is fulfilled, contribute greatly to the acquisition of this skill. Also, the numerous opportunities to make requests in all activities on a daily basis provide considerable practice for the skill to develop.

Students can request to sit in a specific location, to get a drink of water, to write with a certain writing tool (e.g., vibrating pen, marker, glitter pen), to read with a certain partner, to be pushed to lunch or recess by a certain classmate, to use a certain colored paper, or any number of other preferences. Within a reading activity, for instance, the student can request not only a specific book but also whether a peer or teacher should continue reading. The list of possible requests is endless; however, the adults or other children in the classroom must provide opportunities to make requests and must respond to them quickly in order to reinforce the student's acquisition of the skill.

Almost any activity or situation can offer the student an opportunity to practice making requests if those around the student recognize the opportunities. For example, it is easy to assign a student to push a classmate in a wheelchair to lunch. It is just as easy to allow the student in the wheelchair to make the selection. The student can choose a classmate from a group who gathers around the wheelchair or from looking at class photographs. Similarly, rather than just giving a student with a significant disability a particular item to use for a work assignment, the student can be allowed to choose from a selection of items, or the student can be given nothing to work with so that he or she is compelled to request the materials. If a student does not particularly enjoy an activity, then requesting a break from the activity can be quite motivating. Of course, when a student needs help to engage in a specific activity, requesting the necessary assistance provides an opportunity to practice this skill. For example, in Figure 5.1, a fifth grader requests assistance from her classmate to open her milk carton.

For students with limited means of communication, determining when they are making requests instead of merely expressing interest in something can be difficult. To differentiate a student's requesting behavior from behavior meant simply to gain another's attention, it may be necessary to require the student to clarify the intent. The student can learn that a certain behavior (e.g., producing a manual sign, pointing to a generalized symbol for "want") informs the conversation partner that he or she needs something. Once a need has been established, then the partner can help the student specify exactly what he or she is requesting. Reichle and Brown (1986) demonstrated the use of a generalized "want" symbol with an adult with autism. Explicit requests were taught to this individual by requiring him to use the "want" symbol in conjunction with other graphic displays of desired items. Reichle and colleagues achieved similar success with an adolescent who was blind and had mental retardation requiring extensive supports (Reichle, Sigafoos, & Piché, 1989). Given the inability to use graphic symbols, this student was taught to say "want" to draw attention to the fact that something was desired. For objects that were already known, the student was requested to combine the word "want" with the word for the desired item (e.g., "cracker"). If the word for the item was unknown, the student could specify the item that was desired by picking up the object or a tangible symbol that stands for the object.

Combining symbols to clarify communicative intent is always desirable. If the student does not use the symbol for "want," then the communicative behavior may be interpreted in another way. Educators can help teach this skill by honoring requests only when

Figure 5.1.   At lunch a fifth grader asks a classmate to help her open her milk carton by using the carton itself. (Photographer: Margo Taylor)

the student combines the use of the "want" symbol with other forms of communication (e.g., looking at an object, reaching for a picture, leading someone toward something). Of course, teachers need to use sound judgment in determining whether the student is capable of processing this kind of instruction. For example, students who are just learning that small and relatively vague behaviors that they make can be interpreted as requests should continue to have their behaviors reinforced; however, for those students who have clearly learned that certain behaviors can produce desired results, the addition of a symbol specifically stating the request function ("I want") can help clarify their intent.

Rejecting or Protesting

Students with disabilities often exhibit behavior that signifies protest or rejection, but those working with them often fail to recognize the behavior as communicative. Students will protest certain instructional techniques (e.g., hand-over-hand manipulation), certain activities (e.g., large-group lectures), assistance from particular individuals, or certain food items at lunch, to name just a few.

When students do not have or know a conventional way to say "no," they will express rejection in any way that proves effective, which often gains them negative attention. For example, when a student pinches a classmate in an attempt to express disinterest in an activity, classmates may concentrate on the negative behavior and label the student a "pincher" instead of understanding that the student is simply expressing rejection in the only way he or she may be able. Labels such as "pinchers," "kickers," "screamers," "spitters," and "biters" are dehumanizing and do nothing to help students with severe disabilities become welcomed members of a classroom. Furthermore, such labels remove focus from the student's attempts to communicate and place it instead on undesirable behaviors. A real problem can develop if a student is rejected by classmates because of negative behavior (Siperstein, Leffert, & Widaman, 1996).

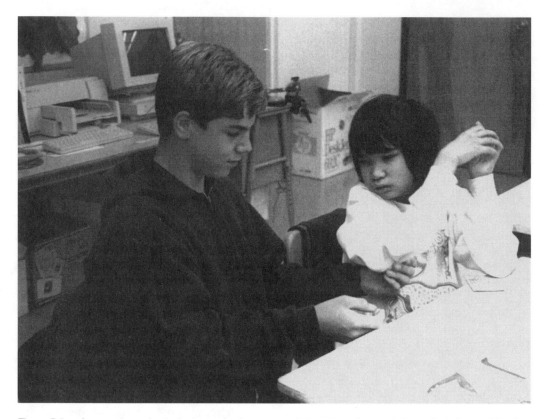

Figure 5.2.   A seventh-grade student uses body movements to let her classmate know that she would rather not have his help. (Photographer: Margo Yunker)

Obviously, all students have a right to say, "No, I don't want to do that," or "No, I don't like that." Students say "no" by shaking their heads, pushing items away, pushing a red "no" button on a simple voice output communicative aid (VOCA), or closing their eyes, to name just a few. In Figure 5.2, a seventh grader who does not speak and cannot see pulls away from a classmate who is offering to help her. These methods of rejecting are all acceptable; however, if the form that a student is using to say "no" is socially undesirable, then intervention requires providing the student with an equally efficient yet more conventional form. Carr and Durand (1985) found that with functional communication training, excess behaviors decreased when socially appropriate behaviors were substituted. Hunt, Alwell, and Goetz (1988) found that instances of unconventional behavior decreased in students with disabilities as their conversational skills developed. In fact, this relationship between the ability to express oneself and one's behavior has been well established (see Mirenda, 1997, for a review of this literature).

To help students with disabilities communicate rejection in more conventional and acceptable ways, those working with these students should anticipate this possibility, watch for the behaviors that lead to unconventional rejections, and provide students with appropriate ways of saying "no." This alternative way to reject must be as efficient (take as much or less energy and be as successful) as the student's customary form of rejection. For example, if Kaneesha, a fifth grader with disabilities, is required to stay at a her task of pasting pictures in her daily journal for more than 10 minutes, she will start to fuss, squirm, refuse to hold the glue stick, and look away from her work. If those working with her do not recognize this behavior as a request to end the activity, she will eventually throw the scissors, glue stick, and pictures off her desk. A paraeducator can intervene in this instance by being responsive to Kaneesha's initial signs of protest, reminding her that she can say "no more" and shake her head to express that she is tired. The paraeducator can then ask Kaneesha if she would like to continue with the task, to which Kaneesha will more than likely vigorously shake her head and say "no." She is then allowed to put her work away and asked to check her schedule to see what activity is next. By anticipating negative behavior, educators can often lessen the behavior and teach more conventional communication skills at the same time.

Gaining Attention

In order to communicate a message, it is imperative that the sender gain the recipient's attention, or the message will probably not be received. Most individuals can easily gain others' attention. Saying the other's name, establishing eye contact, moving close to the individual, or touching the other person all are very acceptable means of gaining someone's attention to initiate an interaction. These same behaviors are also within many students' repertoires, regardless of whether they have severe disabilities. Students who cannot engage in these more conventional means of attention-getting may be able to gain another's attention by making a vocalization, making a movement (e.g., kicking a leg, lifting one's head), or using a BIGmack or other VOCA preprogrammed with an appropriate message (e.g., "Hey, can someone come over here and talk to me?"). Students who are accustomed to gaining attention by screaming, throwing objects, grabbing clothing, hitting, or engaging in a variety of self-injurious behaviors need support and specific instruction to learn more appropriate behaviors that serve the same purpose (Carr & Durand, 1985; Drasgow & Halle, 1995; Durand & Carr, 1991). Because students with disabilities are unlikely to change negative behavior on their own, educators will need to actively teach them more appropriate behavior (Cipani, 1990).

Kaczmarek (1990) stated that there were three components to initiating a conversation: selecting a listener, increasing proximity to that listener, and obtaining the listener's attention. Students with severe disabilities may need specific instruction in each of these three steps to perform this function. Others, because of physical and sensory impairments, may not be able to perform all components and will consequently need adaptations. For example, if a student is not physically able to get closer to a potential communication partner, then potential partners can remain in close proximity to the student, but not initiate an interaction. The student will need to initiate the interaction by following through the other steps (e.g., selecting a potential listener and obtaining that person's attention).

In order to teach a student how to gain someone's attention in a socially acceptable manner, it may be necessary to have three people participate in the learning activity (Goossens' & Crain, 1992). Obviously, it is difficult for a teacher to teach a student to gain his or her attention when that attention has already been gained; therefore, it makes much more sense to have a third party involved. For example, when Tyler, a student with disabilities, needs some paper in his high school typing class, the special educator can tell him that she does not know where it is, which makes it necessary for Tyler ask the typing teacher. Because this teacher is invariably busy with the large number of students in the class, it is relatively easy for her to "ignore" Tyler until he has appropriately gained her attention. The special educator uses a lot of natural gestures to indicate that she does not know where the paper is and then points to the typing teacher. If he does not respond to this suggestion within 5 seconds, then she guides him to the teacher (whose attention is elsewhere) and models (without actually touching) how to tap the teacher on her shoulder to gain her attention. If Tyler does not follow the model (again, within 5 seconds), then the special educator gently pushes his elbow forward until he taps the teacher. The teacher then turns to Tyler and asks him what he wants. At this point, Tyler can either take the teacher to his desk to show her that he has no paper, or he can provide her with a printed/pictorial card requesting paper. Once Tyler has the attention of the typing teacher, the special educator fades back and begins to assist other students to give the typing teacher time to respond to Tyler's request. Obviously, the teacher and special educator have agreed upon this procedure well in advance. As Tyler experiences this situation more frequently, the procedure becomes more routine until, hopefully, he is able to gain the teacher's attention without prompting from the special educator.

The teaching strategy employed with Tyler involved a series of least-to-most intensive prompts coupled with a consistent wait time of 5 seconds. This intervention strategy was determined by the team based on who Tyler is, how he learns, and what seemed to make the most sense given the environment of the typing classroom. Different approaches need to be applied for different students. For example, Cipani (1990) used a least-to-most intensive prompting strategy, but used a wait time of 15 seconds to teach young children with severe disabilities to engage in appropriate attention-getting behavior. For some students, a more intensive or informative set of prompts might be given initially and then faded gradually as the student demonstrated increased mastery (Sigafoos, Mustonen, DePaepe, Reichle, & York, 1991).

Another example of teaching attention-getting skills involves Jacob, a second grader with disabilities. Jacob does not initiate interactions with other children but always looks as if he would like to play. The second-grade teacher verbally suggests that he could approach a student closest to him and ask that student if he would like to play. When Jacob is reluctant, the teacher takes his hand and suggests that they both go. The student to be addressed is playing ball with a few other boys and has his back to Jacob and the teacher. As they get very close to the boys, the teacher communicates to them that they should continue playing—if they stop prematurely, then Jacob does not have the opportunity to practice his attention-getting skills. The teacher then whispers in Jacob's ear to say the boy's name to get his attention. Although Jacob cannot say Bobby's name, he can vocalize, "buh," which he does. Bobby turns to Jacob and asks him what he wants. If Jacob does not do anything within 3 seconds, then the teacher will verbally and physically prompt him to point to the ball and will ask the boys what they think he might want. They guess appropriately and include Jacob in their play. In this way, Jacob learns an appropriate way of gaining his classmate's attention.

Engaging in Greetings, Farewells, and Other Social Niceties

Interacting socially—engaging in greetings, farewells, and other social niceties—is a necessary skill in order to feel welcomed in any given social situation. Students need to be able to greet their peers and teachers, to politely terminate an interaction, and to engage in communicative interaction purely for reasons of social etiquette. Students with severe disabilities, when part of a general education classroom and typical school, have multiple opportunities to engage in such functions of communication. They may use smiles, looks, head movements, waves, or verbalizations (e.g., "hi," "bye"). Although such communication alone does not sustain an interaction, it is such an integral part of social conduct that without this skill, the student with severe disabilities may not be accepted by his or her peers (Chadsey-Rusch, Linneman, & Rylance, 1997; Storey & Horner, 1991). Students who learn to initiate as well as to respond to greetings and farewells can also use these skills to gain others' attention.

Teachers can help shape these behaviors by modeling them, directing the student's attention to others engaged in similar behaviors, and making sure alternative and augmentative communication (AAC) devices, if needed, are readily available. If a student's sociable behavior is not particularly clear to others, the individual teaching this skill may need to serve as an interpreter until the behavior can be more easily recognized by a larger number of people.

Because greetings and farewells occur relatively quickly, a least-to-most intensive prompting strategy would not be the most efficient, especially with a student who is slow to respond. When a classmate of a student with disabilities says, "hi," the adult in closest proximity to the student with disabilities should quickly and directly physically shape the appropriate response. As the student begins to exhibit mastery of the skill, the adult can start to fade the physical prompt.

Commenting

Having the ability to make comments—to let others know what you think and, consequently, who you are—is an essential function of communication that is often overlooked for students with severe intellectual disabilities, perhaps from some belief that they are incapable of actually making comments. When students with severe disabilities are encouraged to make comments, their interactions with others become more balanced and reflective of typical conversations (Hunt, Farron-Davis, Wrenn, Hirose-Hatae, & Goetz, 1997; Light & Binger, 1998).

Often, students with severe disabilities attempt to make comments, but because they do so in unconventional ways, their communication partners usually think that they are making requests. For example, when Wes, a tenth grader, looks at an interesting sculpture made by a classmate, he could very easily be making a comment ("That's cool. I wish I could make something like that"); however, the paraeducator assumes by his glance that he is requesting that the item be brought to him. If this happens repeatedly, it can be extremely frustrating for the individual with disabilities. Reichle, Barrett, Tetlie, and McQuarter (1987) determined that unless students are taught to engage in other functions of communication, they will resort to making requests because it is all that they know. It may be, in fact, that they are engaging in other purposes of communication, but that others are simply misinterpreting them. A student whose efforts to communicate are consistently misinterpreted can become considerably frustrated and may eventually give up trying.

Students with disabilities need creative ways of expressing their thoughts and opinions. For instance, in art class, Julie, a third grader, has a pictorial system that allows her not only to request help and supplies (glue, a specific color of paint) but also lets her say, "I like that," or "I think it needs more stuff," when her classmates show her their art products. Figure 5.3 illustrates this situation-specific augmentative communication device. In order to help Julie make comments, the teacher can cover the pictures that signify requests so that Julie will only have access to the two choices that signify comments. Her attention is drawn to these two pictorial choices (a smiling face for "I like that" and a picture of a pile of items for "I think it needs more stuff") after she is shown her classmate's artwork. The teacher models using the pictorial symbols so that Julie can see what they signify and then asks her to give her opinion. If Julie does not respond after 3 seconds, the teacher applies a physical prompt to her elbow. If Julie still does not respond, the teacher tries to interpret her facial expressions and helps her make a response and states it out loud for her classmate. The teacher might say something like, "I think Julie is trying to tell you that she likes your picture." She then asks Julie to confirm or deny if her

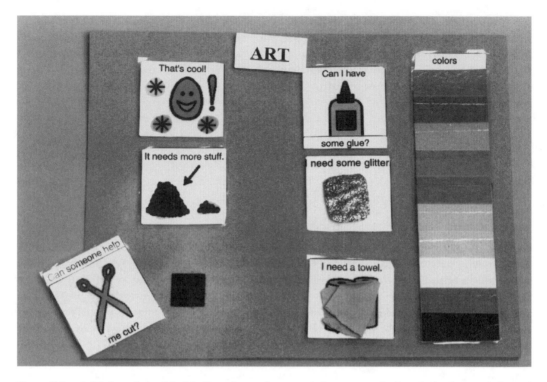

Figure 5.3.   A third grader's pictorial alternative and augmentative communication device for use in her art class. (Photographer: Diane Andres; Designer: June E. Downing)

statement is correct. Julie smiles, looks, and opens her mouth to say "yes" or gives a blank expression if she needs to correct the teacher. In order to help Julie develop this skill, the teacher provides her with several opportunities to comment on different classmates' artwork at the end of each art class.

In a fifth-grade class that includes Kenyon, a boy with severe disabilities, the teacher has developed a creative way to allow him to participate by making comments. Each year, this teacher asks her students to write a certain number of "book reports." She allows students to produce these reports in a variety of ways to acknowledge the different learning styles of students in the class, and she promotes cooperative learning by allowing students who read the same book to work together. Students can write traditional reports or poems, give dramatic or mimed presentations, or create crossword puzzles or artistic projects, such as mobiles or dioramas, that depict the content of the book. Throughout the year, the teacher can encourage students to experiment with different ways of completing this assignment.

Kenyon likes to do the hands-on projects the best, although he also enjoys acting out the books' story lines. He and his classmate, Roger, who read one of the books to him, decide together what kind of project they will do. First, Roger chooses photographic representations of past projects done by other students in the class, and then he gives Kenyon the final decision by asking him to choose from the selected options. They decide to make a mobile, and Roger proceeds to design the project asking Kenyon's opinion throughout. He seeks suggestions for paper color; shapes and size of paper pieces; where to hang the various parts of the mobile; what graphic additions should be added to the written words; and, in general, what Kenyon thinks of how the project is developing. Kenyon points or looks at various options to indicate preferences for colors, shapes, graphics, and so forth. He helps cut out the different shapes by using battery-operated scissors that have been adapted to use with a switch. To express his opinion on how the project is looking, he has a line drawing of a face of a boy smiling on top of two message holders for the Talkback VI (by Crestwood), one of which says, "I think it's pretty cool." On two other message holders for this same device, he has a pictorial drawing of a somewhat disgruntled face with a message that reads, "I don't know. I think we can do better." The two possible message sections in the middle are kept blank, which makes it easier for Kenyon to activate the message he desires. He uses these to respond to Roger's specific questions, but different members on his team (e.g., special educator, paraeducator, speech-language pathologist [SLP], occupational therapist) are teaching him to use the messages as ways of initiating interactions as well. When there is a significant lapse in the interaction between the two boys, a team member will whisper in Kenyon's ear that he could talk to his peer by hitting one of the two messages. They bring the device close to him, point out what the two messages are, and model for him (without actually activating the message) how to initiate the interaction. When he does use the device to say something, his partner responds and asks him more questions. This ability to elicit a response from his classmate tends to prove very reinforcing for Kenyon, prompting him to use the device more often.

Again, conversation partners must allow students with severe disabilities the opportunity to make comments without automatically interpreting their actions as requests. Because students with disabilities have difficulty communicating, their communicative partners must provide them with opportunities that encourage them to make comments. In the following example, Shandra, a ninth grader with disabilities, is asked to participate in a small-group project in her social studies class. The class is studying the social problem of poverty, and their teacher has asked them to work in groups of two or three to develop a photo essay on the topic.

As a member of a group of three students, Shandra participates by using a small, portable pictorial book. She needs a way to interact socially, to express her opinions and make general comments, and to respond to direct questions from her classmates. Her book contains five pictures, each accompanied by a phrase. By pointing to a particular picture, she can say, "That's cool," "I don't like it," "Help me, okay?" "Let's get some more photos," or, "We're done." Most of these phrases are on AAC devices that she uses in other activities, so she is already familiar with them to some degree. She also smiles to communicate "yes" and turns her head to one side to say "no." She is able to grab photographs and place them on the paper to mean "Here, let's put it here," and she shoves photographs away to indicate "No, let's not put it there."

Once the photographs have been taken, Shandra and her partners, Ruthie and Hannah (two ninth graders without disabilities), decide how they will order the photos to create their essay. Ruthie and Hannah offer Shandra two choices at a time (they each select one they would like to see next). She selects one of the photos, and they help to position it in the appropriate place. Ruthie and Hannah add subtitles to each photograph, read these to Shandra, and ask her whether she approves or not. When Shandra tires of the activity, she'll let her partners know that they are done. Although the teacher did not specifically elicit comments from Shandra, the activity was structured so that her classmates asked her to comment in order to complete their project.

Interacting to Achieve Social Closeness

Light (1997) suggested that achieving social closeness is one of the most important functions of communication. Individuals engage in this communicative behavior purely for

Figure 5.4.   Two fifth graders spend some social time together. (Photographer: Margo Taylor)

the purpose of enjoying another's company. Interacting socially is an essential element for forming friendships (see Figure 5.4), the importance of which is discussed in Chapter 1.

Students with severe disabilities, like their peers without disabilities, need to be able to tease, joke, and interact for the sole purpose of having fun. Students who do not have an appropriate way to engage in this type of social interaction may resort to inappropriate and unconventional behavior to meet the same need. Some students will burp, make silly noises, take another's possessions, or run around hoping to be chased in order to tease their teachers and classmates. Collins, Hall, and Branson (1997) reported that, in an effort to make conversation unrelated to the activity, one adolescent with moderate disabilities appeared to intentionally make mistakes to tease his peers. Obviously, it is necessary to provide students like this with more appropriate ways to interact for social closeness.

For example, Leon, a fifth grader who is blind and does not use speech, is encouraged to bring items of interest from home to share with his classmates. Leon's brother has programmed an option on his Mini-Message Mate (by Words+, Inc.) to say, COME SEE WHAT I'VE GOT! When Leon selects that message, a peer close to him comes to him and asks him what he has. Leon is then prompted to show his classmate what he has brought. Sharing items is difficult for Leon because he cannot see where the item is once it has left his hands, so peers have been taught to let Leon keep the item in his hands while they examine it. They will comment on the item and ask him yes/no questions about it, such as, "Did you get it at Toys R Us?" Because another skill that Leon is working on is to respond with a consistent "yes" (head dropped down to his chest) or "no" (head turned toward the side), he receives several opportunities to practice this skill as well.

The tactile symbol on Leon's Mini-Message Mate that he touches to get people to come to him is a denim square because most of his classmates wear denim jeans. A paraeducator or special educator will verbally cue him to push the denim symbol whenever he has brought something to show others. The educator will make sure his device is near him and that he is aware of it and will then ask him if he wants to show anyone what he has brought. If he does not respond within 4 seconds, the educator will remind him that he should touch the appropriate space and will allow him another 4 seconds before physically placing his hand on the correct space and asking him to push it. If Leon does not press the symbol at this point, the educator will ask him again whether he wants to share what he has brought. If he says "no" by turning his head to either side, the educator accepts this response and does not force him to call over a peer. In this example, the educator used a least-to-most intensive or informative prompting strategy because the task is not a new one for Leon and because he can be slow to respond and tends to become overly dependent on physical prompting.

Another example to illustrate how to teach students with disabilities ways to engage in communicative behavior for social purposes involves Melissa, a seventh grader with disabilities. Melissa tries to achieve social closeness by grabbing at her classmates, especially the boys, and then grinning at them. Because she does not have access to an alternative mode of communication, she uses this more physical interaction as a way to gain social closeness. Her severe physical limitations often prevent her from coming in actual contact with her peers, but her attempts are usually treated communicatively. For instance, a boy might see her grab at him and respond with, "Hey, what are you trying to do, Melissa? Keep your hands off the merchandise." Because his response is said good-naturedly, Melissa feels the kind of rapport that she is seeking, and she communicates this by grinning broadly. Although she could benefit from an AAC device that allows her to be more specific in this social interaction (e.g., a BIGmack that she could activate with head movements to say something like, HEY, HOW'S IT GOING?), her own unaided method of interacting seems to provide her with sufficient success. As long as her peers respond appropriately to these efforts, the reason for the interaction is met. If her efforts were ignored or if her peers responded negatively, an AAC device would be more critical.

Educators should try to find creative ways of helping students with disabilities communicate to gain social closeness. Monty, a tenth grader, uses a folder to help him interact socially. When he opens his folder, the left side shows photographs of movie and TV stars he likes, as well as a small Far Side cartoon that represents the question, "Do you want to see a good cartoon?" (The right side of the folder has envelopes that contain items for each of Monty's classes.) Monty particularly likes to initiate interactions with his classmates by pointing to the cartoon. When a peer says "yes" or "sure" in response, he pulls out an envelope from the folder and selects a cartoon to share. In order to keep these interactions stimulating, the cartoons, which are brought from home, are changed daily and are very funny. Monty is positively reinforced by his peers' laughter, so he often initiates interactions in this manner. With a little assistance from his parents (in providing the cartoons) and his teachers (in encouraging him to communicate), Monty is able experience the pleasure of interacting socially with his classmates.

Asking for Information

Students without disabilities often ask questions for information. They seek to clarify assignments, to get permission to engage in certain activities, and to gain understanding. Asking for information is an effective way to initiate an interaction (Newell, 1992). For many students, asking questions is a natural function of communication; however, students with severe disabilities will most likely need the assistance of their teachers to be able to interact in this way.

Some students with severe disabilities ask for information by showing interest in something new and unusual (e.g., reaching for, pointing at, patting, and looking at something in a questioning or puzzled manner). The conversation partner responds by supplying the information (e.g., "Oh, that's an apple core peeler. Here's how it works"). Some students can use a symbol with a question mark on it, and others can use a VOCA to ask WHAT'S THAT? Koegel, Camarata, Valdez-Menchaca, and Koegel (1998) used highly desired items and a delay time to teach students with severe autism to initiate an interaction by asking the question, "What's that?" Not only did students learn how to ask questions but in requesting information about things they also increased their vocabularies. Educators can increase opportunities for students with severe disabilities to develop this communication skill by being sensitive to behavior that may indicate curiosity or interest and by refraining from providing too much information too soon.

Mrs. Leary, a first-grade teacher, has created several methods for encouraging her student with disabilities, Nita, to ask questions. One of these methods is incorporated in a sharing activity that occurs every Monday afternoon and involves the whole class. Students bring items from home and discuss their items with the class, and then classmates are encouraged to ask questions. Nita uses a mercury switch attached to a cassette recorder to ask her question. Her sister tape-records different questions at home every weekend so that Nita can participate in the Monday afternoon activity. The questions are generic enough to be meaningful regardless of what is shared, such as "Where did you say you got that?" or "Can I see it up close?" The teacher calls on Nita first so that other students will hear her question and not repeat it. When Nita starts to raise her hand the teacher is cued to call on her, and when she has finished raising her hand, the mercury switch activates the recording. A paraeducator or parent volunteer first verbally cues Nita to do this when the teacher asks whether anyone has any questions. If a verbal cue ("Remember to raise your hand if you have something to say") is not effective within a 3-second pause, then the educator will touch Nita's arm and give her a more direct verbal cue ("Raise this arm"). If Nita doesn't raise her arm sufficiently to activate the message, the educator can physically support her arm in this upright position. Physical support provided at her shoulder and elbow is faded as long as the message is still activated.

Other students may not need as much physical support to ask questions, but they may need assistance making their questions understood. For example, Helena, a 15-year-old student in the eighth grade is quite verbal but is extremely hard to understand. She can say some one- or two-word combinations that are fairly easily understood, but people unfamiliar with her speech have difficulty understanding her. Her inability to communicate effectively with those unfamiliar to her is frustrating to her and can cause her to engage in inappropriate behavior. To assist Helena in the library, the special educator and SLP converted a coupon holder into a pictorial/word communication device. Some questions were written on pink-colored index cards with a pictorial representation indicating a need for help. For example, "Can you help me find . . . ?" or "Where are the magazines on . . . ?" Specific magazines or categories of books were written on light blue index cards with a corresponding pictorial representation. Helena can choose from these pictured cards to obtain the books or selection she needs. Although she uses speech, the cards make her intent clear for anyone who has difficulty understanding her, such as the librarian.

For students with sufficient physical abilities to sign and point, the teacher can model a question by pointing to something unusual, shrugging his or her shoulders, and maintaining a questioning look. The American Sign Language sign for WHAT? can be paired with this behavior. A student without disabilities can supply the missing information (e.g., "That's a close up I took of the top of my brother's hat"). When students with severe disabilities are asked if they know what something is or if they know what to do, they can be physically prompted to shake their heads "no," point, and sign the question WHAT?

Confirming or Denying

The ability to confirm or deny helps individuals avoid misinterpretations and breakdowns in interactions. This skill is particularly crucial to students who have difficulty making themselves understood. Because students with severe disabilities have difficulty communicating, asking them to confirm or deny whether what they intended to communicate was correctly understood is not only extremely important but it is also a sign of respect, as it lets them know that their attempts to communicate are important enough to be correctly understood.

Opportunities to help students with severe disabilities confirm or deny their communication occur frequently throughout each day; conversation partners simply need to remember to give students this opportunity. Students with severe disabilities can indicate whether they were understood correctly by saying "yes" or "no," nodding or shaking their heads, smiling, frowning, crying, pointing to or looking at a yes/no symbol, turning away from the communicative partner, following through with the desired activity, or resisting, to name just a few possibilities. Educators and peers must remember to ask the student with severe disabilities whether he or she was understood correctly. Figure 5.5 shows sev-

Figure 5.5.   A seventh grader is asked by classmates to respond to yes/no questions in his leadership class by using printed cards. (Photographer: Margo Yunker)

enth graders in leadership class checking to make sure that they correctly understood their classmate. This checking is particularly important when the student is just learning to express him- or herself or has a somewhat vague and obscure means of doing so or both.

For example, Kenny, a twelfth grader with disabilities, is learning to use his eyes to convey his decisions. For many years, Kenny was considered incapable of expressing his thoughts, so he was not given opportunities to do so. When he moved to a new state and school district, the SLP felt he should be given the opportunity to try. This district believes in educating all students together for the benefit of all, so Kenny was placed in a number of general education classes that seemed the most appropriate for helping him develop important skills. For instance, although he cannot sing, he seems to enjoy hearing his classmates, so his educational team outlined opportunities for helping him develop communication skills in choir. One of these is allowing Kenny to choose where he wants his wheelchair positioned. Because the boys sit or stand together depending on their position in the choir (bass or tenor), at the beginning of each class, two stand on either side of Kenny, and he is asked to look at the one he wants to sit by. Initially, it was difficult for Kenny to decide, because he did not know the students well, and for the students to understand his communicative attempts, because his poor head control often makes it difficult to interpret his gaze. Nevertheless, once Kenny makes a choice, the student he selects pushes him to the appropriate position in the choir and asks him whether this is what he had wanted. If Kenny smiles or appears relaxed, then it is assumed that he was correctly understood. If, however, he seems tense or angry, then it is assumed that he was misinterpreted, and he is allowed to choose again using the same two students. All of this occurs at the beginning of class and while the teacher is giving directions. With only three students involved in this interaction, the teacher does not find it overly distracting, especially because it does not take a lot of time. Once Kenny has learned that he can use his eyes to communicate preferences, fewer misunderstandings will likely occur and he will learn to make choices more quickly.

TEACHING STUDENTS CONVERSATION SKILLS

Conversations between people occur when one person initiates the interaction and another responds. Considerable analysis of interactions between those with disabilities and those without shows that students with severe disabilities are often the recipients of the interaction and rarely the initiators (Cipani, 1990; Reichle & Sigafoos, 1991). They must wait until someone approaches them and engages them in conversation. The beginning, duration, and end of the conversation depends, to a large extent, on the conversation partner. The passive role that students with severe disabilities are forced to accept can become extremely frustrating. The fact that these students' conversations are dictated completely by others can be almost unbearable for them. It is, therefore, not surprising when some students attempt to gain attention in any way they can, using bouts of crying or throwing temper tantrums. According to Halle (1987), being able to initiate an interaction spontaneously may be the most important function of communication because of the control it affords. The challenge for educators, then, is to acknowledge the difficulties that these students face and to help them learn conversation skills.

Learning the Parts of a Conversation

Although conversations differ from one to the next depending on an infinite number of factors, they all entail, essentially, initiating, maintaining, and terminating a communicative exchange. Some of the variables that influence conversations are environmental conditions and age, culture, experience, status, and gender of the participants. Although there is no way to control all of these variables, teachers can still utilize general strategies to help students with severe disabilities learn conversation skills.

Initiating

To teach the skill of initiating a conversation, at least two people in addition to the student with severe disabilities need to be involved. One teacher cannot be both the communication partner and the one teaching the communication skill. One person will be needed as the conversation partner for the student to approach while the teacher prompts the desired behavior. The effectiveness of this approach was demonstrated by Frost and Bondy (1996) and Schwartz, Garfinkle, and Bauer (1998). The obvious benefit of a general education classroom is the availability of a number of same-age communication partners for this purpose.

The teacher must ensure that the student has a reason to initiate an interaction (e.g., wants something, wants someone's attention, wants to share information), has some means with which to initiate the interaction, and has easy access to potential communication partners. Anyone in the role of teacher (e.g., general or special educator, SLP, paraprofessional) can then use a variety of prompts to shape the desired behavior. Gestures and direct or indirect verbal prompts can be used to guide the student's attention to the potential communication partner. The teacher can model initiating a conversation by using the student's most effective means of communication (e.g., gesture, manual signs, vocalization, AAC device). Physically guiding the student in performing the behavior may also be necessary, especially if this is a novel behavior or situation or both. Each student will respond best to a unique set of prompts, and members of the student's educational team should be aware of these and use them consistently in order to be effective. If necessary, the teacher can cue the conversation partner to be very responsive to the student's efforts instead of responding to the teacher, which is often a temptation.

For example, in a high school physical education class, the boys shoot baskets in groups of four or five. Scott really enjoys basketball and is eagerly watching his classmates. A work-study student, Glenn, who helps Scott in this class, waits for 2 minutes and then gives Scott an indirect verbal cue if he has not joined in ("Scott, you may want to join a group") and gestures toward the nearest group of boys. If Scott does not approach the boys, Glenn asks Scott to find the single card in his pocket that asks permission to join a group. Glenn may touch Scott's pocket if he seems to have forgotten. Glenn asks Scott what he can do with this card and again gestures toward the group of boys. If Scott does not move within 5 seconds, Glenn walks toward the group as a model for Scott to follow. Once Scott starts moving toward the group, he usually completes the initiation by holding the card out to someone. If he goes for the ball instead, Glenn redirects him to the nearest student in the group with a verbal cue, "Ask (name of student) first," and points at that student while blocking Scott's access to the ball.

When Scott was first learning this skill of initiating an interaction, the prompting strategy was somewhat different. Without an alternative mode of communication, Scott would rush into any group, grab a ball, and run off with it. Although his actions were clear, Scott needed to learn a more acceptable manner of joining his peers. A single pictorial card with a printed request was created that fit easily in Scott's pocket, allowing him free movement and use of his hands (see Figure 5.6). In the locker room, the work-study student and special educator demonstrated the use of the card with verbal instructions.

Figure 5.6.   Scott's symbol for asking to play with friends.

When the class was instructed to get into groups to practice shooting baskets, Scott was encouraged to do this, although he often refused, preferring to watch first. He was physically prevented from running away with a ball that came his way, but when he showed interest in the ball, he was told to take the card out of his pocket (the card was partially removed from his pocket to make it easier for him). The work-study student, Glenn, would say, "Let's go ask this group if we can join them," and point toward the group. The special educator would then physically guide Scott to go with Glenn if necessary (if Glenn were four steps ahead of Scott and he had yet to move). Then Glenn would whisper in Scott's ear for him to give the nearest student the card. If this student was not looking, Scott was told to touch the student with the card. This simplified what Scott had to do to initiate an interaction. As Scott became more adept at approaching and initiating his request, the prompting strategy changed to reflect this progress.

In the preceding example, Scott is physically capable of approaching a peer to initiate an interaction. Students with severe physical impairments who are unable to do this need an alternative method for initiating an interaction. Indeed, it is probably even more critical for students who are physically unable to move to be able to initiate conversation, as the following example illustrates.

Carrie is a second grader who needs a way to initiate conversations during unstructured times to experience a certain degree of social closeness. She is just learning that her actions have definite consequences, which gives her a sense of control in certain situations. Her movements are very limited, so whatever form she is taught to initiate an interaction must be as simple and direct as possible. Because her arms are usually in a flexed position, with a slight downward motion she is able to use her elbow to activate a switch. Due to a severe visual impairment, however, Carrie seems to prefer a vocal output mode. Furthermore, if left alone for awhile, she will resort to crying in order to gain someone's attention. Given these circumstances, Carrie's teachers decided that the best way for Carrie to successfully initiate conversation would be by using a BIGmack that, when activated, would say, CAN ANYONE COME SEE ME? Another little girl in her class recorded the message for her, and Carrie's classmates were instructed to respond to Carrie as quickly as possible in order to reinforce her attempts to initiate conversation.

In order to teach Carrie the skill of initiating interactions with her classmates, her educational team outlined a very specific set of steps to follow. The specialist supporting Carrie brings the BIGmack close to Carrie's left elbow (the movement helps to draw her attention to the switch) and taps the desk next to the switch as an additional cue if she does not detect the movement. The specialist then tells her that she can hit the switch with her elbow when she wants someone to come to her. Her left elbow is physically guided onto the switch at this point, with sufficient pressure applied to activate it. The classmate closest to Carrie, having been taught how to respond, touches Carrie's arm and says, "I heard you, Carrie. I'm right here." The specialist then backs away from the situation, making sure that the BIGmack is suctioned in place and will not move. After a few minutes of being left alone, Carrie will usually begin to squirm. The specialist, recognizing this behavior as an indicator that Carrie wants more contact, approaches her quietly from the side, physically guides her elbow onto the BIGmack until the message is heard, and nods at one of the students close by to respond to her. The specialist does not talk to Carrie during this time, but instead, keeps her interactions minimal and nonsocial in order to encourage Carrie to initiate interactions with her peers. If the specialist interacted more with Carrie at this point (e.g., "Carrie, remember that when you want someone to come to you, use your switch"), then Carrie would learn that fussing and squirming, and eventually, crying, is an effective way to gain attention. Allowing the peers to be more social with her (saying her name, touching her, and appearing concerned and interested in her) reinforces her use of the BIGmack. Of course, once Carrie has mastered the ability to initiate interactions with her peers, her educational team then needs to create a systematic method of teaching her how to maintain these interactions, because simply initiating an interaction falls short of the ultimate goal of conversing.

Maintaining the Interaction

Gaining someone's attention is one thing, but maintaining it is quite another. Students with severe disabilities can be at a distinct disadvantage, especially when they have limited means of expressing themselves. Maintaining conversation falls primarily on the shoulders of the conversation partner, yet the student with disabilities must be able to participate in the turn-taking behavior inherent in conversation. A student's ability to notice things in the environment and to comment on them will largely affect his or her ability to maintain conversation (Reichle, 1991). Obviously, students with a severe visual disability or students who, in general, are not attuned to their environment experience considerable difficulty noticing things on which to comment.

Students with disabilities need to be supplied with communicative aids that go beyond requesting items or activities or saying "yes" and "no." Educators need to be creative in producing conversation books, boards, or boxes of items (see Chapter 6) to facilitate these students' attempts to maintain conversation, and they need to spend sufficient time instructing students how to use the devices (Hunt et al., 1997). Students can use these devices to direct a partner's attention to something of relevance so that the partner can respond and the interaction can be maintained.

Not only do students with disabilities need help finding stimulus for maintaining conversations but they also need assistance learning how to take turns, a critical skill for engaging in conversations (Light & Binger, 1998). Students must learn that one initiation or response is insufficient to engage the other person for any length of time. Teachers can build on the turn-taking skills that students use to play games to teach the kind of turn-taking used to maintain conversations. Students need to understand that when the conversation partner has stopped talking, they need to "say" something in return. Teaching this skill requires the educator to shape a conversation turn at every opportunity, regardless of whether such a turn is actually necessary. Light and Binger (1998) called these turns *obligatory* (when someone asks a question that requires a response) and *nonobligatory* (when a response is not necessary, but can keep the conversation going).

For instance, the question, "Do you like going to Mrs. Claymore's class?" calls for an obligatory response, whereas the comment, "I'm going to show you what we did in art today," could elicit a nonobligatory response, such as, "Great." Davis, Reichle, Johnston, and Southard (1998) were successful at improving the conversation turn-taking of two children with severe disabilities to nonobligatory statements when the statements immediately followed obligatory statements. In their study, they interspersed a nonobligatory statement after a few questions that did require responses and to which the students were capable of responding. They demonstrated that this type of procedure may have built sufficient momentum to keep the conversation going and the student with severe disabilities responding.

The following example illustrates how AAC devices can help students with disabilities maintain conversations. Savannah is a third grader who uses facial expressions, gestures, body movements, objects, and pictures to communicate. To help her maintain social conversations with friends and classmates, she uses a conversation book containing colored Boardmaker symbols, photographs, and pictures from magazines and newspapers with sentences that relate to, but do not just label, the pictures. For instance, a magazine picture of a Barbie doll has the attached sentence "I collect Barbie dolls." The book is a small 6″ × 5″ photo album with a soft cover that fits easily into a fanny pack, making it quite portable. Pictures are different sizes (from 5″ × 3″ to 2″ × 1″), and there are from one to four pictures per side of the book. Two pages of this conversation book are illustrated in Figure 5.7. Pictures and sentences can be changed easily by sliding them in and out of the photo holders. Her parents and siblings change the pictures and conversational statements to reflect her current interests and experiences. Her teacher shows her how to point to pictures of her choice to give her conversation partner something to com-

Figure 5.7.   Savannah's conversation book. (Photographer: Diane Andres; Designer: June E. Downing)

ment on or ask about. Following a response from her partner, Savannah's teacher waits 2 seconds for her to respond before tapping the book to remind her. If Savannah does not respond to this prompt, her teacher verbally directs her to say something to her partner and gently pushes her elbow toward the book at the same time. If Savannah still does not respond, the teacher finds a picture in the book, guides Savannah's hand to it, and tells her to show it to her partner. The teacher allows 2 seconds between each prompt, which gives Savannah time within which to respond without losing her interest in the task or causing the pauses to get so long that they break the rhythm of conversation.

Terminating the Conversation

Although terminating a conversation may be easier than initiating or maintaining one, teaching students appropriate ways to end a conversation can be tricky. Some students end conversations by running away, closing their eyes, or hitting their partners so that the person leaves them. These methods are relatively effective, yet not necessarily socially desirable, and they can have the negative effect of hindering future interactions.

Sometimes students with severe disabilities are not provided the option to end a conversation because of some external factor, such as time constraint. For instance, the school bell rings and the student's conversation partner quickly disappears. This situation can be particularly aggravating for a student with disabilities who requires a substantial amount of time to respond. Teachers can help alleviate this frustration by teaching classmates of these students to notify the student of their need to leave and not just disappear.

Once teachers have solicited the help of classmates and other individuals working with a student with disabilities, opportunities to teach him or her appropriate ways of terminating conversations abound. Students can be reminded to say, "Bye," "See ya," "Gotta go now," or whatever is appropriate for the situation. In order to give these kinds of farewells, the student will probably require an AAC device, such as a message on a VOCA or a pictorial symbol. Students with sufficient physical ability can wave or signal in a manner appropriate for their age.

When others initiate a farewell, students with disabilities can be taught to respond in a manner similar to those just mentioned or in any other way that indicates that they understand, for instance, by giving a smile, nod, or look of acknowledgment. Conversation partners should not just leave the student with severe disabilities without an appropriate conclusion to the conversation, not only to give the student with disabilities a comforting sense of closure but also because expecting a response of some kind from the student with disabilities reinforces the turn-taking nature of conversation.

TEACHING STUDENTS TO GENERALIZE COMMUNICATION SKILLS

Acquiring a communication skill that is used only in one environment or activity and with one person has limited value. Students need communication skills that allow them greater flexibility—skills that they can rely on regardless of environment—yet students with the most challenging disabilities may have extreme difficulty transferring skills learned in one specific situation to another (Calculator, 1988; Duker & Jutten, 1997; Reichle & Sigafoos, 1991). Teachers must vary their instruction sufficiently to provide the student with experiences in as many different situations as possible, while continuing to maintain and demonstrate the desired skill.

Perhaps one of the greatest benefits of *not* perceiving a certain time of day and place (e.g., a speech room) as the only time to work on communication skills is that every environment, time, and activity becomes the appropriate learning environment.

In fact, teaching students using naturalistic language training and distributing that instruction across natural times of the day help students to generalize the skills they learn (McDonnell, 1996).

Because communication is a skill that is needed in almost every situation, most individuals develop the ability to generalize the skills at the same time that they are learning the rudiments of communication. The same dynamic and highly variable nature of communication that forces most of us to generalize communication skills as we acquire them, however, makes it very difficult for students with severe disabilities to master them, despite the fact that the desire and need to communicate would appear to be intrinsically motivating. Individuals working with students with disabilities must continue to remember that, given the extreme variety of communication, these students have great difficulty generalizing the communication skills that they are able to learn; consequently, these skills will not automatically emerge whenever students need them. In fact, one of the reasons that makes it very difficult for students with severe disabilities to generalize communication skills is their tendency to focus on irrelevant stimuli. For instance, if a teacher who is helping students to learn how to say "good-bye" is wearing a bright red dress and the student happens to focus on that, then the student may later misinterpret red clothing as a stimulus rather than whatever communicative prompt the teacher had tried to bring to the student's attention. Students with severe disabilities need specific instruction in order to be able to translate skills acquired in specific situations to more general circumstances, regardless of the conversation partner, the activity, or the environment (Koegel et al., 1998; Mirenda, 1997; Stokes & Osnes, 1989).

Teaching Students to Use Similar Communication Skills in Different Situations

Unlike many self-contained special education rooms, general education classrooms have an abundance of potential and responsive communication partners. In addition, each school day provides many opportunities to practice interacting with a variety of different partners, including classmates, other students, the librarian, cafeteria workers, bus drivers, the principal, and a conceivably large number of teachers (especially for high school students). Teachers need to recognize these opportunities and plan to make use of them so that students with disabilities can learn to respond appropriately to different individuals. Collecting data on successful interactions will help clarify with whom interactions are occurring and whether a student is able to use communication skills with different partners.

For example, Marc, a fourth grader with severe and multiple disabilities, is learning to respond to requests from classmates or teachers to provide information. Students in his class are working on a lesson on nouns and modifying adjectives. They have finished reading a chapter in their books and are supposed to list 10 nouns from this chapter and then add any adjectives they choose to modify the nouns. Marc is working with a partner who has written the nouns on a piece of paper and is ready to add the adjectives. Marc, who is blind, has several textures in front of him representing adjectives such as "smooth," "hard," "rough," "scratchy," and "soft." Because they are also different colors, Marc's partner can decide to use color as an adjective as well. Marc is supposed to pick one texture and hand it to his partner. If he does not do this, his partner specifically asks him for one ("Give me one"). If this does not work, the partner asks again, and the paraeducator gently taps Marc's elbow to bring his hand forward. If necessary, the paraeducator provides more physical assistance to help Marc select, grasp, and extend one to his partner. Marc's partner thanks him and then decides what adjective he would like it to represent (texture or color) and what noun he would like it to modify. He writes the adjective in the space provided and reads the result to Marc. He then asks for another one and the process is repeated until all 10 nouns have a modifying adjective beside them.

To ensure that Marc translates this skill to other situations, his teacher outlines procedures for teaching the same skill during other activities. For example, during spelling, when students are studying for a test by writing sentences using their spelling words, Marc's classmate asks him for a spelling word. Marc selects an item from in front of him that stands for a spelling word and hands it to the classmate. Only the spelling words that are easily represented by objects are presented by Marc (e.g., magnet, ribbon, clothespin, leather, pumpkin). Again, his teacher uses a similar teaching method in social studies, in which students are building igloos out of sugar cubes after reading a story about Eskimos. Marc responds to requests from peers to hand them building materials of sugar cubes and toothpicks. Occasionally, Marc's teacher asks him to hand out materials. Each student asks him for the materials, and he receives many opportunities to practice giving them their materials. Finally, when Marc goes with a peer to take the attendance sheet to the office, the secretary asks him if he has anything to give her, and he responds by handing her the sheet. During each school day, Marc receives many different opportunities to use this same communication skill in different activities and with several different partners, thereby helping him to generalize the skill.

Although each situation will differ, certain communication acts are expected across different environments and activities. These already have been addressed in this chapter. In general, the more opportunities a student has to practice skills, the more chance there is of the student acquiring the skill. If students are taught to engage in specific communicative behaviors in one particular environment only, the overall effectiveness of such skills will be greatly diminished. Students need to understand that their communicative behaviors are expected across all environments.

For example, Whitney (age 15) has severe and multiple disabilities. She is learning to make comments about things she likes and does not particularly like. She uses a voice output device for two messages with graphic designs to represent each remark. She uses this device in different situations and classes that she takes at her local high school. As indicated on her IEP/activity matrix (Figure 5.8), Whitney asks her peers to push her to each class, lets those around her know what position she would like to be in for several classes where there is a choice, and uses her SpeakEasy with two messages and facial expressions to provide feedback to peers across all classes. By documenting how communication skills will be targeted across different environments and social situations, there is less danger that Whitney will learn to communicate only in a certain way in only one situation. This type of generalization across settings must be planned.

SUMMARY

This chapter has targeted the need for students with severe disabilities to learn specific functions of communication; to use these functions in initiating, maintaining, and terminating conversations; and to be able to transfer these skills to various different settings. Students with severe disabilities need to be encouraged to do more than make requests or rejections. Specific examples were provided to illustrate strategies developed by educational teams to teach students with severe disabilities specific communication skills in order for the reader to understand how these strategies translate to real teaching experiences.

Student: Whitney
Level: 9th grade

Skills	Choir	Computers	PE	Drama	Lunch
• Controls environment with the switch	• Turns on music with switch • Records classmates with switch	• Opens chosen software program/file with switch • Chooses program • Chooses graphics	• Operates music for aerobics, exercises • Operates radio during PT (using headphones) • Uses BIGmack to cheer team	• Controls background music for classmates during skits (with switch) • Operates some lights as directed (with switch)	• Activates radio with switch using headphones
• Requests peer to push her to next class	X	X	X	X	X
• Provides feedback to peers	• Uses SpeakEasy (two messages) on practice sessions • Uses facial expressions to comment	• Uses facial expressions to comment on peers' work	• Uses BIGmack to cheer team • Uses SpeakEasy (two messages) to comment on performance	• Uses SpeakEasy (two messages) to comment on peers' performance	• Responds to peers' comments using facial expressions and some gestures
• Decides on position to be in	• Decides to use stander or chair • Decides where to be (if choice provided)		• Decides position in which to do exercises, receive PT, participate in activity of day (if choice provided)	• Decides to be in chair or stander • Decides where to be in room	• Decides whether to get out of chair after lunch • Decides to receive feeding in chair or on wedge • Decides to eat in cafeteria or outside

Figure 5.8.   Whitney's IEP/activity matrix for generalization of communication skills.

REFERENCES

Calculator, S.N. (1988). Promoting the acquisition and generalization of conversational skills by individuals with severe disabilities. *Augmentative and Alternative Communication, 4,* 94–103.

Carr, E., & Durand, V. (1985). Reducing behavior problems through functional communication training. *Journal of Applied Behavior Analysis, 18,* 111–126.

Chadsey-Rusch, J., Linneman, D., & Rylance, B.J. (1997). Beliefs about social integration from the perspectives of persons with mental retardation, job coaches, and employers. *American Journal on Mental Retardation, 102,* 1–12.

Cipani, E. (1990). "Excuse me: I'll have . . .": Teaching appropriate attention-getting behavior to young children with severe handicaps. *Mental Retardation, 28,* 29–33.

Collins, B.C., Hall, M., & Branson, T.A. (1997). Teaching leisure skills to adolescents with moderate disabilities. *Exceptional Children, 63,* 499–512.

Davis, C.A., Reichle, J., Johnston, S., & Southard, K. (1998). Teaching children with severe disabilities to utilize nonobligatory conversational opportunities: An application of high-probability requests. *Journal of The Association for Persons with Severe Handicaps, 23,* 57–68.

Drasgow, W., & Halle, J.W. (1995). Teaching social communication to young children with severe disabilities. *Topics in Early Childhood Special Education, 15,* 164–186.

Duker, P.C., & Jutten, W. (1997). Establishing gestural yes-no responding with individuals with profound mental retardation. *Education and Training in Mental Retardation and Developmental Disabilities, 32,* 59–67.

Durand, V.M., & Carr, E.G. (1991). Functional communication training to reduce challenging behavior: Maintenance and application in new settings. *Journal of Applied Behavior Analysis, 24,* 251–264.

Frost, L., & Bondy, A. (1996). *PECS: The picture exchange communication system training manual.* Cherry Hill, NJ: Pyramid Educational Consultant.

Goodman, J., & Remington, B. (1993). Acquisition of expressive signing: Comparison of reinforcement strategies. *Augmentative and Alternative Communication, 9,* 26–35.

Goossens', C., & Crain, S.S. (1992). *Utilizing switch interfaces with children who are severely physically challenged.* Austin, TX: PRO-ED.

Halle, J. (1987). Teaching language in the natural environment: An analysis of spontaneity. *Journal of The Association for Persons with Severe Handicaps, 12,* 28–37.

Hunt, P., Alwell, M., & Goetz, L. (1988). Acquisition of conversational skills and the reduction of inappropriate social interaction behaviors. *Journal of The Association for Persons with Severe Handicaps, 13,* 20–27.

Hunt, P., Farron-Davis, F., Wrenn, M., Hirose-Hatae, A., & Goetz, L. (1997). Promoting interactive partnerships in inclusive educational settings. *Journal of The Association for Persons with Severe Handicaps, 22,* 127–137.

Kaczmarek, L. (1990). Teaching spontaneous language to individuals with severe handicaps: A matrix model. *Journal of The Association for Persons with Severe Handicaps, 15,* 160–169.

Koegel, L.K., Camarata, S.M., Valdez-Menchaca, M., & Koegel, R.L. (1998). Setting generalization of question-asking by children with autism. *American Journal on Mental Retardation, 102,* 346–357.

Light, J. (1988). Interactions involving individuals using augmentative and alternative communication systems: State of the art and future directions. *Augmentative and Alternative Communication, 4,* 66–82.

Light, J. (1997). "Communication is the essence of human life": Reflections on communicative competence. *Augmentative and Alternative Communication, 13,* 61–70.

Light, J.C., & Binger, C. (1998). *Building communicative competence with individuals who use augmentative and alternative communication.* Baltimore: Paul H. Brookes Publishing Co.

McDonnell, A.P. (1996). The acquisition, transfer, and generalization of requests by young children with severe disabilities. *Education and Training in Mental Retardation and Developmental Disabilities, 31,* 213–234.

Mirenda, P. (1997). Supporting individuals with challenging behavior through functional communication training and AAC: Research review. *Augmentative and Alternative Communication, 13,* 207–225.

Newell, A. (1992). Social communication: Chattering, mattering, and cheek. *Communication Outlook, 14*(1), 6–8.

Reichle, J. (1991). Developing communicative exchanges. In J. Reichle, J. York, & J. Sigafoos (Eds.), *Implementing augmentative and alternative communication: Strategies for learners with severe disabilities* (pp. 133–156). Baltimore: Paul H. Brookes Publishing Co.

Reichle, J., Barrett, C., Tetlie, R., & McQuarter, R. (1987). The effect of prior intervention to establish generalized requesting on the acquisition of object labels. *Augmentative and Alternative Communication, 3,* 3–11.

Reichle, J., & Brown, L. (1986). Teaching the use of a multi-page direct selection communication board to an adult with autism. *Journal of The Association for Persons with Severe Handicaps, 11,* 68–73.

Reichle, J., & Sigafoos, J. (1991). Establishing spontaneity and generalization. In J. Reichle, J. York, & J. Sigafoos (Eds.), *Implementing augmentative and alternative communication: Strategies for learners with severe disabilities* (pp. 157–171). Baltimore: Paul H. Brookes Publishing Co.

Reichle, J., Sigafoos, J., & Piché, L. (1989). Teaching an adolescent with blindness: A correspondence between requesting and selecting preferred objects. *Journal of The Association for Persons with Severe Handicaps, 14,* 75–80.

Schwartz, I.S., Garfinkle, A.N., & Bauer, J. (1998). The picture exchange communication system: Communication outcomes for young children with disabilities. *Topics in Early Childhood Special Education, 18,* 144–159.

Sigafoos, J., Mustonen, T., DePaepe, P., Reichle, J., & York, J. (1991). Defining the array of instructional prompts for teaching communication skills. In J. Reichle, J. York, & J. Sigafoos (Eds.) *Implementing augmentative and alternative communication: Strategies for learners with severe disabilities* (pp. 173–192). Baltimore: Paul H. Brookes Publishing Co.

Siperstein, G.N., Leffert, J.S., & Widaman, K. (1996). Social behavior and the social acceptance and rejection of children with mental retardation. *Education and Training in Mental Retardation and Developmental Disabilities, 31,* 271–281.

Stokes, T.F., & Osnes, P.G. (1989). An operant pursuit of generalization. *Behavior Research and Therapy, 20,* 337–355.

Storey, K., & Horner, R.H. (1991). Social interactions in three supported employment options: A comparative analysis. *Journal of Applied Behavior Analysis, 24,* 349–360.

6

Augmentative and Alternative Communication Techniques

Pat Mirenda

Augmentative and alternative communication (AAC) techniques are used to supplement (i.e., augment) or replace speech. AAC techniques are of two types: unaided and aided. Unaided techniques, which do not require any external equipment, include manual signing, pantomime, and gestures. Aided techniques incorporate devices that are external to the individuals who use them, such as computers, microswitches, or voice output communication aides (VOCAs). Most people use a combination of both unaided and aided techniques to communicate in different situations or with different people. For example, a teacher may use speech, gestures, and body language (unaided techniques) together with videotapes, words written on overhead transparencies, and pictures or diagrams (aided techniques) to illustrate the class topic. That same teacher, however, when working alone in his or her office may use a variety of aided techniques, such as a computer, printer, telephone, and fax machine, and only one unaided technique (speech) when someone enters his or her office. Imagine what it would be like to be restricted to only one or two communication techniques in most situations—even though communication may occur, it would probably not be very efficient or effective.

The fact that people communicate in a variety of ways is important to remember when supporting students with severe disabilities. One AAC technique will never meet all of a student's communication needs, and each student will almost always use a combination of unaided and aided techniques. Furthermore, students will need AAC devices updated continuously to accommodate changing skills and needs. In this chapter, the combination of all of the techniques used by an individual student is referred to as his or her AAC system. This chapter reviews the most commonly used AAC techniques (both unaided and aided) and discusses some of the basic processes for making decisions about when each might be incorporated into a student's system.

UNAIDED COMMUNICATION

The most commonly used unaided communication techniques (aside from speech) are manual signs, gestures, body language, vocalizations, and pantomime. Except for manual signs, most individuals acquire unaided techniques on their own and need little or no practice in order to use them, which is a real advantage for teachers. Classroom support personnel need to be attuned to how each student communicates and what his or her various gestures, vocalizations, and other unaided techniques mean. When teachers are not attuned to their students' nonverbal communication, scenarios such as the following are likely to occur.

> It is math time in Ms. Harris's fourth-grade class. All of the students are working in pairs on their multiplication worksheets. Marv, a student with autism, and his partner Fred are working together as a pair. Marv is learning to use a calculator to find the answers, while Fred is multiplying the "old-fashioned" way. After working for about 5 minutes, Marv dashes to the door of the classroom and vocalizes loudly. Ms. Harris asks him to be seated, but he persists, increasing the volume of his sounds. Ms. Harris asks him to be seated again, but Marv falls to the floor, kicking and yelling loudly. Finally, after yelling for almost 10 minutes, Marv calms down, walks back to his desk, and continues with his math. During lunch time, Ms. Harris comments to a colleague, "Marv had another episode today, this time during math class. I wish I could figure out what he's trying to tell me when he runs to the door and yells like that."

Often, students who have difficulty communicating resort to nontraditional modes of communication to try to express their needs and wants, which can be easily misunderstood by those trying to help them. The basic scenario in which a student uses one or more unaided communication techniques to try to get a message across is very common. When the message is easily understood (as when a student nods his head to say "yes" or shakes his head to say "no"), this form of communication can be quite efficient and effective, but when the message is unclear, such as Marv's, some type of additional communication support may be necessary. A gesture dictionary, for example, may have allowed Marv to communicate his desires to his teacher.

Gesture Dictionary

A gesture dictionary helps individuals who are not familiar with someone's unaided communication signals to understand their meanings. It acts as a translation aid by describing a student's gestures along with their meanings and suggestions for appropriate responses. The dictionary may be in the form of a wall poster in the classroom or home or may be an alphabetized notebook with cross-referenced entries. For example, if Marv had a gesture dictionary in the above situation, then Ms. Harris could look up "runs to the door" under "R" (for "run") or under "D" (for "door"). She might then find an entry that looks like this:

What Marv Does	What it Means	How to Respond
Runs to the door	"I want a drink of water from the water fountain in the hall."	Let him go for a drink or set a timer to ring when he can go.

If Marv had had a gesture dictionary, then his teacher could have discovered that running to the door is Marv's way of saying, "I'm thirsty; can I have a drink of water?" Perhaps this entry in the gesture dictionary was made by the classroom assistant who knows him quite well and has learned to "read" his communicative gestures over the years, or perhaps his parents added the entry at the beginning of the year when Ms. Harris asked them for input about how Marv communicates. Regardless, the idea is to document the meanings behind the various gestures, vocalizations, and other unaided communication modes a student uses, so that these meanings can be determined easily in order to prevent communication breakdowns. Here are some additional entries in Marv's gesture dictionary:

What Marv Does	What it Means	How to Respond
Makes an "uh-uh" sound	"I want some help."	Show him the manual sign for "help" and then provide help.
Grabs another student's hand or arm	"I like you."	Explain the meaning to the student's classmate and help them work together, if possible.
Bangs or taps the desk	"I'm bored; I don't understand what's going on."	Quietly explain to him what is happening, using simple language and graphics if needed.

As you can see from these entries, Marv has a lot to say and has developed some rather creative ways to communicate. Imagine how frustrated he would be if Ms. Harris were to treat his communicative attempts as problem behaviors and try to eliminate them, instead of using the gesture dictionary to understand and support him.

When Is Unaided Communication Appropriate?

As apparent in the story of Marv and Ms. Harris, some type of unaided communication—gestures, body language, vocalizations, and so forth—will almost always be used when students have no other way to get their messages across. As long as their unaided communication is socially acceptable and intelligible to both familiar and unfamiliar listeners, there is no reason to be concerned about it. For example, if Marv nods his head to say "yes" and shakes his head to say "no," his communication is both socially acceptable and easily understood. However, if he touches or grabs his genitals to say, "I need to go to the bathroom," he needs to learn a more socially acceptable form to communicate this. He also needs to learn a better way to say, "I want a drink of water from the fountain," because his running to the door and vocalizing will not be understood by anyone without access to his gesture dictionary. One way of accomplishing this is through the use of manual signs.

Manual Signs

Most North Americans are probably familiar with American Sign Language (ASL) (Sternberg, 1994), which is the language system of manual signs used by people who are deaf or hard of hearing. Some individuals who are able to hear but have difficulty communicating through speech can also use manual signs. The advantage of manual signing is that it requires no external equipment such as communication books or boards. The disadvantage, of course, is that many people do not understand manual signs, which limits the communication partners by whom a signing student can be understood. Furthermore, students with motor impairments may not be able to make the hand and arm motions required for manual signing. Students with severe visual impairments will not be able to see others using signs, which may make sign acquisition very difficult for them. Nevertheless, manual signs can be very useful for students with competent fine motor skills and in situations in which the teacher and classmates are willing to learn to sign as well.

Several different manual sign systems have been used successfully by students who can hear. Some students learn signs from ASL, the language system used by the Deaf community. Others may learn signs from the Signed English (Bornstein, Saulnier, & Hamilton, 1983) or the Signing Exact English (Gustason, Pfetzing, & Zawolkow, 1980) systems, which are widely used in schools to teach students who are hearing impaired. The differences between these systems has to do with the complexity of the signs themselves as well as the language structure that governs their use. Selection of a manual sign system for a student with multiple disabilities is a complex decision that will require input from many members of a student's educational team. Often, manual signs are used in conjunction with aided communication techniques such as those discussed in the next section.

AIDED COMMUNICATION

Many different types of aided communication can be used by students in schools, some of which are quite simple and inexpensive, whereas others (e.g., those that are electronic) require considerable expertise to use and operate. This section discusses some of the considerations for using nonelectronically aided communication techniques and reviews some of the most commonly used electronic options as well. First, however, it is important to provide some introductory information about symbols and how they can be used for communication.

Symbols for Communication

A symbol is something that stands for something else. In general, people are surrounded by symbols every day. The golden arches are a symbol for McDonald's; the Coca Cola logo reminds those who see it to drink Coke; the maple leaf flag stands for Canada; and the "V" sign made by spreading two fingers apart stands for either peace or victory. All of these symbols are commonly understood by most people who live in North America, although they may be unfamiliar to people in other parts of the world. When we use them, we communicate messages to each other without using speech.

In order to communicate, students with disabilities can utilize a variety of symbols. Some of these symbols are easy to learn to use, while others are more difficult. The sections that follow examine the most common types of communication symbols, from those that are easiest for students with disabilities to use to those that are more difficult.

Real Objects   The easiest type of symbol to learn is a *real object symbol*. This is simply a three-dimensional object (or partial object) that stands for a person, activity, place, or thing. Real object symbols are created specifically for each person who uses them, depending on the person's experiences. For example, Marcia uses real object symbols to ask for what she wants and to share information with others. If she's thirsty, she brings her teacher a cup to ask for something to drink. If she wants to go out in the car, she brings her mom the car keys. After she goes to the park, she can tell her friends what she did by showing them the tennis ball that she enjoys using there. For Marcia, the cup, keys, and tennis ball are symbols for specific messages—"I'm thirsty," "I want to go out in the car," and "I went to the park." Those specific symbols were selected for Marcia because she always drinks from a cup, sees her mom use the car keys, and carries the tennis ball to the park. She has learned from experience to associate the symbols with the activities they represent. The advantage of real object symbols is that most students, including those with no useable vision, can learn to use them quite easily. The disadvantage is that many messages, such as, "I'm sad" or "Thank you," cannot be represented by real objects. In addition, students with motor impairments may have difficulty manipulating real object symbols. Finally, objects are less portable than other types of symbols, which makes it difficult to ensure that they are readily available to students who need them in all environments.

Tangible Symbols   Tangible symbols are like real objects but are used primarily with students who have severe visual impairments or are blind (Rowland & Schweigert, 1989). Tangible symbols are real objects or parts of objects that *feel* or *sound like* what they represent. For students who cannot see very well or at all, they can be used to represent people, places, activities, or things through the sense of touch or the sense of hearing. For example, Vincent is a third-grade student who is blind and uses tangible symbols. When he goes out to recess with his pals, they offer him a choice between going on the slide and going on the tire swing by having him feel a flat piece of metal and a piece of chain. They use the first symbol because, to Vincent, the slide feels flat and cold, like the piece of metal. They use the chain because, when Vincent sits on the tire swing, he holds onto the chain from which it hangs. He recognizes the activities according to how they *feel*, not according to how they look, because he cannot see them. He chooses the symbol that represents what he wants to do.

Sometimes the tangible and real object symbols may be the same, and sometimes they might be different. Like Marcia (who can see), Vincent uses a cup to mean "I'm thirsty" and a set of car keys to mean "Let's go someplace in the car." He recognizes the *feel* of the cup and the jingling *sound* of the car keys. Vincent, however, does not use a tennis ball like Marcia does when she goes to the park. Instead, he wears a special baseball cap every time he goes to the park, and he has learned to associate it with this activity. For Vincent, the baseball cap means "going to the park" just as the tennis ball means this for Marcia.

Photographs   Students with vision can also use photographs as symbols. These are more difficult to learn than either real object or tangible symbols, but they can still be very useful. Colored photographs are easier to learn than black-and-white photos because the colors provide more information. Colored photographs can be taken with a high-quality camera or can be bought as postcards that represent specific places. They can also be cut out of magazine advertisements, coupons, or menus, or can be scanned into a computer graphics program from various Internet sites and then printed. Black-and-white photographs can also be taken with a camera but are harder to find from other sources. Photographs can be used to represent specific people, places, activities, or items. For example, Mai Lee uses photographs of food items to ask for her lunch in the high school cafeteria. She can talk to her classmates about her family by using photographs and can tell her teachers that she went to San Francisco for her holiday by showing postcards and photographs of the places she visited. The advantage of photographs is that they are easier to carry around than are real objects or tangible symbols. The disadvantage is that they have to be taken with a camera, bought, or cut out of magazines or other media, so they can be time-consuming to produce (downloading them from the Internet reduces the time requirements dramatically). Furthermore, students with visual impairments may have difficulty recognizing photographs unless they are enlarged and very clear.

Black-and-White Line Drawing Symbols   Sets of commercially available symbols made of black-and-white line drawings are available in many sizes and forms and can be bought from a number of different companies (see Appendix). The symbols in these sets usually include those for people, places, activities, and items, as well as those for action verbs (e.g., eat, sit, sleep), feelings (e.g., happy, angry, bored), descriptors (e.g., hot, little, up, down), and social etiquette messages (e.g., please, thank you).

The most commonly used sets of symbols are called Picture Communication Symbols (PCS) (Johnson, 1994). There are more than 3,000 of these symbols that come in three books of 1- and 2-inch square symbols, which can be cut out and then glued to a page. They can also be bought as 1-inch stamps that can be licked and stuck to a page. A software program for computers called Boardmaker can also be used to produce communication displays of PCS symbols (Boardmaker, 1998). Figure 6.1 shows some examples of PCS symbols.

The advantage of commercially available symbols is that they represent many types of messages that cannot be communicated with objects or photographs. The disadvantage is that they need to be purchased, so funding must be available for this purpose, and students with visual impairments may have difficulty recognizing them unless they are enlarged or otherwise enhanced (e.g., colored). Students with severe cognitive disabilities may have difficulty interpreting the black-and-white symbols.

Textured Symbols   Textured symbols may be constructed on an individual basis and used by students with severe visual impairments who have proficient fine motor skills. Textured symbols may be either logically or arbitrarily associated with their referents. A logically associated textured symbol may be a piece of spandex material to symbolize a bathing suit because many suits are made of this material. Alternatively, a square of velvet might be arbitrarily selected to represent a favorite snack. The word or phrase represented by the texture would be added to this symbol to clarify its intent for those who do read. Several case studies have documented the successful use of textured symbols with individuals with one or more sensory impairments in addition to severe intellectual disabilities (Locke & Mirenda, 1988; Mathy-Laikko et al., 1989; Murray-Branch, Udvari-Solner, & Bailey, 1991). The advantage of textured symbols is their portability, but the disadvantage is that they need to be constructed on an individual basis and may be difficult to learn because they are relatively abstract.

Letters and Words   Letters and words, considered *orthographic* symbols, also can be used to help students with disabilities to communicate. People use words to represent many ideas and things every day—in fact, one must interpret orthographic symbols in order to read this book. Students who know how to read and write can also use words and letters to communicate. Even if a student does not know how to read or write *everything* he or she needs to communicate, words and letters might be useful to communicate *some* things. For example, Jordan can recognize the words of many foods he eats regularly,

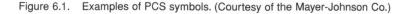

Figure 6.1.   Examples of PCS symbols. (Courtesy of the Mayer-Johnson Co.)

such as "Kellogg's Rice Krispies" and "peanut butter." He has several pages of these food words in a communication book that he carries around with him. When he wants to ask for some type of food or tell someone what he ate or what he likes, he simply points to the word in his book. The advantage of orthographic symbols is that many of them can be placed on a single page, and they are easily understood by people who can read. The disadvantage is that students with disabilities usually have difficulty learning to read and write well enough to use them.

Selecting Symbols   The symbols discussed previously are the ones that classroom support personnel will most likely use with the students they assist. It is important to think carefully about what type(s) of symbols to use with each person because the same symbols are not necessarily best for everyone. Many variables come into play when determining which symbols to use. Perhaps the most important of these variables is that the symbol selected should make sense to the user as well as to potential communicative partners. Although the symbols selected may make perfect sense to those developing the device, the student for whom the device is intended may not share the same vantage point. If at all possible, the student who will be using the symbols should help to select them. In order to find a symbol that makes most sense to the student, the educational team can present a range of choices for each message (e.g., a real object symbol, a colored photograph, a PCS symbol) in a relevant context to see which symbol the student appears to respond to the most. If this procedure is repeated a few times, it may become clear which of the three symbols is preferred. If no preference is observed, then the team can select the one that seems most appropriate.

For students who are just learning to use symbols, the similarity between the symbol and what it represents (i.e., its *referent*) should be as obvious as possible. Symbols should be based on a student's life experiences so that he or she is able to determine readily what the symbol represents. Obviously, a student's ability to acquire information through the sensory modalities is also critical in determining appropriate symbols. A student who is unable to obtain visual information at all will need to use tangible symbols or a technique called *partner assisted auditory scanning* ("20 questions"), in which the partner verbally lists message options and the user responds "yes" or "no" to make choices among them (e.g., "Do you want the red crayon? the blue one? green? yellow?"). Students with limited vision may need symbols to be larger or smaller, spread out with more space between them or brought closer together, or placed within a particular visual field. Color added to symbols may be helpful, as well as strong contrast between foreground and background. Bailey and Downing (1994) have articulated certain features of symbols that may help to gain an individual's visual attention.

Finally, symbol use should be introduced gradually, especially for a student who is just beginning to use symbols to communicate. Building on current communication skills, adding new vocabulary as needed, and following the student's lead are all recommended practices when introducing aided communication to students who are beginning communicators. The following section discusses some of the specific ways symbols can be used for communication in the classroom.

Nonelectronic Communication Displays

Most students with little or no speech can learn to use some type of nonelectronic communication display with symbols on it to communicate. (Some people also refer to these as "low-tech" or "light-tech" displays because they do not utilize computer technology.) The display may be a Velcro board with a few pictorial symbols that a student points to with a finger, fist, or hand (Figure 6.2), or it may be a Plexiglas eye gaze display that is

Figure 6.2.   A Velcro clipboard serves as a flexible device for a student to use in different classes. (Photographer: Diane Andres: Designer: Anita Daudani)

held up at eye level in front of a student, who uses his or her eyes to "point" to symbols to send messages. The display may be a communication book or wallet that an ambulatory student carries around on a strap or waist pouch, or it may be a vertical board attached to a wheelchair with symbols that are selected via a light pointer of some type. Clearly, communication displays can take many forms, depending on the abilities and needs of individual students.

The sections that follow describe some of the basic considerations for designing simple communication displays for students with severe and multiple disabilities. This task requires the input of teachers as well as team members, including speech-language pathologists, occupational and/or physical therapists, and teachers of students with visual impairments, among others. Together, the team must decide on the messages that are needed, the symbols to be used, and how the symbols will be displayed and organized. Because many possibilities exist for designing an appropriate communication display, it is recommended that, whenever possible, the individual student also play a major role in all aspects of its development.

Messages   Perhaps the most important decision to be made in designing a communication display is deciding which messages are needed. What does the student need to be able to say in various contexts? Communicative messages can be divided into four main categories, according to their purposes: wants and needs, information sharing, social closeness, and social etiquette (Light, 1988). *Wants and needs* messages are the easiest to learn how to communicate. Young children first communicate about wants and needs when they learn to say things such as, "I want. . ." "Give me. . ." "No," and "I don't want. . . ." Communication displays usually contain symbols that can be used to make requests for food, activities, or people or to let others know when the person *does not* want something to occur.

Information-sharing messages enable people to share information with classmates, teachers, family members, and others. For example, two of the most popular information-sharing questions that students ask each other focus on weekend activities. On Mondays, students are likely to ask each other, "How was your weekend?" or "What did you do over the weekend?" Similarly, on Fridays, they tend to ask each other, "What are you doing this weekend?" or "Do you have any plans?" In addition, the school environment itself often necessitates that students exchange more complicated information, such as when they want to ask or answer questions in class. For these reasons, symbols for information sharing are especially important for individuals who have difficulty communicating.

A third function of communication is *social closeness*, which has been discussed in length in previous chapters. Often, the purpose of communication is not to get what we want or to share information but simply to connect with other people and to enjoy each other. Students do this when they chat during recess or when they tell each other jokes. Students who have communication difficulties also need to be able to interact to achieve social closeness. They need to have ways of getting the attention of others, interacting in positive ways, and using humor to connect to other people. At least some of the symbols on their communication displays should be related to messages for social closeness.

Finally, a fourth purpose of communication deals with the routines for *social etiquette* that are important in specific cultures. In North America, for example, people are expected to say "please," "thank you," and "excuse me" in certain situations. It is also considered polite to say "hello" or "good-bye" when meeting or leaving someone, to face other people when talking to them, and to shake someone's hand if it is extended. Students who use communication displays need to be provided with symbols that enable them to interact with others in ways that are culturally acceptable and respectful.

How can you determine exactly which messages from these four categories should be included on a display? Some guidelines for making these decisions follow:

- Which messages will the student need to communicate on a regular basis (i.e., daily) or frequently (i.e., several times in a day)? Some examples might include greetings, requests for help, "yes" or "no" responses, requests related to basic wants and needs (e.g., bathroom, water, food), social etiquette messages (e.g., "please," "thank you"), and messages related to regular classroom routines (e.g., reciting the class poem).
- Which messages will facilitate educational participation (e.g., information sharing) in specific classroom activities or lessons? For example, a second grader might participate in a math game by saying, "Your turn," to his classmates at the appropriate times, or a high school student might need to give a report about insects to his science class on behalf of his study group. Messages for educational participation will need to be identified on an ongoing basis for specific activities or classes as they occur.

- Which messages will enable the student to participate in social interactions with other students? For example, a high school student at a pep rally might need a message that says, "Go, team, go!" Students of any age might want to talk about their family; fun events from the past; favorite topics such as basketball stars, cars, dogs, or Barbie dolls; or a host of other topics.
- Which messages are important and *cannot* be communicated by the student using unaided communication (e.g., gestures, body language, facial expressions)? For example, a student who smiles broadly to indicate "yes" and frowns to indicate "no" probably does not need symbols for "yes" and "no" on her display, but she might need symbols for messages such as "help me," "leave me alone," and so forth.

You can see from these guidelines that most students probably need to communicate hundreds of messages during each school day. Team members need to work together to identify the *most* important messages that a student with disabilities needs to communicate throughout the day. A common mistake is to design displays that are too limited in terms of the number and types of messages available. For example, students are often provided with communication displays that have only symbols for concrete wants and needs messages, such as *eat, drink, toilet, juice, cookie, puzzle,* and so forth—how boring! The display design must be able to accommodate a sufficiently large number of messages to meet students' social, learning, and other needs as well.

Symbols   The types of symbols and basic guidelines for selecting them were discussed previously in this chapter. Depending on the individual and the messages required on a communication display, symbols of several types can be used. The symbols do *not* have to be all of the same type; indeed, students will generally benefit most from communication displays containing symbols that are mixed and matched on an individual basis. For example, a communication display might consist of colored photographs, printed words, and line drawing symbols to represent various messages. At least in the beginning, most messages will probably be represented by single symbols accompanied by printed words that act as translation aids for communication partners. Another reason to pair printed words with other types of symbols is that there is some evidence from research that many students can learn to recognize printed words over time when they are introduced in this manner (Romski & Sevcik, 1996). Some examples of single- and multiword PCS symbols are displayed in Figure 6.3.

Design of the Display   How symbols are displayed for individual students can be as varied as the symbols themselves. Some of the options include booklets, notebooks, large boards, photograph albums, eye gaze displays, handkerchiefs, aprons, kickboards, wheelchair trays, incline boards, computer screens, and rotary scanners. The development of the communication display will depend on a number of variables unique to each student. These include a student's visual skills (both acuity and field); physical skills (e.g., range

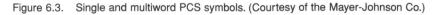

Figure 6.3.   Single and multiword PCS symbols. (Courtesy of the Mayer-Johnson Co.)

Figure 6.4.   A few line drawing symbols attached to a wristband serve as a portable communication aid for a young elementary school student at recess. (Photographer: Diane Andres; Designer: June E. Downing)

of motion, best control of a body part); cognitive abilities, especially the ability to handle a number of symbols at one time; and, perhaps most important, personal preference. Together, these variables will determine the type of display to design (e.g., an eye gaze display versus a communication book), how many symbols to put on a display, the size of the symbols, how far apart they need to be, and how they are arranged (e.g., in a half-circle; in rows accessible to a student's right hand, left hand, or both).

How symbols are displayed also will depend on each situation. When an ambulatory student needs to be moving around a lot instead of confined to any one spot, as in recess, the display must be portable (e.g., in a small photo album that fits in a fanny pack, on a fold-up display attached to the waist, on a wristband) (see Figure 6.4). Of course, symbols displayed in restrooms, in shower stalls, by sinks, or in pools need to be waterproof. When a student needs working space, the display cannot take up that space but must still be accessible to him or her.

Decisions about display design are often quite complex, especially for students with severe physical or sensory impairments or both. Because limited space makes it impossible to provide detailed information related to the decision-making process, this chapter offers just a few basic guidelines. The design of a display will require coordinated input from team members who represent all of the therapeutic disciplines that are relevant to each student, but following are some guidelines that might prove useful to the team:

• Displays cannot be designed adequately for students who are poorly positioned or uncomfortable in their wheelchairs or other adaptive equipment. Good positioning and support is an important first step to good system design.

- However they are displayed, symbols should enable a student to select messages in an accurate, efficient, and nontiring manner. If the display design results in frequent message inaccuracies, is too physically difficult for a student to use, or results in a student becoming easily fatigued, the student will eventually refuse to use it.

- Finally, if at first you do not succeed, keep on trying. It is not at all uncommon to design a display and then realize that it limits a student in some way and needs to be revised or even discarded completely. This is the case especially when students have complex needs that require trade-offs when it comes to system design. For example, Eric is a boy with cerebral palsy whose first communication display consisted of an electronic communication device with 32 symbols on it that he was supposed to point to with his fist. It seemed like a good idea at first, except that it took him at least 2 minutes to get his hand to the symbol he wanted. After a week of intense frustration, he simply refused to use the device at all. Fortunately, his team then designed a second display, an eye gaze chart mounted vertically in front of him, that was quite successful. His team was dedicated to finding a way for him to communicate, and they did not give up until they designed something that worked.

Organizing Symbols on a Display   Many considerations go into the design of individualized nonelectronic communication displays. Sometimes, such displays are *generic* in nature, providing one or two displays designed for use in different contexts to enable a student to communicate a limited number of predictable and frequent messages. In other cases, communication displays are more *specific*, offering multiple displays designed for use in specific environments, activities, or situations. An advantage of the specific display strategy is that students have access to a greater number of messages. A disadvantage is that multiple displays take more time to create and implement. Nonetheless, this strategy has become increasingly popular over the years as it has become evident that generic displays often unnecessarily limit students' language and communication development. Environment or activity displays are usually created with messages that are specific to an environment (e.g., a class, such as home economics or language arts) or an activity (e.g., playing at recess, going to the cafeteria for lunch). Mirenda (1985) described a variety of strategies for designing and organizing activity displays for students who are ambulatory. For example, divider tabs in communication books can separate activity sections and facilitate accessibility. Such strategies provide a wide range of messages while allowing a student to find a desired display quickly. Several authors have also discussed the construction of activity displays for children who use eye gaze, rotary scanners, communication books, dynamic display devices, and other display formats (Burkhart, 1993; Goossens', 1989; Goossens' & Crain, 1986; Goossens', Crain, & Elder, 1994). Figure 6.5 provides an example of an activity display designed to assist a student to participate in his fifth-grade science class during a unit on plants.

Displays can also be designed for specific purposes, such as for sharing information or interacting socially. Information in the next sections discusses the use of communication techniques designed for such specialized use.

Calendar or Schedule Systems   Calendar or schedule systems can be excellent communication aids. They provide an overview of upcoming activities, so that students know exactly what will happen next. They are also a vehicle for introducing new symbols that represent activities or classes in the school day. They can also provide a means for students to respond to direct questions (e.g., "What's next?") and can be used expressively to request desired activities (e.g., "Is it lunchtime yet?") Finally, they can help students who engage in behavior problems during transitions to move from one activity or class to

Figure 6.5. Activity display for a fifth-grade unit on plants. (Courtesy of the Mayer-Johnson Co.)

the next with fewer problems by making upcoming activities more predictable (Beukelman & Mirenda, 1998).

The premise of these systems is to use symbols to represent the activities or classes in a student's school day. Several types of symbols can be used in a calendar or schedule system. If the symbols used are real object symbols or tangible symbols, they are placed in a series of calendar or schedule *boxes* (see Figure 6.6). If photos, small objects, line drawings, or other graphic symbols are used, they can be located in a calendar or schedule *book*.

Once the appropriate type of symbol has been determined, specific symbols are selected for each of the activities or classes in the school day. The symbols are then laid out in the box or book in sequential order from the first to the last activity or class. Figure 6.7 provides an example of one page in the school schedule book used by Dan, an adolescent with autism.

Those working with a student with disabilities should help the student use the system in a dynamic manner throughout the day. At the beginning of each activity or class, the student should examine the related symbol (either visually, tactually, or both), with assistance as needed, while being provided with verbal or signed information about what activity is about to take place (e.g., "Look, here's the symbol that tells you it's time for art class"; "Feel the apron? That means it's time for foods class"). Afterward, the student should be assisted to put the symbol "away" to indicate that the activity or class is finished. Real object or tangible symbols can be placed in a "finished" box (see Figure 6.6), and

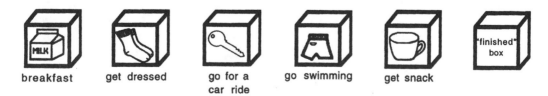

breakfast | get dressed | go for a car ride | go swimming | get snack

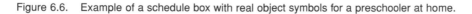

Figure 6.6. Example of a schedule box with real object symbols for a preschooler at home.

Figure 6.7. School and after-school schedule for Dan, an adolescent with autism.

symbols in a schedule book can simply be turned over when activities or classes have ended. Then, the student can be directed toward the symbol for the next activity or class and so on throughout the day. A simple calendar or schedule system can be a very effective way to teach symbol meanings to many students who are beginning communicators, because they get to experience the relationship between symbols and the activities they represent in natural contexts throughout the day. Many students who have a high need for predictability may also show evidence of reduced behavior problems during transitions when symbols are used to help them predict what will happen next.

Remnant and Conversation Displays   Remnant and conversation displays can be used to enable students both to share information and to achieve social closeness. *Remnants,* or scraps left over from different activities, provide a way for students to share information with others about past events, such as those that occurred over the weekend. Remnants are simply saved, rather than discarded, and then fastened or inserted into a display such as a communication book or board. For example, a student might use a worksheet completed in math class, the program from a drama club play, or the leftover scraps from an art project as remnants. He or she can then answer questions such as, "What did you do in Mr. James's art class?" or "What did you do over the weekend?" by pointing to the relevant remnants. The student can also initiate topics of conversation about interesting past events by referring to the remnants. Figure 6.8 represents such a

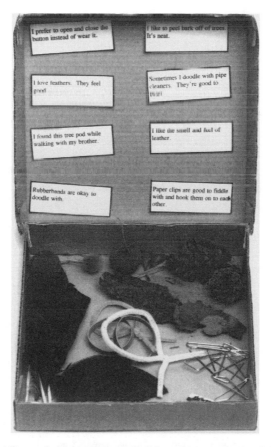

Figure 6.8.   A tactile box that fits easily into a student's desk is used as a conversation box by a student with no vision or speech. Items are changed periodically and statements written for conversation partners to respond to. (Photographer: Diane Andres; Designer: June E. Downing)

device for one elementary school student who is blind and does not use speech. Following are some guidelines for using remnants:

- Let the student help in selecting the remnant, if possible. The remnant should be something that is meaningful to the student so that he or she will be able to associate it with the activity from which it came.
- With the student's participation, put the remnant in or on his or her communication display.
- Be sure that the display with remnants is available to the student during times when social interactions usually occur, such as before class, at recess and lunch, during transitions between classes, and so forth.
- Encourage classmates to converse naturally with the student, rather than asking question after question about the remnants. Instead, classmates can use the remnants to spark engaging conversation (e.g., "Oh, I see you went to Chinatown. Did you have a good time?").

Conversation displays, based on the work of Pam Hunt and her colleagues at San Francisco State University (Hunt, Alwell, & Goetz, 1988, 1990, 1991a, 1991b), are usually made from small, portable albums of some type that contain photographs of a student engaged in his or her favorite activities. They can also contain favorite items that a student might collect, such as hockey cards, pictures of rock stars, or political buttons. Recent events for which photographs are unavailable can also be represented with remnants, as discussed previously. The pictures and items should be accompanied by captions that both give information and ask questions. For example, in Jennifer's book, there is a postcard of the Vancouver Aquarium, along with a note that reads, "I went to the aquarium last week. I loved the beluga whales! Have you ever been there? What kind of fish do you like best?" The captions should be written in a friendly and age-appropriate way that suggest things for the conversation partner to talk about. The point is to create an interesting collection of photographs, remnants, and other items that the student will enjoy discussing with others. The items in the book should be kept current, so that the student can always talk about whatever is new and different in his or her life. Figure 6.9 provides one example of such a device that was created by a student and her peers using spelling words and familiar items from home.

Electronic Communication Devices

Numerous communication devices that are operated by rechargeable batteries are also available. Some of these devices are quite complex and expensive, whereas others are relatively simple to program and use. The primary advantage of electronic communication devices is that they "talk"—that is, when a student touches a symbol on the device, the device provides voice output for the message that has been stored under that symbol. For example, a student might touch a photograph (symbol) of her dog and the device might say, THIS IS MY DOG SHARMA. SHE'S A GERMAN SHEPHERD. DO YOU LIKE DOGS? As one might imagine, there are many advantages to such voice output, especially in busy, noisy classrooms.

Types of Electronic Communication Devices   The three main types of voice output devices are single-level devices, multilevel devices, and comprehensive devices. *Single-level devices* are designed to deliver a limited number of messages, usually not more than 20, and are very simple to program and operate. For example, a device called a BIGmack (AbleNet, Inc.) is a small device with a built-in microswitch that, when activated, plays a single recorded message up to 20 seconds long.

Figure 6.9.   A small book with familiar items that was made by a pair of students to represent spelling words in sentences serves as a tactile conversation book for a student without vision. (Photographer: Diane Andres)

Recording a message into the BIGmack takes only seconds, and new messages can be recorded over old ones throughout the day. With the assistance of an aide or peer who is responsible for recording the messages, a student in kindergarten could use a BIG-mack to greet his teacher and classmates on arrival at school (HI, HOW ARE YOU TODAY?), to recite the Pledge of Allegiance with his classmates, to participate in a language arts lesson by "reciting" the repeating line of a story the teacher is reading (BROWN BEAR, BROWN BEAR, WHAT DID YOU SEE?), and then to call out DUCK, DUCK, DUCK, DUCK, GOOSE! while a classmate touches each child's head in a circle. As is apparent, the BIGmack might not do very much, but with some creativity and planning, it can be a very useful tool for helping a student with disabilities to participate. Additional examples of single-level devices and the number of messages they can store include the Talk Back (6) and Messenger (1), both by the Crestwood Company; Hawk (9; ADAMLAB); MessageMate (8–20; Words+, Inc.); Parrot (16; Zygo Industries, Inc.); SpeakEasy (12; AbleNet, Inc.); and Voicemate/Switchmate/Scanmate devices (4–8; Tash, Inc.). The Appendix lists complete contact information for these and all other devices mentioned in this chapter.

Multilevel devices are capable of delivering more than 20 messages (in some cases, thousands) and are more difficult both to program and use because they are more complex. Of course, the advantage of multilevel devices is that they can contain a greater number of preprogrammed messages. Usually, these devices utilize multiple symbol displays that are placed on the device to allow access to messages programmed on two or more "levels." In most cases, either the user or an assistant must manually change these displays. Some of the best-known examples include the Black Hawk, Whisper Wolf, and Wolf (ADAMLAB); Macaw (Zygo Industries, Inc.); and Say-It-Simply Plus (Innocomp). In addition, some multilevel devices use various electronic techniques that allow users to access multiple message levels without having to change the symbol displays manually. These include the AlphaTalker and Walker Talker (Prentke Romich Co.), and the Digivox (DynaVox Systems, Inc.).

Finally, *comprehensive devices* are designed to deliver multiple messages using a variety of rate enhancement techniques to increase efficiency and speed. Many of these devices have additional features as well, including printers, calculators, large memory capacities for storing lengthy text and speeches, and the ability to interface with standard computers. Some examples include the DeltaTalker, Liberator, and Vanguard (Prentke Romich Company); DynaVox (DynaVox Systems, Inc.); Lightwriter (Toby Churchill, Ltd.); Speaking Dynamically (Mayer-Johnson Company); and Talking Screen (Words+, Inc.). These devices are appropriate primarily for students with multiple disabilities who do not have significant cognitive or visual impairments.

Using Electronic Communication Devices in Conjunction with Other Techniques   One
of the major disadvantages of electronic devices is that, because of their very nature, they are more cumbersome and more vulnerable to simple wear and tear than nonelectronic displays. They can break down, their batteries can run down or fail, the switches used to operate them can fail to function, they can be impractical to transport, and the rapid pace of the classroom sometimes does not allow the time to program messages. Obviously, whenever these devices malfunction or are not available, a student's *need* to communicate remains the same, but his or her *ability* to do so is restricted.

In such situations, it becomes imperative for classroom support personnel to resort to other communication strategies. An immediate assessment of the environment is needed to determine which communication interactions will be expected and how to support these interactions. Other students can be recruited as potential communication partners, or other adults can be asked to provide specific types of support. Following are some of the options that are available to classroom support personnel in such circumstances.

- Give the student choices presented two to three at a time (e.g., "Do you want the red crayon?" [hold it up] "or the blue crayon ?" [hold it up]). The student can then point to or look at his or her choice.
- Use a multiple-choice format by verbally listing the available options so the student can respond "yes" or "no" (e.g., "What did the wolf say to the three little pigs? Did he say, 'Hi, I sure like you'?" [pause for yes/no response]; "'I'm going to eat you all up'?" [pause for yes/no response]; "or, 'I'll huff and I'll puff and I'll blow your house down'?" [pause for yes/no response]).
- Use objects or pictures that are readily available, or use the symbol display from the electronic device, but without the voice output. For example, Angel typically uses about 25 words or phrases programmed into her AlphaTalker to participate in her fifth-grade class. During a field trip to a cave as the final phase of a unit on bats, her AlphaTalker is inadvertently left on the school bus. Given the rough trail and the physical difficulty involved in getting Angel and her wheelchair to the cave, it is decided not to return to the bus to retrieve the AlphaTalker. Instead, the paraprofessional and the fifth-grade teacher decide to help Angel communicate by using available objects (dried bat droppings, bats) and pictures in a brochure from the cave (bats, cave, baby bat). They also ask her specific yes/no questions, as they do for the other children. In addition, they encourage Angel's classmates to ask her similar types of questions or make statements to which she can agree or disagree. Because of these impromptu adaptations, Angel is an active and involved participant in the bat cave experience, even though she is unable to ask for help or make spontaneous comments.

When she returns to the bus, she uses her device to ask questions and recount what she saw with the rest of the class.

SUMMARY

As is obvious from the information in this chapter, there are a multitude of ways to provide effective communication support to students with multiple disabilities. Fortunately, the two most important ingredients—commitment and creativity—are already part of the repertoires of teachers and others who support these students in schools and other settings. In addition, a number of excellent books are available that discuss AAC for students with disabilities in more detail. I recommend the texts by Beukelman and Mirenda (1998); Glennen and DeCoste (1997); Johnson, Baumgart, Helmstetter, and Curry (1996); Lloyd, Fuller, and Arvidson (1997); and Reichle, York, and Sigafoos (1991).

REFERENCES

Bailey, B., & Downing, J. (1994). Using visual accents to enhance attending to communication symbols for students with severe multiple disabilities. *RE:view, 26*(3), 101–118.

Beukelman, D.R., & Mirenda, P. (1998). *Augmentative and alternative communication: Management of severe communication disorders in children and adults* (2nd ed.). Baltimore: Paul H. Brookes Publishing Co.

Boardmaker [Computer software]. (1998). Solano Beach, CA: Mayer-Johnson Co.

Bornstein, H., Saulnier, L., & Hamilton, L. (1983). *The comprehensive Signed English dictionary*. Washington, DC: Gallaudet University Press.

Burkhart, L. (1993). *Total augmentative communication in the early childhood classroom*. Solana Beach, CA: Mayer-Johnson.

Glennen, S., & DeCoste, D. (1997). *Handbook of augmentative and alternative communication*. San Diego, CA: Singular Publishing Group.

Goossens', C. (1989). Aided communication intervention before assessment: A case study of a child with cerebral palsy. *Augmentative and Alternative Communication, 5*, 14–26.

Goossens', C., & Crain, S. (1986). *Augmentative communication intervention resource*. Wauconda, IL: Don Johnston Developmental Equipment.

Goossens', C., Crain, S., & Elder, P. (1994). *Communication displays for engineered preschool environments* (Books 1 & 2). Solana Beach, CA: Mayer-Johnson.

Gustason, G., Pfetzing, D., & Zawolkow, E. (1980). *Signing Exact English* (3rd ed.). Los Alamitos, CA: Modern Signs Press.

Hunt, P., Alwell, M., & Goetz, L. (1988). Acquisition of conversation skills and the reduction of inappropriate social interaction behaviors. *Journal of The Association for Persons with Severe Handicaps, 13*, 20–27.

Hunt, P., Alwell, M., & Goetz, L. (1990). *Teaching conversation skills to individuals with severe disabilities with a communication book adaptation.* (Available from P. Hunt, San Francisco State University, 612 Font Boulevard, San Francisco, CA 94132)

Hunt, P., Alwell, M., & Goetz, L. (1991a). Establishing conversational exchanges with family and friends: Moving from training to meaningful conversation. *Journal of Special Education, 25*, 305–319.

Hunt, P., Alwell, M., & Goetz, L. (1991b). Interacting with peers through conversation turntaking with a communication book adaptation. *Augmentative and Alternative Communication, 7*, 117–126.

Johnson, J.M., Baumgart, D., Helmstetter, E., & Curry, C. (1996). *Augmenting basic communication in natural contexts*. Baltimore: Paul H. Brookes Publishing Co.

Johnson, R. (1994). *The Picture Communication Symbols combination book*. Solana Beach, CA: Mayer-Johnson.

Light, J. (1988). Interaction involving individuals using augmentative and alternative communication systems: State of the art and future directions. *Augmentative and Alternative Communication, 4*, 66–82.

Lloyd, L.L., Fuller, D., & Arvidson, H. (1997). *Augmentative and alternative communication*. Needham Heights, MA: Allyn & Bacon.

Locke, P., & Mirenda, P. (1988). A computer-supported communication approach for a nonspeaking child with severe visual and cognitive impairments: A case study. *Augmentative and Alternative Communication, 4,* 15–22.

Mathy-Laikko, P., Iacono, T., Ratcliff, A., Villarruel, F., Yoder, D., & Vanderheiden, G. (1989). Teaching a child with multiple disabilities to use a tactile augmentative communication device. *Augmentative and Alternative Communication, 5,* 249–256.

Mirenda, P. (1985). Designing pictorial communication systems for physically able-bodied students with severe handicaps. *Augmentative and Alternative Communication, 1,* 58–64.

Murray-Branch, J., Udvari-Solner, A., & Bailey, B. (1991). Textured communication systems for individuals with severe intellectual and dual sensory impairments. *Language, Speech, and Hearing Services in Schools, 22,* 260–268.

Reichle, J., York, J., & Sigafoos, J. (1991). *Implementing augmentative and alternative communication: Strategies for learners with severe disabilities.* Baltimore: Paul H. Brookes Publishing Co.

Romski, M.A., & Sevcik, R.A. (1996). *Breaking the speech barrier: Language development through augmented means.* Baltimore: Paul H. Brookes Publishing Co.

Rowland, C., & Schweigert, P. (1989). Tangible symbols: Symbolic communication for individuals with multisensory impairments. *Augmentative and Alternative Communication, 5,* 226–234.

Sternberg, M. (1994). *American Sign Language dictionary* (Rev. ed.). New York: HarperCollins.

7

The Role of Communicative Partners

V. Mark Durand, Eileen Mapstone, and Lise Youngblade

How a person responds to the communicative initiations of another greatly determines the outcome of the conversation. The "wrong" response generally limits the interaction, whereas the "right" response usually encourages more interaction. Furthermore, successful conversations are likely to encourage more interactions in the future, possibly leading to more meaningful relationships such as friendships (Gaylord-Ross, Haring, Breen, & Pitts-Conway, 1984; Hunt, Alwell, & Goetz, 1991).

Given the importance of conversations to social relationships, how can educators encourage such interactions between children with severe disabilities and their peers in the classroom? Does this require simply teaching the appropriate skills (e.g., teaching a person to respond, "Hello, how are you?" when someone says, "Hello"), or are other experiences necessary? Is it reasonable to just place a child with disabilities in general education environments and expect their peers to facilitate conversations, or do teachers need to provide specific intervention with these peers? In addition, what are the obstacles to successful conversation-skills training for this population of children and adolescents? These questions served as the foundation for a 3-year project on conversation-skills training for students with severe disabilities and their general education peers conducted by our research group; this chapter describes the results of this work. Specifically, it outlines procedures for encouraging conversations between students with disabilities (by teaching them to use voice output communication aids, or VOCAs [see Chapter 6]), and their peers in general education classes, and it describes the lessons learned from our successes and failures.

ENCOURAGING MEANINGFUL CONVERSATION

Three essential components are necessary for creating meaningful conversations between students with and without severe disabilities. First, both partners need to possess and recognize *basic communication skills,* whether verbal, symbolic, or nonsymbolic (Downing & Siegel-Causey, 1988). Other chapters in this book thoroughly describe how to teach children with severe disabilities these skills (e.g., see Chapters 4 and 5). Second, the participants need to have *the motivation to interact* with each other. Just knowing *how* to converse does not guarantee that a conversation will take place. Third, conversation is much easier when participants share *a common repertoire of experiences.* For meaningful conversations to last for any reasonable length of time, the partners must have something to talk about—shared experiences that form the basis of ongoing discussion. Each of these three components is integral to sustained conversations between two people.

Formal Communication Skills

Each child in any communicative exchange serves an important role. Reciprocal sharing of information requires that all partners be able to express themselves and understand the messages sent by others. The first step, then, in facilitating conversations between children with and without severe disabilities is to establish a method of communication. In this project, we identified children who had no formal communication strategies and for whom augmentative communication would be appropriate. Our goal was to use VOCAs to allow the child with severe disabilities to communicate with peers. (In this chapter, *peer[s]* refers to the student[s] without disabilities, while *the student[s]* refers primarily to the students with disabilities.) The decision to use these devices rather than some other method of communication was guided by previous research. For example, Bedrosian (1997) and Light (1988) found that children interacting with students with disabilities may be more likely to respond to VOCAs than other systems (e.g., communication boards). It has been estimated, for example, that less than two thirds of the initiations made by students with communication boards (e.g., picture books) receive responses (Calculator & Dollaghan, 1982). Clearly, if individuals do not respond to the communicative efforts of these students, the applicability of such a system for classroom and community environments is limited (Bedrosian, 1997; Heller, Allgood, Davis, Arnold, Castelle, & Taber, 1996; Rotholz, Berdowitz, & Burberry, 1989). We describe the selection and training in the use of these devices later in this chapter.

Just establishing a method for a student to communicate messages to others, however, does not appear to be sufficient to guarantee meaningful conversation (Hunt, Staub, Alwell, & Goetz, 1994). Experience suggests that additional facilitative strategies are required to bring about significant exchanges between children with severe disabilities and their peers (Davis, Reichle, Johnston, & Southard, 1998). Classroom practices and research suggest several general strategies, including putting students together and hoping for interactions (Kuder & Bryen, 1993), teaching basic communication skills (Hughes, Harmer, Killian, & Niarhos, 1995; Hughes, Killian, & Fischer, 1996), and structuring conversations using techniques such as communication books (Hunt et al., 1994; Kuder & Bryen, 1993). Again, for students with severe disabilities, just placing them with their peers does not regularly lead to meaningful communication. Additional steps must be taken to teach and encourage these interactions.

In an important series of studies, Hughes and colleagues taught conversation skills to students with moderate disabilities (Hughes et al., 1995, 1996). Using primarily a skills-training approach—which involved modeling "correct talking" as well as teaching self-evaluation (e.g., "I did it—I talked!") and self-reinforcement (e.g., "I did a good job")—this research group found that peers without disabilities could successfully teach their classmates with disabilities conversation skills that generalized to other peers. It is not clear, however, whether this teaching strategy will be equally successful for students with more limited skills, such as those with multiple and severe disabilities. These students may need more direct instruction that does not rely so heavily on self-management strategies such as self-evaluation and self-reinforcement.

Working with high school students with severe disabilities, Hunt, Alwell, Goetz and their colleagues used conversation books to help structure conversations between these students and their peers (Hunt, Alwell, & Goetz, 1991; Hunt, Alwell, Goetz, & Sailor, 1990). By using these books and teaching students how to take turns communicating, the researchers found that students would engage in more sustained conversations. This series of studies demonstrated that conversation instruction can facilitate more elaborate interactions between students with and without severe disabilities.

It is important to note that this work focused primarily on high school students, which raises this question: How does the developmental level of the students involved affect the ability to encourage such interactions? In other words, are there *developmental differences* in students that predict the outcomes of these interactions? Would peers in elementary school, for example, be able to facilitate conversations with their partners having severe disabilities? We examined the influence of students' levels of development on conversation-skills training in the present project by working with students from elementary school through high school, and this chapter discusses the differences that we observed in children of different ages.

Motivation

As described previously (Chapter 4), people need to be motivated to converse. Usually, when two or more people are together for any length of time, they typically engage in conversation; however, this is not always the case. Sometimes the context dictates the likelihood of people engaging in conversation. For example, strangers sitting in a reception area waiting for a medical appointment often do not converse. Similarly, people riding in an elevator or on an escalator often do not engage in any meaningful interactions, despite their close proximity. Indeed, putting children next to each other in a classroom for the first time can sometimes resemble these situations. Children will often work or play in parallel until some aspect of the situation changes. Unfortunately, very little discussion in the literature guides how to structure classroom situations in order to encourage conversations between students with disabilities and their peers. One excellent exception to this omission was the work of Hunt and colleagues, which examined how cooperative learning groups could facilitate interactions between students with severe disabilities and their peers (Hunt et al., 1994). This group used the communication books described previously in the context of a cooperative instructional format and found that the students with severe disabilities improved in a number of academic measures.

In a similar manner, our project sought to examine how a strategy that could be incorporated into any classroom could be used to encourage conversations. Specifically, we examined how providing a project for students to work on together encouraged conversation. Students were given choices in order to increase their motivation and interest in the project and, consequently, stimulate conversation (Houghton, Bronicki, & Guess, 1987; Kearney, Durand, & Mindell, 1995; Peck, 1985). By allowing both partners to have significant input into the nature and design of the project, we anticipated greater student interest.

Shared Experiences

The fact that people engage in conversation because they have something to talk about is another important aspect of communication that is often taken for granted (see Chapter 1). A common background between partners is extremely helpful for initiating and maintaining social interactions. Two people in a store may strike up a conversation about their children. Teachers may talk about their upcoming vacation and how they will spend their free time. Children may start to talk about their interests in similar toys, movies, and television shows. Unfortunately, however, the lives of children with disabilities are sometimes very different from their peers. Because of motor, sensory, or cognitive differences, these children may not share many of the same experiences or interests as their peers (e.g., hanging out at the mall with friends, listening to the latest music, recalling statistics from last night's baseball game). Without these shared experiences, students may have difficulty engaging in conversation.

The projects that we constructed to help motivate students to converse were designed to address students' need for shared experiences. We believed that putting students together on a task over several weeks would create a number of experiences that students would then have in common. This was viewed as especially important for students who may not have shared many other experiences. More elaborate *content* for conversations would develop naturally given the significant amount of interaction.

PROJECT ACTIVITIES

To examine these important issues, the project identified 37 students with severe disabilities, ages 5–18, and their peers without disabilities in 10 different school districts. The program began by screening the students with disabilities to determine eligibility for participation. For example, all of the students needed to have adequate visual and auditory skills in order to participate. Following the screening, student pairs participated in several activities. After a baseline phase in which students with disabilities and their peers were placed together randomly, the pairs were then exposed to the VOCAs but were not provided with any training. This phase was designed to assess whether students could make use of the devices without formal instruction. After this assessment (in which few of the pairs used the VOCAs, and none used them in any meaningful ways), the pairs were randomly divided into two groups. The first group received conversation-skills training first and then participated in shared experiences; the second group participated in shared experiences first and then received conversation-skills training. This design was used to assess the effects of each approach separately as well as combined.

Conversation-Skills Training

The conversation-skills training of our research project had two goals. The first was to teach students to use VOCAs. The second was to teach students with disabilities and their peers to converse. In order to achieve these goals, the trainers worked actively with the students by modeling conversation, teaching and prompting conversation, and reinforcing attempts made by students and their peer partners. Eventually, as the pairs began to converse on their own, the trainers faded their participation.

We programmed the VOCAs with a combination of statements in order to facilitate their use. Several buttons were programmed with conventional conversation units designed to get an interaction going (e.g., "HI," "HOW ARE YOU?" "MY NAME'S JOHN," "WHAT WOULD YOU LIKE TO DO NOW?"). There were also several buttons programmed with basic communication statements or requests (e.g., "I'M HUNGRY," "I HAVE TO GO TO THE BATHROOM," "I NEED HELP PLEASE") (Durand, 1990). Pictorial Communication Symbols (Johnson, 1984) and photos were used for the devices. Finally, to help motivate students to use their machines, several buttons were programmed with the student's favorite activities (e.g., "LET'S BOWL," "LET'S READ A BOOK").

Training generally began by showing the student where the favorite activities buttons were located and then prompting the student to use one of those buttons. Peers were instructed to respond quickly to the initiation by providing verbal praise and permission to engage in the activity, thereby reinforcing the students' use of the VOCA. Once the student learned the connection between specific VOCA messages and their subsequent outcomes, the task was broadened to generate conversation about what the pair wanted to do. Thus, the peer was instructed to initiate the conversation about what they would do and then discuss with the student various choices of activities. The trainer prompted or physically assisted the student as needed, eventually fading his or her prompts and assists as the student demonstrated mastery of specific communicative behaviors.

The second part of our conversation-skills training involved teaching students to engage in conventional polite conversation. Student pairs were trained to use a sequence of statements in a variety of settings to get a conversation going. For example, a prototypical sequence might be as follows:

Student: Hi.

Peer: Hi.

Student: My name's John. What's yours?

Peer: Steven.

Student: How are you?

Peer: I'm fine. How are you?

Student: Fine.

Peer: Goodbye.

Student: Bye.

As students became more adept at this interchange, which was trained via prompting and role-playing, the trainer faded back. In addition, once the students were proficient at this, additional steps were included, such as discussing what activity the pair would like to do, what either child might have done over the weekend, and so on. Once the pair could negotiate such additional steps with minimal intervention by the trainer, this particular phase of conversation-skills training ended.

Shared Experiences

As a collaborative effort, the student, peer, teacher, and trainer decided on a project for the pair to work on for a period of 4–6 weeks. During this phase, the trainer and teacher were available to the students and their peers to assist them in any situation that would occur in a routine educational activity. Trainers, however, did not instruct the children in conversation skills nor prompt either conversation turns nor use of the VOCAs. We discuss this kind of instruction in more detail later in the chapter.

ISSUES RELATED TO CONVERSATION-SKILLS TRAINING

Peer Selection

It should be clear that the peer selected to be paired with the student with disabilities serves a crucial role in the success (or failure) of attempts to encourage conversation

(Haring & Green, 1992); however, there are many issues to be addressed when selecting peers, and some of these may not be under our control.

The students with disabilities in our study were paired with peers of similar age whenever possible. This practice was based on modeling research, which suggests the value of matching children of similar age and gender to facilitate optimal social interactions. Nonetheless, despite the desire to keep the pairs as similar as possible, they were often of mixed gender, particularly among the younger children. Peers were recruited based on the recommendations of special or general education teachers. In some cases, there was a preexisting peer tutoring program from which peers were selected. Typically, students without disabilities who were known by special educators to be responsible and at least minimally interested were recruited for participation in the project.

Unfortunately, in one school district, students without disabilities were given the option of participating in the project as an alternative to detention. Including these particular students in the project had obvious limitations, but given the demands of conducting a large-scale study, we often had limited control over the peers who were nominated for inclusion. Despite our initial concerns, however, some of the peers who chose to participate in the study rather than sit in detention appeared to benefit substantially from their participation. They reported looking forward to spending time with their partner and demonstrated an appreciation that what they were doing was important. For some of these peers, their participation may have offered them something to be proud of and helped them feel useful (Williams & Downing, 1998). In addition, they received quite a bit of positive attention rather than the attention they typically received for their problematic behaviors. As the experience for the peer became increasingly positive, so did the experience of the student with disabilities.

The pairs of students worked together primarily in the general education classroom during all phases of the project, although some pairs spent significant time in other areas of the school as part of their shared experiences. Typically, the participants were immersed in a large, busy classroom with other students who were able to observe them participating in the project. Often these other classmates would comment on the activities in which the project participants were engaged and frequently expressed an interest in using the communication device to interact with the student.

The peers who participated in the project were typically excused from the activity in which the rest of the class was participating in order to focus on our project; however, no students were allowed to miss any portion of math, English, or science class. Scheduling time to work on the project was often challenging. Frequently, the student with disabilities would have a certain number of scheduled activities outside the classroom that could not be missed, such as speech-language therapy and physical therapy. In some cases, the peer who had been nominated for participation was ultimately not included because of scheduling difficulties. Having the support and cooperation of all teachers involved was often crucial to the successful scheduling of the sessions. Teachers who could be flexible and include the peer in different classes on occasion or meet with the peer at a different time greatly facilitated the consistency with which the students were able to meet.

The peers that were selected were varied in their experiences with other children or adults with disabilities. Most of the peers in the project had limited exposure to individuals with disabilities prior to the start of classes. Among the peer participants were honor roll students, students who were involved in many volunteer organizations, students who were shy and had difficulty making friends among their other classmates, students who were experiencing academic and behavioral difficulties, as well as students who were considering careers in psychology or special education and were looking for some experience relevant to those professions. Clearly, the peer partners in our project represented a heterogeneous group of students. Informal observations suggested that the peers who had their own difficulties to overcome, such as shyness or academic struggles, were often able to establish a meaningful relationship with their peer who had disabilities more quickly and with greater ease than other peers. Perhaps these students' experiences of being different from the "norm" may have enhanced their ability to connect with their partners with disabilities.

As with relationships between any two people, some of the pairs of students were more successful in developing meaningful conversation and establishing friendships. Certain peer variables, such as gender or age, may have influenced successful outcome. Certainly, one factor that likely affected the success of the project was the consistency with which the pairs actually met. Sessions were scheduled to take place at least twice a week, sometimes more often. Peers who consistently attended the training sessions as well as the sessions during the project phase were more likely to develop a relationship with their peer with disabilities.

Developmental Issues

One of the factors affecting the success rate of our project was the developmental stage of the participants. Peers in junior high grades were often the most inconsistent in their attendance. These students appeared quite concerned with their classmates' opinions and perhaps, as a result, were less motivated to participate in activities that their class-mates might find different or strange (see Williams & Downing, 1998). This observation is consistent with the developmental stage of early adolescence, in which the opinions of peers become particularly important (Elkind, 1984). The junior high peers reported feeling particularly uncomfortable during the conversation-skills training sessions that involved a lot of repetition. They would often say statements such as, "This is stupid," or "I look like a dork doing this." The peers in this age group, however, did report enjoying the stage of the project that focused on shared experiences. Indeed, working on projects with the students with disabilities often appeared to be fun for them. Perhaps future conversation-skills training would be more effective if the training were to be conducted in a more "natural" fashion or if it took place in an area where the peers would not feel as if they not are being watched and evaluated by their classmates.

In one particular case, the student with disabilities, Mandy, had two peer partners, Lisa and Katy, who each participated in some portions of all the phases of the project. The general and special educators both felt that, given certain time constraints, using two peers would make the most sense for Mandy. This situation highlighted some issues that may be important when working to establish meaningful relationships between students with disabilities and their peers.

> Mandy was selected for participation in our research for a number of reasons. She was already placed in general education classes, and, although she had expressed interest in conversing with the other students and they in her, because of her limited communication skills, she had no avenue by which to successfully interact. Mandy was 18 at the time she participated in our study. She was enrolled in her local high school and spent part of her day in a self-contained special education classroom and the other part of her school day in general education classrooms with her peers. Mandy had no consistently effective means of communication, although she did know and occasionally used some sign language. She had adequate sensory

abilities and relied on the use of gestures and idiosyncratic signs to communicate with those around her. Mandy had been diagnosed with severe multiple disabilities and had always been placed in special education classrooms.

The research sessions took place during art class when Mandy was fully included with the other students. She was provided with a 16-square Introtalker to use during the training and to keep thereafter. Prior to participation in our project, Mandy had never had consistent access to an augmentative communication device (ACD), and she had certainly never had an ACD of her own. Unlike most other students who participated in our projects, Mandy had two peers, Lisa and Katy, who worked consistently with her, and occasionally other students in the art class would participate in sessions as well. The students worked together to create an art portfolio that included an image made by tracing and enlarging a picture, textured prints, paintings, sketches, and collages.

Lisa and Katy were both 16-year-old females in the eleventh grade. They had each indicated a willingness to interact with Mandy and had expressed a desire to spend more time with her. Prior to participation in the project, the peers indicated on a questionnaire that they would like to talk with and do things with Mandy, but they were unsure whether Mandy was interested in spending time with them. After the intervention, the same questionnaire indicated that the peers felt confident that Mandy wanted to interact and engage in activities with them. Providing Mandy with a means to communicate apparently allowed Lisa and Katy to understand that Mandy did want to spend time with them but had previously been unable to communicate this.

Mandy and her peers participated in the shared experience phase first and then the conversation-skills training. During the shared experience phase of the project the peers expressed a great deal of enthusiasm when working with Mandy on their art projects. In addition, the other students in the class expressed interest in Mandy's communication device and in using the device to communicate with her. Furthermore, Lisa and Katy received a lot of positive attention from their classmates and reported feeling supported and encouraged to spend time with Mandy.

During the training phase of the project, the peers reported feeling somewhat uncomfortable with the conversation-skills training that focused so much on the repetition of turn taking. They reported feeling embarrassed by the training and expressed relief when it was over so that they could return to "hanging out" with Mandy. In addition, the classroom was often chaotic and loud, which made training difficult to conduct. The noise in the classroom was often distracting for students and the trainer, and the art teacher also complained that the training phase interfered with her efforts to conduct class. Balancing the desire to teach skills in their natural context (e.g., the classroom) with competing concerns (e.g., desires of a teacher) can be quite challenging, as this scenario indicates.

Through the course of their involvement in the project, Mandy and her peers demonstrated an increased capacity to communicate with one another. Mandy in particular expressed an increased number of appropriate verbal turns, an increased range of topics, and an increased number of initiations and expansions. She learned to use her Introtalker to make appropriate verbal turns during conversations with her peers, to communicate about increasingly more topics, and to initiate conversation as well as expand upon initiations from others. The shared experience with her peers likely increased the number of topics about which the students were able to communicate.

The situation with Mandy and her peers highlights many important issues in the selection of the peer partners and the factors that may affect the success of assisting students to establish friendships with each other. Providing Mandy with two partners appeared to enhance motivation and enjoyment for all of the students involved. Mandy was afforded the opportunity to interact closely with two different peers and the peers were able to rely on one another for support. Perhaps the success of these peer relationships is a reflection of the tendency for friendships to develop within small groups of people rather than within an isolated pairing. One needs only to glance around a crowded school cafeteria to notice that students usually spend time together in groups rather than isolated pairs. Having three students interact together may have been a much more typical scenario for friendships to develop.

The project staff who worked with Mandy, Katy, and Lisa had to be careful to structure sessions so that interactions would take place among all of the students. Taking into consideration Mandy's unique personality characteristics when structuring activities made the interaction more meaningful for everyone. For example, Mandy was known to have a rather quirky sense of humor. Activities that evoked this sense of humor, such as drawing caricatures of classmates, greatly facilitated interactions among Mandy, Katy, and Lisa. Achieving the balance between providing structure and letting the students just spend time alone was challenging for the project staff, but when they were able to do so, the students appeared to have meaningful interactions.

Another factor that likely contributed to the development of a more meaningful relationship among Mandy, Lisa, and Katy is that Lisa and Katy had indicated a desire to get to know Mandy better. In many instances, teachers selected students based on the teacher's belief that the student would be responsible and do well within the project and not necessarily because the peer had indicated a desire to get to know the student with disabilities. A larger-scale recruitment, preferably schoolwide, might increase the number of peers who are sincerely interested in developing meaningful relationships with students who have disabilities. Furthermore, attempting to match students with peers based on similar interests (i.e., sports, art, outdoor activities) may yield greater success.

Creating Shared Experiences

In order to facilitate meaningful interactions between students, we designed the project so that the student with disabilities and his or her peer partner would engage in some kind of shared experience. As discussed previously, students with disabilities often have very little in common with their peers without disabilities. Whereas students without disabilities have social networks composed primarily of students their own age, students with disabilities tend to have social networks composed of adults (Lewis, Feiring, & Brooks-Gunn, 1987). In addition to the kind of large-scale life differences that exist between students with disabilities and their peers without disabilities, such as major health problems and extreme difficulty communicating, they also experience many differences on a smaller scale. For example, they sometimes ride different school buses and have different teachers, different classrooms, and different friends. Placing children together with the hope that they will develop a meaningful relationship without first providing them a means of communication and second, and perhaps more important, providing them something about which to communicate is likely to fail.

Selecting the experience to be shared by the students was difficult for several reasons. The children's input in the selection was essential to the success of the shared experience, but certain factors often limited the amount of control the students had. Some teachers, for example, insisted that the shared experience be something consistent with the student's educational program. For instance, in one classroom the children were working on electronics in science and the teacher insisted that the shared experience consist of building a light board. The children in this pair were often bored with this project, which may have affected their desire to spend time together. In addition, sometimes the students were interested initially, but their interest waned before the designated time for the completion of the study. The younger children in particular had difficulty maintaining interest, not only for the duration of the study but sometimes for the duration of the 20-minute session.

Some of the shared experiences, however, worked very well toward facilitating a meaningful connection between the students. One pair worked on building a terrarium with soda bottles. They planted plants in their terrarium and watched as the plants grew or decayed over time. The children who participated in this shared experience demonstrated an increase from baseline in their range of conversation topics as well an increase in unprompted verbal turns, increases that were observed prior to any conversation-skills training. Perhaps one factor that contributed to the success of this shared experience was that the students had the terrarium to work on throughout the duration of the study, which provided the consistent experience, but once the terrarium was built and the plants planted, they spent their time together participating in activities of their choosing. For example, they would begin by noticing and discussing any changes in the terrarium, and then they would choose a preferred activity for the remainder of the session. They had the common bonding experience of having built the terrarium but were then allowed to choose and participate in fun activities each time they were together.

The children who participated in this study did appear to enjoy their time together more when they were allowed to choose the shared experience. What would typically occur in these situations is that the children would be presented with choices at the beginning of the session, and they would select which one they wanted to do. For example, students working on a nature book were given the choice to 1) go outside to collect leaves, grass, and so forth; 2) design a cover; 3) work on the narrative; or 4) produce relevant drawings. Frequently, the peer would make the decision, although the child with disabilities would participate in the decision-making process to the extent possible.

As mentioned previously, the younger children had more difficulty maintaining interest in a project and appeared to enjoy the time they spent together much more when they were allowed to just play. Perhaps this observation reflects a natural inclination toward developing friendships through unstructured play during early childhood. Children may very well know what is best as far as how to make friends and may do much better without the intrusion of an adult. Children may need *scaffolding,* for example, which is arranging the environment such that there are many activities from which to choose but not a highly structured activity which may interfere with spontaneity. Some of these factors were very evident with a pair of young children whose spontaneous, unprompted communication increased when they were allowed to simply play together, as evidenced in the following example (Knapcyzk, 1989; Marcovitch, Chasson, Ushycky, Goldberg, & MacGregor, 1995).

Christie, a 7-year-old with Williams syndrome, and Aaron, a second grader without disabilities in Christie's class, were given a project based on structured activities in which the rest of the class was participating. Christie's special education teacher developed a rather elaborate animal unit complete with baby chicks for the pair to take care of. Christie and Aaron were engaged in this shared experience, but informal observations indicated that there was more spontaneous communication between them when they were allowed to play freely or allowed to choose their activities. Again, perhaps it is important to let children be children and play with one another rather than have them participate in structured activities that are not of their choosing. Some structure may be necessary to facilitate interactions, but in order for children to develop meaningful relationships, it may be important for adults to give children freedom to make choices and play together the way they want (e.g., Giangreco, Edelman, Luiselli, & MacFarland, 1997).

Working With the Teachers

The full inclusion of students with disabilities is often hotly debated by parents and educators. The sometimes widely discrepant attitudes regarding inclusion of students with disabilities are reflected by the teachers and staff who participated with us in this project. There were teachers, both general educators and special educators, who felt strongly that children with disabilities should be fully included in the general education environment, and there were also teachers who felt strongly that children with disabilities should be educated in a separate environment. Most of the teachers we worked with fell somewhere in between, believing that students with disabilities should be integrated into the general education environment for portions of the day.

These attitudes about inclusion often became exceedingly important when conflicts emerged around issues such as peer, project, and device selection; where the students would work together; and even scheduling. One of the primary goals of this study was to explore the factors that may influence the development of meaningful relationships between students with severe and multiple disabilities and those without in order to facilitate a more successful inclusion experience. Clearly, the goals of this project were consistent with the belief that students with disabilities should be fully included in the general education environment. Success in this kind of training, however, may require intervention with teachers beyond the immediate issues involved with teaching conversation skills.

The project staff worked primarily with the special educator, although in some situations, the speech-language pathologist (SLP) played the most active role. The special educator coordinated the project within the school, and, as a result, there was minimal contact between the project staff and the general educators. In retrospect, this was a mistake. The general educators were often somewhat confused about the goals of the project, and the importance of the peer's participation was often misunderstood. The general educator was at times reluctant to allow the peer to miss the scheduled activity in order to participate in the research sessions. On occasion, the general educator expressed concern about the student with disabilities disrupting or otherwise distracting the other students. Perhaps some of these difficulties could have been avoided if we had met with all the school staff involved at one meeting and taken more of a team approach (see Chapter 8). Had we taken such an approach, we could have ensured that the objectives of the study were understood by all of the school staff who were involved, and we could have at that time openly addressed concerns regarding the project as well as inclusion in general.

DEVICE SELECTION

Selecting the most appropriate and effective augmentative communication system for children with disabilities can be a challenge (see Chapter 6). The durability, transportability, flexibility, and cost of the device, as well as quality of the speech, all need to be considered when making a selection. More important, the communication needs of the children and their ability to access an augmentative communication system need to be assessed prior to providing the child with a communication system. The devices used in our project were selected with input from the child's teacher and SLP, as well as our own experience with augmentative communication. The selection of the VOCAs was also somewhat regulated by budgetary constraints.

Many issues surrounding the use of augmentative communication systems emerged during the study. One of the requisite criteria in the selection of a communication system was that the system utilize vocal output. Children with disabilities and communication impairments need a voice of their own, particularly when developing relationships with peers (e.g., O'Keefe, Brown, & Schuller, 1998; Schepis & Reid, 1995; Schepis, Reid, & Behrman, 1996). As discussed previously, a distinct advantage of using a device with vocal output is that another can recognize the student's communicative attempt even when the student is not in the other's visual field. This becomes particularly relevant when children are playing together and the likelihood of missed communicative intents is high because of the activity level. VOCAs provide individuals with the ability to get a partner's attention as well as express a desired message. All of the students in our project had VOCAs with the exception of Nancy.

> Nancy was a 14-year-old girl with cerebral palsy and mental retardation. Her limited mobility prevented her from using her hands to activate a vocal output device. She also had limited ability to use a scanning device because of her severe spasticity. She did, however, have very good control of her eye movements and was able to hold a purposeful gaze for an extended period of time. It was decided that the best communication system for Nancy (and one within our budget) was to use a laser head pointer and a communication board with Mayer-Johnson picture symbols on it. Nancy was also provided with a single-switch VOCA programmed with a single message to get the attention of those in her environment. She was able to reliably access this single-switch device, and after getting the attention of her intended listener, she would proceed to communicate with the light pointer. Although it would have been ideal to have a complete vocal output system for Nancy, we were able to provide her with an alternative and affordable system, which she used to effectively communicate with her peer partner and others in her environment.

Deciding what communicative messages would be included on the student's vocal output device was also a critical issue. The majority of vocal output devices have limitations on the number of messages that can be programmed. The devices used in this project typically had the capacity for 16 messages. Determining what those 16 messages would be and how they would be represented (e.g., pictures, photos, size) required the input of the student, the peer partner, the teacher, the SLP, and the parent. Typically, the devices were programmed with messages for initiations such as, "HOW ARE YOU?" "WHAT DID YOU DO LAST NIGHT?" "WHAT WOULD YOU LIKE TO DO TODAY?" AND "LET'S PLAY A GAME." The devices were also programmed with messages the child could use to express basic needs, such as, "I NEED A DRINK" or "I'D LIKE A BREAK." The messages on each device were tailored specifically to the needs of the student. Some of the messages were specific to the shared experience. For example, one pair of students applied dried flowers to straw wreaths with a glue gun. The student's device was programmed with messages such as, "I

NEED MORE GLUE" and "WOULD YOU LIKE ANOTHER FLOWER?" The messages could be changed based on the student's varied needs. We also made every attempt to have the voice used in the messages match the gender and approximate age of the student.

The durability and transportability of the device was also an important consideration. It is extremely important that individuals have unlimited access to their communication systems. Unlimited access included being able to carry the device easily so that it was always within reach. Unlimited access meant that the device needed to be reliable and that a back-up communication system for those days when the device was not working needed to be available. VOCAs' batteries often need frequent recharging, a responsibility that would occasionally be overlooked resulting in a "dead" device. Back-up communication systems were typically communication boards with the same symbols but without the vocal output. Clearly, back-up systems are less desirable, but they were necessary for those days when the vocal output device was malfunctioning. The device also needed to be able to withstand certain "mishaps," such as being dropped occasionally or even thrown.

Teachers and SLPs sometimes raised the concern that a VOCA could be considered a "step backward" for some children. Teachers expressed concern that if a student already used some speech or sign language to communicate, he or she would stop when provided with a device and would lose those communication skills. What typically happens, however, is that as students become more competent communicators, which frequently occurs with vocal output, they experience an increase in all of their communication skills. It is not uncommon for speech or sign to increase after the individual becomes successful at communicating with his or her vocal output device (Beukelman, 1987; Cregan, 1993).

We learned a great deal about practical issues relevant to vocal output devices over the 3 years of the study; consequently, we recommend the following regarding their use:

1. Have a back-up system available for all individuals who rely on augmentative systems as their primary means of communication.
2. Stress the importance of unlimited accessibility of the communication system to the individuals in the student's environment. This means ensuring that batteries are charged and that the system is always with the student.
3. Include messages students can use to initiate conversations, not merely responses to questions such as "YES" and "NO."
4. Choose a device that is relatively easy to program and whose messages are easy to change.
5. Use a voice that matches the gender and approximate age of the child.

The Role of Adults

The staff who worked on this project played an integral role in the development of meaningful relationships between the participating students. The project staff often served as a resource to educate peers about their partners' disabilities as well as to emphasize the children's similarities. It was important to have the same project staff work with each pair of students for the duration of the project in order to facilitate a positive, trusting relationship. In addition, project staff needed to have an understanding for how much structure and direction the pair needed, an understanding which could come only through knowing the children well. Clearly, this would be achieved more easily by the adults who are typically present in these situations (e.g., teachers, aides).

As part of the research design, the staff were instructed to interact minimally with the pair during the shared-experience phase of the project. The project staff person would set up the materials and bring the students together but would then only interact with the students as needed. Some pairs needed more structure and support than others, often depending on the age of the students and the shared experience. Staff would help with an activity if requested, but not instruct or prompt the students to communicate with each other. Although the students would be encouraged to work things out together without the help of the adult when at all possible, there were times when project staff did need to become involved in the activity. For example, activities involving safety issues, such as cooking, required a bit more supervision than painting or arts and crafts.

During the conversation-skills training phase, the project staff were much more involved. Staff educated the children and modeled conversation turns and appropriate initiations and responses. Staff prompted the student with disabilities and the peer to use the vocal output device to interact with one another. Project staff worked with the peer partner to develop an understanding of the communicative attempts of the child with disabilities. The peer partners typically had no previous experience with alternative methods of communication, such as vocal output devices and sign language. The project staff and the children discussed the various ways in which people express themselves, beginning with a discussion of the ways people express different feelings nonverbally, such as smiling when happy and crying when sad. The staff member and pair of students would then compare the ways in which each student in the pair communicated nonverbally. Emphasizing the common ways in which the children communicated, such as facial expressions and gestures, appeared to make the peers more comfortable using a device to communicate. They began to recognize there were many more similarities in their ways of communicating than there were differences. Through project staff modeling, peers became very adept at understanding the gestures, vocalizations, and facial expressions of the students with disabilities, interpreting the intent and prompting them to use their devices. We recommend that teachers conduct the same types of discussions in their classrooms at the beginning of the year to help facilitate communication among their students.

Many of the peer partners also became very competent at understanding the challenging behaviors of their partners with disabilities and were able to work with them to replace those behaviors with communicative responses. The communicative interactions between one pair, Dana and Tracy, illustrate how peer partners could be an integral part of functional communication training (Durand, 1990).

> Dana was an 18-year-old with autism. She attended her local high school and was included with her peers for portions of the day. Her peer partner, Tracy, was also 18 and a senior. Tracy was nominated to participate in the project as Dana's peer because she expressed an interest in spending time with Dana. Dana had very limited expressive language skills. She used vocalizations, idiosyncratic signs, and gestures to communicate. Dana also engaged in frequent challenging behaviors, such as tantrums, and could be self-injurious.
>
> Tracy initially expressed some confusion about Dana's challenging behaviors. She often feared that she may have done something to upset Dana. When Tracy expressed these concerns, the project staff member would try to help her understand Dana's behavior as attempts to communicate. Although Tracy understood Dana's behavior to be communicative, she still assumed that she had done something to upset her. Tracy worked with the project staff to assess the motivation for Dana's challenging behavior. She was quite surprised when she discovered, based on assessment information and her own observations, that Dana did seem to be engag-

ing in problem behavior when she was tired of doing something or when she needed to escape from a demanding situation.

Once Tracy had a better understanding of Dana's behavior, she was more encouraged to spend time with her. She began to notice when Dana was getting restless and would spontaneously suggest they do something different, like take a walk or read a magazine. With some prompting from project staff, Tracy learned to encourage Dana to use her VOCA to request a break when she needed it. Dana began to exhibit fewer problem behaviors, and the pair was able to spend more time together having fun.

Dana and Tracy were able to establish a meaningful relationship over the course of the project in part because Tracy developed an understanding of the different ways in which Dana communicated. The researcher who worked with Dana and Tracy was essential to this process by helping Tracy reformulate her ideas about Dana's behavior. The staff person also served as a model for responding to Dana's nonverbal communications while simultaneously prompting her to use her vocal output device.

RESULTS AND OVERVIEW

One of the successes of the project was that *all* of the students with disabilities who participated increased their ability to maintain conversations with peers as well as the range of topics they discussed. We continue to analyze our data further, but it appears that providing students with shared experiences prior to formal training in conversation skills may have resulted in better results than providing training first.

As we have discussed, there were many issues raised beyond simply teaching conversation skills that potentially affected the ability of students with and without disabilities to converse with each other. Important developmental differences, for example, seemed to influence the outcomes. When structuring sessions for students, educators need to take into account the students' development stages. For example, students in early adolescence appear most sensitive to the opinions of their peers, and this should influence how sessions are conducted. Younger children may need less structure and more play-oriented activities to encourage conversations.

Another factor to take into consideration when planning similar activities is the children's rather negative response to the formal conversation-skills training. Many students with and without disabilities found these sessions boring, despite the best efforts of the staff. In light of this, educators should perhaps spend significantly less time with formal training and more time in student-directed activities. These findings suggest that simply teaching conversation skills may not be the best approach to increasing these skills in children.

We have tried to emphasize the complex nature of conversations in general and the additional concerns that arise when trying to encourage these interactions between students with and without severe disabilities. Clearly, teaching only conversation skills is insufficient to ensure meaningful interaction. In order to facilitate communication among students with disabilities and their peers, educators should focus on developing relationships among these students based on shared experiences.

REFERENCES

Bedrosian, J.L. (1997). Language acquisition in young AAC system users: Issues and directions for future research. *Augmentative and Alternative Communication, 13*, 179–185.

Beukelman, D. (1987). When you have a hammer everything looks like a nail. *Augmentative and Alternative Communication, 3,* 94–96.

Boardmaker [Computer software]. (1989). Solano Beach, CA: Mayer-Johnson.

Calculator, S., & Dollaghan, C. (1982). The use of communication boards in a residential setting. *Journal of Speech and Hearing Disorders, 14,* 281–287.

Cregan, A. (1993). Sigsymbol system in a multimodal approach to speech elicitation: Classroom project involving an adolescent with severe mental retardation. *Augmentative and Alternative Communication, 9,* 146–160.

Davis, C.A., Reichle, J., Johnston, S., & Southard, K. (1998). Teaching children with severe disabilities to utilize nonobligatory conversational opportunities: An application of high-probability requests. *Journal of The Association for Persons with Severe Handicaps, 23,* 57–68.

Downing, J., & Siegel-Causey, E. (1988). Enhancing the nonsymbolic communicative behavior of children with multiple handicaps. *Language, Speech and Hearing Services in Schools, 19,* 338–348.

Durand, V.M. (1990). *Severe behavior problems: A functional communication training approach.* New York: Guilford Press.

Elkind, D. (1984). *All grown up and no place to go.* Reading, MA: Addison-Wesley.

Gaylord-Ross, R.J., Haring, T.G., Breen, C., & Pitts-Conway, V. (1984). The training and generalization of social intervention skills with autistic youth. *Journal of Applied Behavior Analysis, 17,* 229–247.

Giangreco, M.F., Edelman, S.W., Luiselli, T.E., & MacFarland, S.Z.C. (1997). Helping or hovering? Effects of instructional assistant proximity on students with disabilities. *Exceptional Children, 64,* 7–18.

Haring, T.G., & Green, C.G. (1992). A peer-mediated social network intervention to enhance the social integration of persons with moderate and severe disabilities. *Journal of Applied Behavior Analysis, 25,* 319–333.

Heller, K.W., Allgood, M.H., Davis, B., Arnold, S.E., Castelle, M.D., & Taber, T.A. (1996). Promoting nontask-related communication at vocational sites. *Augmentative and Alternative Communication, 12,* 169–178.

Houghton, J., Bronicki, G.J.B., & Guess, D. (1987). Opportunities to express preferences and make choices among students with severe disabilities in classroom settings. *Journal of The Association for Persons With Severe Handicaps, 12,* 18–27.

Hughes, C., Harmer, M.L., Killian, D.J., & Niarhos, F. (1995). The effects of multiple-exemplar self-instructional training of high school students' generalized conversational interactions. *Journal of Applied Behavior Analysis, 28,* 201–218.

Hughes, C., Killian, D.J., & Fischer, G.M. (1996). Validation and assessment of a conversational interaction intervention. *American Journal on Mental Retardation, 100,* 493–509.

Hunt, P., Alwell, M., & Goetz, L. (1991). Establishing conversational exchanges with family and friends: Moving from training to meaningful communication. *Journal of Special Education, 25,* 305–319.

Hunt, P., Alwell, M., Goetz, L., & Sailor, W. (1990). Generalized effects of conversation skill training. *Journal of The Association for Persons with Severe Handicaps, 14,* 250–260.

Hunt, P., Staub, D., Alwell, M., & Goetz, L. (1994). Achievement by all students within the context of cooperative learning groups. *Journal of The Association of Persons with Severe Handicaps, 19,* 290–301.

Johnson, R. (1994). *The Picture Communication Symbols combination book.* Solana Beach, CA: Mayer-Johnson.

Kearney, C.A., Durand, V.M., & Mindell, J.A. (1995). It's not where you live but how you live: Choice and adaptive/maladaptive behavior in persons with severe handicaps. *Journal of Developmental and Physical Disabilities, 7,* 11–24.

Knapcyzk, D.R. (1989). Peer-mediated training of cooperative play between special and regular education students in integrated settings. *Education and Training in Mental Retardation, 24,* 255–264.

Kuder, S.J., & Bryen, D.N. (1993). Conversational topics of staff members and institutionalized individuals with mental retardation. *Mental Retardation, 31,* 148–153.

Lewis, M., Feiring, C., & Brooks-Gunn, J. (1987). The social networks of children with and without handicaps: A developmental perspective. In S. Landesman, P.M. Vietze, & M.J. Begab (Eds.), *Living arrangements and mental retardation* (pp. 377–400). Washington, DC: American Association on Mental Retardation.

Light, J. (1988). Interaction involving individuals using augmentative and alternative communication systems: State of the art and future directions. *Augmentative and Alternative Communication, 4,* 66–82.

Marcovitch, S., Chasson, L., Ushycky, I., Goldberg, S., & MacGregor, D. (1995). Maternal communication style with developmentally delayed preschoolers. *Journal of Children's Communication Development, 17,* 23–30.

O'Keefe, B.M., Brown, L., & Schuller, R. (1998). Identification and rankings of communication aid features by five groups. *Augmentative and Alternative Communication, 14,* 37–50.

Peck, C.A. (1985). Increasing opportunities for social control by children with autism and severe handicaps: Effects on student behavior and perceived classroom climate. *Journal of The Association for the Severely Handicapped, 10*(4), 183–193.

Rotholz, D., Berdowitz, S., & Burberry, J. (1989). Functionality of two modes of communication in the community for students with developmental disabilities: A comparison of signing and communication boards. *Journal of The Association for Persons with Severe Handicaps, 14,* 227–233.

Schepis, M.M., & Reid, D.H. (1995). Effects of a voice output communication aid on interactions between support personnel and an individual with multiple disabilities. *Journal of Applied Behavior Analysis, 28,* 73–77.

Schepis, M.M., Reid, D.H., & Behrman, M.M. (1996). Acquisition and functional use of voice output communication by persons with profound multiple disabilities. *Behavior Modification, 20,* 451–468.

Williams, L.J., & Downing, J.E. (1998). Membership and belonging in inclusive classrooms: What do middle school students have to say? *Journal of The Association for Persons with Severe Handicaps, 23,* 98–110.

8

Working Together to Ensure
Integrated Service Delivery

The responsibility of ensuring that all students have an effective means of communicating cannot fall to any one person. The task is too complex and requires the efforts of many individuals. The most effective collaboration takes a transdisciplinary approach, wherein contributing members of a team could include a student, the student's parents or other family members or both, friends, teachers (both special and general), paraeducators, a speech-language pathologist (SLP), an occupational therapist, a physical therapist, a vision specialist, a hearing specialist, an orientation and mobility instructor, an adaptive physical educator, an administrator, a nurse, and a school psychologist. All of these individuals can contribute unique and important information to help the student learn better ways to communicate. The more individuals on a given team, the greater the number of ideas generated to solve problems and the lighter the workload for any one team member. The benefits, however, that can come from individual team members with different experiences and backgrounds collaborating with one another can also pose a challenge to cohesiveness (Bauwens & Hourcade, 1995). Certainly, the benefits of having several people on a team must be weighed against potential negative consequences, such as lack of time and difficulties scheduling meetings (Rainforth, York, & Macdonald, 1992; Villa & Thousand, 1994). In fact, Giangreco, Edelman, and Nelson (1998) suggested that the question is not how many people could be on a given team, but what services are needed by the student. Because several people on a team could have similar knowledge and expertise, shifting the focus from who can be on a team to who can provide needed support is recommended.

PROBLEMS WITH A TRADITIONAL PULL-OUT APPROACH

Lack of a Holistic and Cohesive Program

When professionals stay within clearly defined boundaries and work independently without knowledge of what other team members are doing with a student, the cohesiveness of a student's program is placed in jeopardy. Each discipline (e.g., general education, special education, occupational therapy, speech-language therapy) works separately with a given student, concentrating its efforts on remediating weaknesses. Instead of being guided by one overall plan for the student as a member of a community, the agenda consists of separate programs that target specific skills based on independent assessment results. Students are removed or pulled out from their typical classrooms to work on an individual basis with different specialists. Skills being targeted may or may not have any direct relation to what is being learned in the student's class. The teachers who feel that a student's difficulties fall beyond their own expertise and responsibility may prefer a pull-out model of service delivery (Jordan, Kircaali-Iftar, & Diamond, 1993). For those who suffer from the "Little Red Hen" syndrome, otherwise known as the "I can do it myself" syndrome, being forced to collaborate with other team members can be aggravating; nonetheless, a strong rationale does exist for a more collaborative approach.

When a student receives special services outside the classroom, communicating among professionals as well as parents can become extremely difficult. Schedules demand that professionals move quickly from one student to another, which makes sharing information very difficult. Keeping up with students' progress becomes extremely challenging when different specialists work with students in different environments, with different materials, and for different purposes. Professionals and paraprofessionals are not able to watch each other work with a particular student and are thus deprived of the opportunity to learn from one another.

Heavy Workload

When professionals are expected to work independently and remain within the boundaries of their own disciplines, the workload can be more intensive. Meetings can take longer if individual team members have not been working together closely and interacting on a regular basis. Considerably more effort must be spent exchanging information about goals, progress, intervention techniques, and challenges. In fact, Reed (1993) noted that more comprehensive and coordinated recommendations could be made more efficiently when assessment teams used a transdisciplinary approach.

Individual team members will spend more energy writing separate individualized education program (IEP) goals and short-term objectives and collecting data on those objectives. In addition, separate goals and objectives based on discipline-related assessment tools create a confusing, fragmented, and lengthy document that may not reflect the family's or student's desired goals. Many parents known to the author have expressed confusion over the length of these documents, their overlapping objectives (two or more specialists writing similar objectives), and their extremely varied criteria. The IEP simply did not reflect a holistic approach to a student's education. In some cases, different specialists vie for control and ownership over the same goals and objectives, forgetting the fact that the goals and objectives belong to the student and not the specialists.

Missed Education for Students

When students are pulled from general education classrooms to receive specialized services, such as speech-language therapy, in a separate location, they miss what is happening in the general education classroom. Perhaps the class is conducting a science experiment that day, and the student missing class really needs the extra exposure to science to master the material; or perhaps students are giving presentations, an in-class activity in which the student with disabilities really enjoys participating. When that student returns to class, he or she not only feels left out but is also lacking a vital building block to the lesson at hand. Pulling students with disabilities out of the classroom deprives them of the opportunity to absorb information, extra exposure to the material, and the support they require to understand the curriculum. Furthermore, the instruction they received from the specialist may have been totally unrelated to the instruction in the classroom, so the student has the added difficulty of trying to make sense out of the fragmented curriculum.

In a study by Giangreco, Dennis, Cloninger, Edelman, and Schattman (1993), general educators expressed their frustrations with having specialists pull students from their rooms to engage in therapy. They felt that their day was disrupted by these pull-out periods and expressed concerns about how they would help the student catch up. A second study by Giangreco, Edelman, and Nelson (1998) produced similar findings, with general educators thinking that having all specialists on the team did not necessarily help the student progress. Parents also have expressed concerns about specialized services not being provided in typical classes, especially for young children (Wesley, Buysse, & Tyndall, 1997). Listening to such concerns expressed by individual team members is a first step to a holistic services delivery approach.

Specialists may complain that they cannot work on all of *their* IEP objectives without pulling the student to an environment free of distractions (Rainforth & York-Barr, 1997). Because it is doubtful whether any student will experience much time in such environments and because the transfer of learned skills from one environment to another is not often observed (Warren & Yoder, 1994), perhaps such goals and objectives need to be reexamined in light of their real value to the student.

DIFFICULTIES WITH CREATING CHANGE

Changing the way that services are delivered is not a simple task. Professionals who have received training that advocated isolated skills training in special, pull-out contexts may not feel particularly comfortable providing services in another format. Certainly, the way schools are structured (with one teacher in control of his or her classroom) has encouraged professionals to work independently and has supported their relative isolation (Janney, Snell, Beers, & Raynes, 1995; Skrtic, 1991; York, Giangreco, Vandercook, & Macdonald, 1992). Not knowing how students can benefit from receiving services in alternative and integrated ways can be a real deterrent to change. Sharing information and helping professionals see different ways of providing services can be very beneficial to the process of change. Of course, change takes time, and completely understanding and mastering a new practice will take extensive time. Joyce and Weil (1986) claimed that it takes approximately 12–14 applications to feel comfortable with a new practice. Certainly one problem in the field of education (and in particular, special education) is insufficient time to properly explore a new approach. The search for a quick fix can be a real problem when working with individuals who have complex needs. Allowing for sufficient time to develop appropriate ways to deliver services may be critical in creating effective intervention strategies.

Professionals need to feel that what they contribute to a child's learning is important and worthwhile. They also need to feel that their contributions are valued by other team members, even when there are disagreements. Working together as a team can be awkward if certain team members do not feel comfortable with what they have to contribute. Some studies have found a correlation between how teachers feel about their effectiveness and their willingness to collaborate (Morrison, Wakefield, Walker, & Solberg, 1994). Those with a sense of high self-efficacy were more likely to want to work collaboratively with other team members. Such findings have clear implications for personnel preparation programs.

Recognizing that everyone wants to help the student helps to ease hard feelings that develop over differences regarding intervention. Because there is never just one correct way to help a child learn, remaining open to the ideas of others is a critical collaborative skill. Team members need to listen to each other so that everyone can learn. Certainly being respectful of every member's ability and right to share ideas and responses is a critical component of collaboration. Sometimes a compromise may be the best solution for all concerned. If a consensus truly cannot be reached, then perhaps an effective strategy may be to consider more than one approach if they are not incompatible. For instance, an adversarial situation could occur if parents advocate for speech-language training as the major focus of intervention, but professionals insist that an alternative to speech should be the focus. There is no evidence to suggest, however, that concentrating on both speech and alternatives to speech at the same time would be detrimental (De-Viveiros & McLaughlin, 1982; Romski & Sevcik, 1992). In fact, teaching both makes a great deal of sense as long as it is done in a natural manner that meets the needs of the student. Compromise is essential for collaboration among team members, and it often succeeds in enhancing the student's educational program at the same time.

STUMBLING BLOCKS TO COLLABORATION

Transient Nature

Members of a team can be an extremely diverse group, united only by their interest in helping a child. Furthermore, this union can be a relatively tentative grouping as team members change jobs and switch to different schools or as the student moves to a new grade or school. Members of any given team can change and often do change frequently, depending on a wide range of variables. The dynamic makeup of any team adds an additional challenge to the already difficult task of cooperatively supporting a child with a disability.

Whenever a team member leaves and is replaced by another person, the dynamics of the group are disrupted, and members must start again to form a cohesive unit. For example, Brandon's team of eight individuals took almost 6 months of regular meetings to feel as if they were truly functioning in as a cohesive unit. Three months later, when Brandon graduated from fifth grade and prepared to enter middle school, his grandmother realized that only she, Brandon, and one of Brandon's friends would remain on his team. Such a situation could be repeated many times during a student's progress in any school system. Each time this happens, Brandon's grandmother feels that it is her responsibility to bring everyone up to date, but she is tired of this role. Using a decision-making process, such as Making Action Plans (MAPs) (Vandercook, York, & Forest, 1989) that keeps the focus on who the student is, his or her strengths and goals, and a plan to meet those goals can help to alleviate the burden from any one person in bringing a team together for a student. Updating this information on a regular basis can serve as a valuable starting point for new team members.

Different Experiences

Another difficulty with working collaboratively is that all team members have had different experiences. Although sharing different experiences with teammates can be beneficial, it sometimes makes it difficult to understand others' perspectives. For example, if a paraprofessional's experiences have only been in a special education room, then that person may have great difficulty conceiving of supporting the student in a general education classroom and may feel uncomfortable at such a prospect.

When individuals have different experiences that color their perceptions of what is and is not possible, arriving at an agreed-on decision regarding placement or intervention may be difficult. Providing information about realistic possibilities and their benefits for all involved (teachers and students alike) is extremely important. Of course, information needs to be shared in such a way that does not make team members feel ignorant or inferior.

Differences in Training

Not only do team members bring different experiences to the group but they also come with different training backgrounds. The education one receives in pursuit of a professional credential can have a marked effect on knowledge and skills and how that knowledge will be applied (Ferguson & Ryan-Vincek, 1992).

Professionals on any given team can be educated in completely conflicting philosophies of assessment, placement, and intervention. Individuals cannot be expected to know what was not part of their professional training. Because institutions of higher education (colleges and universities) do not share a universal philosophy of how different administrators, teachers, and specialists are to be trained, the chances of working on a team with members sharing similar knowledge and skills is unlikely. Each team member must be able to keep an open mind in order to learn new ideas while sharing information with others at the same time.

SLPs who are trained exclusively in speech articulation, fluency, and language difficulties and not at all in augmentative communication systems may feel particularly at a disadvantage when trying to support a student who does not use speech. Murphy (1997) found that SLPs felt uncomfortable with a number of issues related to augmentative communication—in particular, positioning, mounting, and repairing the equipment. The tendency may be to say that the student cannot benefit from intervention instead of looking at ways to change the intervention to make it beneficial. It can be disconcerting, to say the least, when confronted with situations that one's training never addressed. This situation can be particularly awkward if the other team members expect the SLP to assume total responsibility for communication issues. Team members will probably be more successful if they can work together without specific regard to titles, professional training, and degrees.

In addition, professionals trained in the belief that the student must display certain cognitive prerequisites prior to receiving intervention will approach the situation completely different than a professional or parent who does not share this view. Although the need to delay instruction until certain developmental skills emerge has not been substantiated (Kangas & Lloyd, 1988; Romski & Sevcik, 1988; Zangari, Kangas, & Lloyd, 1988), many professionals still hold to this belief. (For a discussion of this controversy, please see Chapter 1.) Individual team members, however, who come to a team meeting believing that students should demonstrate certain skills before receiving intervention can expect to meet with some resistance.

Finally, many SLPs may have had little or no training in working with teachers in general education classrooms (Friend & Cook, 1996). Their entire training and experiences may have been completely clinical in nature. Alternatively, general educators have had little experience working with other adults in their room and may find the experience quite uncomfortable. As a result, it is not surprising that efforts at collaboration are difficult.

Differences in Expectations

Often, team members' different expectations for a student can present a challenge to the team functioning as a cohesive unit. These different expectations may be based on different cultural backgrounds, religious beliefs, family values, training, experiences, as well as a host of student characteristics (e.g., age, skill level). Some individuals will expect the student to communicate and will respond to different behaviors as communicative, while others will view the behaviors as noncommunicative and will not see their communicative possibilities. For example, direct services providers at a group home were interested in helping Mathew, a man with severe disabilities, acquire and use communication skills. Although Mathew was attempting to interact with those around him, the service providers did not recognize his behavior as communicative. He pulled his body back and turned his head away from unwanted food with a look of disgust on his face. He either physically reached for items or turned his head and looked steadily at items of his choice when presented with a selection to choose from. The direct services providers were shown how Mathew was attempting to communicate, but they did not see the behavior as communicative. Their perception of Mathew as an individual with severe and multiple disabilities may have prevented them from seeing fairly obvious communicative behavior. Indeed, although Mathew could benefit from an augmentative communication device to enhance his efforts, those supporting him on a daily basis did not consider him capable of using an augmentative system. Clearly, different expectations and perceptions can have a profound impact on an individual's communication instruction and success.

A study by Soto (1997) suggested that special educators' perceptions of their students' abilities to learn to communicate were associated with their intentions to provide and teach augmentative and alternative communication (AAC). Surveying 317 special educators, Soto found that teachers who believed that their students could learn to communicate were more inclined to consider using AAC. Soto also found that teachers' perceptions of their students' abilities to learn were closely tied to their perceptions about their own ability to teach communication.

Need for Control

The need to feel in control is a common human trait. Not only is it a strong reason for communication but it is also a desire of professionals and paraprofessionals in their daily work. True collaboration, however, requires individuals to compromise, which means relinquishing control, yet the need to feel in control is a powerful inducement to avoid collaboration. In fact, most professionals have been trained to take control—to assess the student, diagnose the problem, carry out an intervention, and evaluate the student's progress in relative isolation from other professionals (Friend & Cook, 1996). Given the complexity of assisting students with severe disabilities to communicate effectively in general education classrooms, it is unlikely that any one professional will have the expertise, time, and energy to assume sole responsibility.

Lack of Time

Perhaps the biggest stumbling block to effective collaboration is the lack of time available to team members (Gallagher, 1997; Ryan & Paterna, 1997; Utley, 1993). Collaboration takes time, which is a rare commodity with teachers. Finding time to explore different options, solve difficulties, and share information on progress and techniques can be extremely challenging, especially when schools are structured with professionals working in isolation from one another, in their own rooms or offices (Friend & Cook, 1996). The more members on the team, the more difficult it becomes to arrange a time to meet. This scheduling difficulty is even worse at the secondary level, where teams may include all of the general educators involved in a student's education; however, Ryan and Paterna (1997) stated the importance of weekly meetings despite complaints from team members of lack of time.

Administrators who support inclusive education must find ways to give team members time to meet. Some possibilities for creating time for team members to meet include early release and late arrival time for students, similar preparation times for general and special educators, use of professional development days, and breaks during year-round schooling (National Staff Development Council, 1994; Raywid, 1993). Sometimes administrative personnel, substitute teachers, or parent volunteers can take over a class, allowing teachers the time to meet. Most of these suggestions affect educators in the school but do little to bring related services providers into the team. In fact, Friend and Cook (1996) warned that the very nature of related-services providers' jobs may make it nearly impossible for them to find the necessary time to work effectively on a team.

To make the best use of very limited time, members need to find convenient ways to share information between meetings (Robertson, Haines, Sanche, & Biffart, 1997). Respect for each member's time is necessary to collaborate effectively; therefore, using available technology may be quite advantageous. For example, using videotape to document student behavior can become a convenient way to share information, brainstorm strategies, and seek answers to questions while making effective use of each team member's time as can using e-mail to disseminate information and updates.

Another way for team members to use time more effectively is by making their messages more specific. Leaving messages for team members that specifically state concerns, ask questions, or relate progress is much more efficient for all involved than leaving vague messages merely stating the need to get in touch. When the message (left as a telephone contact or placed in someone's mailbox) is specific, the response can be equally specific and save each member valuable time. For example, instead of leaving a message for the SLP that the teacher needs to see her as soon as possible, the teacher can state that a particular student was not using the augmentative communication device as stated on his or her IEP. The message briefly describes the difficulty and requests the SLP to observe the student at a particular time. The SLP can then rearrange his or her schedule to meet the student's (and teacher's) needs and can quickly confirm these plans with the teacher by telephone. In addition, because the SLP has some idea of the concern, he or she will be able to give the difficulty some thought prior to her visit, again, saving valuable time.

BENEFITS OF COLLABORATION FOR INTEGRATED SERVICES DELIVERY

The many benefits of working collaboratively have been well documented (Giangreco, Edelman, Luiselli, & MacFarland, 1996; Rainforth et al., 1992; Villa & Thousand, 1994). Sharing the responsibility of helping students, getting feedback on ideas from others, acquiring new skills and knowledge, having access to different resources, and giving and receiving emotional support are all very positive attributes of collaboration. Giangreco et al. (1996) found that team members liked the greater coordination, less overlap of services, and greater input from other professionals that working on a team afforded. Perhaps most important, collaboration provides students with more effective programs.

Increased Skills for Professionals

Collaboration among professionals, as mentioned previously, is beneficial for the team members as well as the students (Villa & Thousand, 1994). Working effectively with adults can prove at times much more challenging than working with students, perhaps because children are more flexible or have less invested in one particular approach. Teachers complaining that "It's not the kids—it's the adults!" is a fairly common refrain in this field. Although adults may want to resist collaboration, they often find that working as part of a team helps them to hone their communication skills and gives them access to a variety of resources outside their specific disciplines. As with any new undertaking, the benefits must be clear to everyone involved to warrant the expenditure of time and energy that will be required.

Improved Student Programs

Professionals working together as part of a team should provide greater consistency and a more concentrated effort at improving a student's targeted skills. Furthermore, collaboration among professionals and individuals providing integrated services should improve the overall quality of programs as individuals contribute their expertise. For example, Giangreco et al. (1996) reported that as a result of using the Vermont Interdependent Services Team Approach (VISTA), team members reported less gaps in service delivery, less overlaps of instruction, increased parental involvement, and increased agreement on what services were to be provided and how.

Not only do students with disabilities benefit from a collaborative and integrated approach but students without disabilities benefit as well. When professionals work together in a general education classroom, there is more support for all students. For example, when the SLP comes into Carmen's high school health class to work with her on increasing her interactions with her classmates, she also assists other students in the group with Carmen at the same time. Such assistance not only eases the teacher's work but also allows the teacher to be more available to other students in the class.

Greater Equality for Team Members

True collaboration equalizes team members' roles and positions, recognizing the expertise and interest of all. Credentials are less important than interest, commitment, and willingness and ability to work together to support a student. For example, students without disabilities' opinions regarding their classmates needs for communication are just as important as the other members' opinions. Contributions to a student's educational program are not tied solely to one's official area of expertise but to what the individual has to offer and how that individual shares the information (York et al., 1992).

When team members feel as if they are valuable constituents, they are more likely to feel comfortable and committed to contributing to a student's program, making the implementation of the program more likely. The effect that personal ownership has on facilitating the implementation of a student's program cannot be underestimated.

FACILITATING A STUDENT'S BELONGING IN THE GENERAL EDUCATION CLASSROOM

A basic premise of this book is that students with severe disabilities are full-time members of their age-appropriate classroom, either at their local neighborhood schools or at schools of their choice. These students do not go to special education rooms but belong to typical classrooms just like their peers without disabilities. Depending on the situation, however, some students more than others appear to belong to a class. This sense of belonging may not necessarily occur unless facilitated by those involved with a student's education.

Students with severe disabilities often require additional aids and services to receive an appropriate education in the general education classroom. As a result, a paraprofessional may be in the room to help out. Although this support is beneficial to the student's education, it can lead to minimal interactions between teacher and student. Although well-intentioned, some paraeducators contribute to this problem by taking over for the general educator. The teacher may feel that the paraprofessional is there solely for the purpose of supporting one student. Giangreco, Edelman, Luiselli, and MacFarland (1997) found from their interviews with various team members that at times paraeducators physically separated the student with severe disabilities from others in the class and hindered the student's interactions with both the teacher and the other students. Team members need to try to guard against this all-too-common pitfall.

As a critical member of the student's educational team and as the central figure in the classroom, the teacher does need to assume responsibility for interacting with a student with disabilities as with any student in the room. In addition to helping the student belong, some researchers have found a positive relationship between student progress and teacher involvement (Giangreco et al., 1998). Some teachers will interact naturally and easily with students with disabilities, but others will need instruction and support to gain the skills to feel comfortable in this role.

Helping the teacher interact effectively with a particular student does not have to be complicated or time consuming, yet there are certain skills that the teacher will want to have (Downing, 1996a). Teachers need to learn to feel comfortable initiating an interaction even when there is a strong possibility that a student may not respond or may respond incorrectly. Teachers should know how to handle incorrect responses from other students. Teachers also need to know how to interact when a student is not performing as desired. Instead of looking to the special educator or paraeducator to deal with the student, the teacher needs to speak directly to the student. If the student fails to respond, another adult in the room can assist. The adult providing assistance should not feel compelled to second guess a teacher's ability to handle a student's unique behavior, otherwise he or she may intervene when it really is not necessary. Inclusion is much more successful when the teacher deals with the student as she would with any student in the class, and the support person (e.g., paraeducator, special educator, SLP) provides back-up only when necessary.

Other adults in the room can undermine the general educator's interaction with the student by assuming full responsibility for the student's program. Once the teacher sees that the student is "being taken care of," he or she is likely to back off and concentrate on the other students in the room. Because general educators do not necessarily like other adults in their classrooms (Wood, 1997), those providing support to the student should be particularly mindful of the way in which they provide that support. For instance, other adults should move around the room to work with all students, not just the student with severe disabilities. Planning with the teacher and co-teaching lessons support the teacher and reduce the tendency to focus additional service only on one student. The teacher–student relationship also can be supported if other adults in the room avoid intervening unnecessarily.

PROVIDING COMMUNICATION INTERVENTION IN A HOLISTIC AND INTEGRATED MANNER

Without a truly collaborative effort by all team members, providing services in an integrated manner will be difficult. Certain rules should govern the team's efforts so that the overall goals for the student are not lost.

Develop a Shared Vision

"To function effectively as a team, members need to develop a shared framework, including a set of core beliefs, values, and assumptions about education, children, families, and professionals to guide their practice" (Giangreco, Edelman, MacFarland, & Luiselli, 1997, p. 341). Efforts to work as a team are greatly facilitated when all members are aware of the overall vision for the student. In Chapter 2, a functional-ecological assessment process (Downing, 1996b) is recommended as a means of identifying the daily practical needs of a particular student. The initial step of such an assessment is to determine the hopes and dreams for the student. The MAPs and Person-Centered Planning (Mount & Zwernick, 1988) processes help the team maintain its focus on meaningful life goals for a student and form the basis for his or her educational program (see Table 8.1 for an example). Having a shared vision for a student can serve as a guide to intervention for all team members and can help prevent the kind of fragmentation that results from individually determined goals.

Obviously, an integrated approach to intervention will be hampered if team members disagree over most important outcomes. For example, when one member of the team thinks that it is important for a 7 year-old child to say "ba, ba, ba" upon request, and another member thinks that it is important for the child to turn toward a peer when a peer taps him on the arm, the student's intervention program can become fragmented. Because other second graders are not working on saying "ba" repeatedly in class (or anywhere else for that matter), to work with this student on that particular skill may necessitate removing the student from the class (or at least the activity). Otherwise, working with the student could be quite disruptive and, at the very least, distracting for other students. Furthermore, it does little to raise the student's self-esteem or enhance participation in most typical second-grade activities.

Table 8.1.   Sample of a MAPs process for Joshua, a second grader

---

Who is Joshua? 7 years old; fun; very active; persistent; silly; in second grade; strong; loves computers, fans, and most machinery; has a great family; collects strings; has lots of allergies; has a short fuse

What are Joshua's goals (dreams)? to make friends, to understand and to express himself better, to play well with others, to finish things, to control his temper, to occupy his time in a meaningful way, to learn to read

What are Joshua's strengths? has clear preferences, likes to explore, can read some words, responds to pictures, learns by doing, has good coordination

What should be avoided (fears)? being alone, not being able to communicate what he wants to, boredom, being taken care of by people who don't like him, eating things that are bad for him

What supports are needed for Joshua to reach his goals? proximity to same-age peers, friends, augmentative communication devices (ACDs), educators who know how to facilitate interactions, behavioral specialist, communication specialist, paraeducator who wants to work with him, schedule he can use

What would an ideal day be like? all day with same-age peers in second grade, lots of opportunities to make choices and express himself, visual input to aid his understanding, friends to play with after school, structured after-school activities such as Cub Scouts, soccer

IEP Goals and Objectives from Joshua's MAP

Goal: To increase interactions with others by 50% and make at least two friends

Objective: When working in cooperative groups during the day, Joshua will respond appropriately to at least two direct questions from his peers by using natural gestures or pictorial symbols for 10 consecutive cooperative groups (a total of 20 responses).

Objective: When Joshua needs assistance from a classmate during highly motivating classroom activities, Joshua will initiate the interaction by gaining the classmate's attention in an appropriate manner and making his request clear using pictures or objects. He will do this at least once a day for two weeks.

Goal: To demonstrate greater self-control when frustrated in 70% of all interactions

Objective: When Joshua starts to become frustrated by a task, instead of screaming or hitting, he will get the attention of an adult by signing a modified HELP 8 out of 10 times this happens.

Objective: When Joshua wants items that a classmate has, instead of kicking, screaming, and trying to grab the item, Joshua will respond to the cue ("Joshua, remember to ask") by pointing or touching the desired item and placing a hand on his chest (MINE) within 2 seconds of the cue for 7 of 10 times this happens.

If practice of a particular skill must be fabricated and has to occur in a special environment (e.g., saying "ba ba" repeatedly), then chances are the skill is not overly critical in the student's daily life. Team members will need to reexamine these kind of skills in light of the agreed-upon shared vision for the student. Members may need to ask specific questions to clarify whether the skill in question is an important one. Why is this skill perceived by a team member to be important? To what end is it leading? How will it help the student reach desired outcomes, and is there a more direct route to take? Perhaps a team member has misunderstood the purpose and goal of teaching a particular skill. For example, a student's intervention program suggested that the student be taught to say "ba" in order to request a ball, which is something that the student desires. This intervention was to occur during recess and after lunch on the playground where other students who wanted to play ball were gathered. Clearly, this particular skill was important to the student because it facilitated interaction with others. The skill of vocalizing "ba" is important only within a particular context, which was not understood by one of the team members. This is why a shared vision by team members helps to clarify intervention practices.

Create an Individualized Education Program with Equal Input from All Team Members

Once team members have established a shared vision for a student's education, then they can create a meaningful IEP. As everyone's input is needed to determine a vision for the student, everyone's input is also needed in the development of the IEP. The teacher should not write one set of IEP goals and objectives and the speech-language pathologist another. Giangreco, Edelman, and Dennis (1991) found seven professional practices that interfere with integrated services delivery, and discipline-specific goals and objectives that were written separately by individuals on the team was one of them. The team as a whole uses the desired outcome for a student to determine IEP goals and objectives. Objectives should be activity-based, with everyone contributing input. The team decides what skills must be taught within activities and what accommodations will be needed for the student's successful participation. Instead of writing objectives that are based on isolated skills (e.g., making a specific sound on request), the team focuses on a student's full participation in meaningful activities to determine which skills to teach. Many skills can be embedded within a particular activity. Table 8.2 provides examples of IEP goals and objectives that have been written from an isolated skill perspective. In contrast, Table 8.3 provides examples of IEP goals and objectives written from an integrated and holistic approach.

Understand All Goals and Objectives

Not all goals and objectives on the IEP will be related to communication, although this could be a major part of the IEP for some students. Every member of the team must understand the student's entire program, not just the aspects that relate to one's area of expertise. If done correctly, the IEP reflects an attempt to meaningfully engage the child in important activities rather than to teach the child isolated skills outside of any relevant context.

Even if some IEP objectives do not necessarily fall within a team member's area of expertise or interest, each person on the team should assume some responsibility for helping the student successfully meet all objectives. Furthermore, the IEP represents only a small part (the accountable part) of a student's total education program. The student will be involved in a considerable number of activities each day that may not be directly reflected on the IEP. Giangreco, Cloninger, and Iverson (1993) described this "extra" instruction that went beyond stated IEP objectives as the "breadth of curriculum." Giangreco and colleagues thought that teachers should be aware of these larger, more

Table 8.2.   Examples of nonintegrated and non–activity-based IEP goals and objectives

Goal: To improve intelligibility of speech
Objective: Kris will correctly imitate /k/ when saying words that begin with this sound 70% of the time.
Objective: Kris will put his tongue on the back of his front teeth to make the /th/ sound when requested to do so 75% of the time.

Goal: To improve receptive communication
Objective: Martin will follow two-step directions 75% of the time.
Objective: Martin will point to the correct photograph from a field of three when shown the object represented in the photograph with 80% accuracy.

Goal: To increase vocalizations
Objective: Katrina will vocalize in response to hearing her name 60% of the time.
Objective: Katrina will vocalize in response to hearing loud noises 60% of the time

encompassing objectives so that a student's educational program would not be unnecessarily narrow and restricted. Being familiar with a student's complete IEP can help all service providers identify opportunities to teach important skills.

Determine the Most Critical Times to Intervene

Given the relatively fast pace of the general education environment and the many details involved in the process of teaching, it is unlikely that teachers will be able to take advantage of every opportunity to provide communication skills instruction. The next best option, however, is to identify the most critical or meaningful times to do so. As a collaborative effort, team members can identify when and where they can focus their attentions on a student's communication goals. The following example illustrates the benefits of this kind of collaboration.

A twelfth-grade ceramics class has been identified as a potentially good learning environment for Logan. Although Logan does not speak, he does hear. Logan is learning to use some signs and pictures as part of his alternative communication system. He likes to watch other students and likes brightly colored things. The teacher has iden-

Table 8.3.   Examples of integrated and activity-based goals and objectives

Goal: To increase initiations with classmates by 50% during school activities
Objective: During cooperative group activities, Roberto will touch a peer to gain that peer's attention to obtain necessary materials for the project or to obtain help for 8 of 10 opportunities.
Objective: At lunch or recess, Roberto will touch a classmate's hand or arm and show that classmate an item brought from home or in his tactile scrapbook for 7 of 10 opportunities.

Goal: To be actively involved in partner learning activities by following 80% of all directions in math and science
Objective: Blenda will give her partner a problem to work on when requested by selecting one colored envelope from a basket and handing it to her partner for 10 of 12 consecutive opportunities.
Objective: Blenda will follow a classmate's direction to perform at least one step of an activity using manipulatives within 5 seconds of being asked for 8 of 10 opportunities.

Goal: To express at least six preferences in an appropriate manner for different items, people, or activities across the school day for 1 month
Objective: Prior to going to his next class, Raoul will choose a fellow student to push him in his wheelchair by looking at one of two or three students who volunteer for every period of the day for 1 week.
Objective: When given the opportunity to work on different tasks for a drama class, Raoul will look at one of three representative objects and reach for that object for 2 weeks of drama class.

tified several topics that will be covered in class and shares this information with the SLP and special educator so that they can help in planning the intervention. The team works together to make sure they have the necessary pictures and know which signs to teach Logan and his entire class. They identify times Logan will be expected to greet classmates and respond to their greetings. The teacher agrees to teach some American Sign Language as part of the lessons, which then creates opportunities for Logan to respond to questions from the teacher and classmates concerning how to produce a certain word in sign. The team decides to use a pictorial sequence chart of steps needed to get materials and put them away. Logan reads the list with a peer and can respond to the question, "What's next?" by pointing.

Every member of a team's input will be necessary because each individual will be with the student at different times of the day and in different activities. Keeping team members informed of different opportunities as they emerge will be important. It may be equally important to avoid interrupting the flow of an activity to stress communication skills if the focus for the student is on other skills. For example, the team may decide that for a particular student, efforts should concentrate on helping the student bring food to her mouth and consume food rather than on interacting socially with peers despite the opportunities during lunch to focus on communicating for social closeness. Of course, parents may decide to focus on food intake when they help their child eat at home and prefer for the teachers and paraeducators to work on social interaction skills with peers while at school. In Tables 8.4 through 8.7, specific examples are provided of both a pull-out strategy used to address communication skills and an alternative and integrated approach. Collaborative teaming forms the basis for all such alternative approaches.

Understand and Know How to Intervene

All team members will need to know the best strategies for helping a student communicate more effectively. Considerable discussion may be needed so that everyone is clear on the strategies to use. Otherwise, the student may become confused regarding expectations. Family members will need to provide information about strategies that have been successful in the past as well as the strategies with which they feel most comfortable. If family members are unable or unwilling to interact with their child in a certain way, then

Table 8.4.   Two examples of service delivery for a preschool student

A pull-out approach
On Wednesdays at 8:30 A.M., Jake, a preschooler, receives his speech-language therapy from the speech-language pathologist (SLP) in her speech room. Jake is fun-loving, curious, and very interactive. He is profoundly deaf and has additional intellectual impairments. He has had a difficult time learning American Sign Language (ASL) as a result. For his speech-language therapy, Jake sits with the SLP at a table and drills on individual words using ASL vocabulary. Words signed include hat, shoes, shirt, toilet, play, and jump. The SLP signs the words and asks him to repeat it. She physically manipulates his hands to make the signs. This continues for 25 minutes. Then Jake returns to his class.

An alternative, integrated approach
The SLP arrives at the preschool at different times to help support Jake during snack, good morning circle, centers, and sometimes outdoor play. She encourages his classmates to use gestures and facial expressions with a few signs to invite Jake to play or to share toys. She shows them how to use the item itself to catch Jake's attention and find out if Jake is interested in playing with them. Occasionally she leads the entire class in learning some signs that they can use during their morning songs. The children are eager to learn signs for animals, numbers, and colors and to learn the same words in Spanish. The SLP encourages Jake to use his gestures, facial expressions, and objects, as well as some signs, where needed.

Table 8.5.   Two examples of service delivery for an elementary student

A pull-out approach
On Tuesdays, at 10:45 A.M., the speech-language pathologist (SLP) comes into the fifth-grade classroom and takes Miranda to another room to work for 30 minutes on language skills. They work in this small room on sequencing pictures and identifying objects and pictures on command. Miranda is then taken back to her class where she tries to participate in the activity, which is half finished. Miranda's teacher is not told what happened during this time because the SLP has to hurry to another student.

An alternative, integrated approach
The SLP supporting Miranda comes to her fifth-grade class at different times in order to see Miranda in different class activities. Sometimes she is there for language arts, recess, science, or lunch. The SLP observes Miranda in her interactions with the teacher and classmates; looks at some data on interactions taken by her fifth-grade teacher, paraeducator, and special education teacher; and determines how much Miranda is using her pictorial and object devices. She also works with Miranda as part of partner or small group work. She helps to shape Miranda's appropriate attention-getting behavior with peers (e.g., appropriate touch on the hand or arm) and her responses to classmates (facial expressions, gestures, and use of her pictorial/tactile systems). When any student in the small group or working close to Miranda needs assistance, this specialist provides support as needed. The social-communication demands of the various activities determine what the SLP addresses and how the interventions occur. Instead of spending time developing artificial activities for Miranda to do twice a week in her speech-language therapy room, the SLP utilizes the activities occurring in the fifth-grade class as a basis for teaching Miranda the skills she needs to acquire.

that information needs to be shared with everyone. For instance, one family prefers to interact with their child using speech (for receptive purposes), natural gestures, and facial expressions instead of requiring the child to use her Words+ augmentative communication device. Knowing this, school personnel can ensure the family that they will encourage and support the child's use of the communicative strategies that the family prefers, while they also teach the child how to use her augmentative communication de-

Table 8.6.   Two examples of service delivery for a middle school student

A pull-out approach
Kathleen, an eighth grader, receives speech-language therapy twice a week from the speech-language pathologist (SLP) in the speech room. She leaves her language arts class early so she can work with the SLP on a one-to-one basis on ways to greet people (e.g., extending her hand, waving) and producing a vocalization in response to having her name called. These are taught by means of role playing and repetitive practice.

An alternative, integrated approach
The SLP meets Kathleen in her eighth-grade language arts class to facilitate her involvement in class activities. Sometimes the paraeducator supporting Kathleen stays to observe how the SLP works with Kathleen, or she helps support other students or prepares for upcoming lessons. When a lecture, class discussion of a topic, or independent reading is taking place in the class, the SLP organizes Kathleen's pictorial/photographic symbols to be used following the present activity. She will remind Kathleen to use the symbols under certain conditions (e.g., to initiate an interaction, to make a comment, to request help), and she will model the use of these symbols. The SLP begins to work with Kathleen on the activity she knows will follow the lecture or independent reading, which gives Kathleen some additional practice time. For instance, following the reading of an early Elizabethan poem, students have the option of working independently, in pairs, or in small groups to analyze the poem and try to determine the author's intent. Usually a few students wish to work with Kathleen because they enjoy working with her and they receive extra help from the SLP or paraeducator. A student rereads part of the poem to Kathleen and anyone else in the group and they discuss what it means. They ask Kathleen what she thinks of the poem or of their analysis and point to her potential comments. Kathleen can indicate messages of IT'S OKAY. I LIKE IT and NAH, THAT'S DUMB, or she is learning to shrug her shoulders to express that she does not know. The students write down their analysis and include an illustration of how the poem makes them feel. Kathleen assists in the development of the illustration by selecting pictures (e.g., flowers, clouds, stars) and colors. She requests help to cut out pictures from magazines using a pictorial/written symbol for CAN YOU HELP ME? A classmate guides the picture and scissors while she activates the adapted scissors with a switch.

Table 8.7.   Two examples of service delivery for a high school student

A pull-out approach
Cisco, who is in eleventh grade, leaves his Spanish class to see the speech-language pathologist (SLP) twice a week for 40-minute sessions. Cisco is totally blind and only makes some sounds. In the speech-language room they work on imitating certain sounds, such as the beginning of his name, "ma" for mother, and "ya" for yes. The paraeducator assigned to Cisco during this time period accompanies them to the SLP room and watches for the 40 minutes.

An alternative, integrated approach
The SLP goes to Spanish with Cisco twice a week. At the beginning of each week, Cisco brings familiar items from home. The teacher incorporates these items into the lessons, adding the words to new vocabulary for the week. Students must incorporate these words into phrases and sentences that they are learning. They learn how to ask Cisco to see a particular item in Spanish. Different students serve as Cisco's partner during each class period. They touch him on the arm, say "hi," and give him their names in Spanish. They also ask him for a particular item that he has. The SLP provides some feedback to them regarding their interactions with Cisco, monitors their Spanish for the general educator, and helps Cisco shape the appropriate response. Cisco seems to enjoy hearing Spanish, has an opportunity to interact with a lot of students on a daily basis, is learning who some of the students are, and is learning to turn toward a student who introduces himself or herself and respond to a request. Occasionally, the class learns some songs in Spanish. Cisco records these on his tape recorder and plays them back to the class. He is encouraged to vocalize along with the class when they sing. One day a week the paraeducator stays to work with the SLP and receives some new information as well as feedback. The other day that the SLP is with Cisco, the paraeducator either works with another student needing support in another classroom or uses the time to prepare for upcoming lessons in Spanish. If the special educator is working with Cisco at this time, she stays with the SLP to exchange information, observe their interactions, and receive some feedback.

vice at necessary times during the school day to clarify her intent. The family's needs and desires are valued, and, at the same time, the child is provided with yet another mode with which to communicate.

ENSURING CONSISTENCY ACROSS TEAM MEMBERS

Students may become confused if each member of the team interacts with them differently and, in general, has different expectations. Despite the special education label assigned to a given student, it has been the author's experience that even students with the most complex and challenging disabilities are able to distinguish fairly quickly how they need to respond to certain individuals on their team. If, for instance, they know that by waiting and not responding, a direct service provider will inevitably provide a cue, then students will invariably wait. Some students quickly discover what behaviors make certain adults react negatively and then will exhibit those behaviors in the presence of those adults but not others. This can be particularly aggravating to individuals on the team who are struggling to do what is best for a given student. For instance, one student that the author knows has a habit of spitting on certain individuals more than others to communicate that he does not want to finish a task and would prefer to be left alone. Every time the student used this behavior with these individuals, they would stomp off angrily saying, "I'm not going to help you if you do that," thereby reinforcing the behavior. Other adults essentially ignored this behavior but made it clear at the beginning of every activity how the student could indicate his desire to stop (e.g., by touching a BIGmack switch with the voice output message, I'VE HAD ENOUGH. I NEED A BREAK). Having this alternative and being reminded periodically of how to use it greatly reduced the student's need to resort to spitting to express his feelings.

Of course, it is quite possible that each student has particular likes and dislikes when it comes to working or being with a certain adult. In our quest to help students express themselves more effectively, we must not overlook the real possibility that what they might want to say (e.g., "I don't like you") is contrary to what we want to hear. Individuals using facilitated communication have demonstrated this several times (Biklen, 1993; Biklen & Duchan, 1994). Respecting the student's preference for working with a certain person could be very important and could help to promote more effective interaction. Although it may not always be possible to comply with students' preferences, when there are options, preferences should be respected.

SUMMARY

All members of a team must assume responsibility for a student's educational program. Because communication is critical to the student's ability to learn, all team members must play an active role in helping the student acquire effective communication skills for both receptive and expressive purposes. Furthermore, *all* team members does not mean only the professionals on the team, but everyone who cares about the student, regardless of age, credentials, education, or role. Working together in a collaborative fashion not only benefits the student but helps everyone involved. When everyone contributes and is aware of overall program goals, the team will be more able to effectively use limited resources and to successfully capitalize on potential learning opportunities.

The success of a team depends on the dedication, commitment, and hard work of its members. Keeping the focus on the student and not on the desires of individual team members will help to create the necessary climate for true collaboration.

REFERENCES

Bauwens, J., & Hourcade, J.J. (1995). *Cooperative teaching: Rebuilding the schoolhouse for all students.* Austin, TX: PRO-ED.

Biklen, D. (1993). *Communication unbound.* New York: Teachers College Press.

Biklen, D., & Duchan, J.F. (1994). " 'I am intelligent' ": The social construction of mental retardation. *Journal of The Association for Persons with Severe Handicaps, 19,* 173–184.

DeViveiros, E.C., & McLaughlin, T.F. (1982). Effects of manual sign use on the expressive language of four hearing kindergarten children. *Sign Language Studies, 35,* 169–177.

Downing, J.E. (1996a). *Assessing the school-age student with dual sensory and multiple impairments (age 6–15).* Columbus, OH: Great Lakes Area Regional Center on Deaf-Blindness.

Downing, J.E. (1996b). *Including students with severe and multiple disabilities in typical classrooms: Practical strategies for teachers.* Baltimore: Paul H. Brookes Publishing Co.

Ferguson, D.L., & Ryan-Vincek, S. (1992). Problems with teaming in special education: From the technical solutions to reflective practice. *Journal of Learning about Learning, 5*(1), 66–81.

Friend, M., & Cook, L. (1996). *Interactions: Collaboration skills for school professionals* (2nd ed.). White Plains, NY: Longman.

Gallagher, P.A. (1997). Teachers and inclusion: Perspectives on changing roles. *Topics in Early Childhood Special Education, 17,* 363–386.

Giangreco, M.F., Cloninger, C.J., & Iverson, V.S. (1993). *Choosing outcomes and accommodations for children (COACH): A guide to educational planning for students with disabilities* (2nd ed.). Baltimore: Paul H. Brookes Publishing Co.

Giangreco, M.F., Dennis, R., Cloninger, C., Edelman, S., & Schattman, R. (1993). "I've counted Jon": Transformational experiences of teachers educating students with disabilities. *Exceptional Children, 59,* 359–372.

Giangreco, M.F., Edelman, S., & Dennis, R. (1991). Common professional practices that interfere with the integrated delivery of related services. *Remedial and Special Education, 12*(2), 16–24.

Giangreco, M.F., Edelman, S.W., Luiselli, T.E., & MacFarland, S.Z.C. (1996). Support service decision making for students with multiple service needs: Evaluative data. *Journal of The Association for Persons with Severe Handicaps, 21,* 135–144.

Giangreco, M.F., Edelman, S.W., Luiselli, T.E., & MacFarland, S.Z.C. (1997). Helping or hovering? Effects of instructional assistant proximity on students with disabilities. *Exceptional Children, 64,* 7–17.

Giangreco, M.F., Edelman, S.W., MacFarland, S.Z.C., & Luiselli, T.E. (1997). Attitudes about educational and related service provision for students with deaf-blindness and multiple disabilities. *Exceptional Children, 63,* 329–342.

Giangreco, M.F., Edelman, S.W., & Nelson, C. (1998). Impact of planning for support services on students who are deaf-blind. *Journal of Visual Impairments and Blindness, 92*(1), 18–29.

Janney, R.E., Snell, M.E., Beers, M.K., & Raynes, M. (1995). Integrating students with moderate and severe disabilities into general education classes. *Exceptional Children, 61,* 425–439.

Jordan, A., Kircaali-Iftar, C., & Diamond, C.T.P. (1993). Who has a problem, the student or the teacher? Differences in teacher beliefs about their work with at risk and integrated exceptional students. *International Journal of Disabilities, Development, and Education, 40,* 45–62.

Joyce, B., & Weil, M. (1986). *Models of teaching.* Needham Heights, MA: Allyn & Bacon.

Kangas, K.A., & Lloyd, L.L. (1988). Early cognitive skills as prerequisites to augmentative and alternative communication use: What are we waiting for? *Augmentative and Alternative Communication, 4,* 211–221.

Morrison, G., Wakefield, P., Walker, D., & Solberg, S. (1994). Teacher preferences for collaborative relationships: Relationship to efficacy for teaching in prevention-related domains. *Psychology in the Schools, 31,* 221–231.

Mount, B., & Zwernick, K. (1988). *It's never too early, it's never too late: An overview of personal futures planning.* St. Paul, MN: Governor's Planning Council on Developmental Disabilities.

Murphy, J. (1997). Direct work with adults who use AAC: Comparison of attitudes and activities of speech and language therapists and non-speech and language therapists. *Augmentative and Alternative Communication, 13,* 92–98.

National Staff Development Council. (1994, April). Finding time for reform. *School Team Innovator, 8.*

Rainforth, B., York, J., & Macdonald, C. (1992). *Collaborative teams for students with severe disabilities: Integrating therapy and educational services.* Baltimore: Paul H. Brookes Publishing Co.

Rainforth, B., & York-Barr, J. (1997). *Collaborative teams for students with severe disabilities: Integrating therapy and educational services* (2nd ed.). Baltimore: Paul H. Brookes Publishing Co.

Raywid, M.A. (1993). Finding time for collaboration. *Educational Leadership, 51*(1), 30–34.

Reed, M.L. (1993). The revised arena format (RAF): Adaptations of transdisciplinary evaluation procedures for young preschool children. *Education and Treatment of Children, 16,* 198–205.

Robertson, G., Haines, L.P., Sanche, R., & Biffart, W. (1997). Positive change through computer networking. *Teaching Exceptional Children, 29*(6), 22–31.

Romski, M.A., & Sevcik, R.A. (1988). Augmentative and alternative communication systems: Considerations for individuals with severe intellectual disabilities. *Augmentative and Alternative Communication, 4,* 83–93.

Romski, M.A., & Sevcik, R.A. (1992). Developing augmented language in children with severe mental retardation. In S.F. Warren & J. Reichle (Series and Vol. Eds.), *Communication and language intervention series: Vol. 1. Causes and effects in communication and language intervention* (pp. 113–130). Baltimore: Paul H. Brookes Publishing Co.

Ryan, S., & Paterna, L. (1997). Junior high can be inclusive: Using natural supports and cooperative learning. *Teaching Exceptional Children, 30*(2), 36–41.

Skrtic, T.M. (1991). *Behind special education: A critical analysis of professional culture and school organization.* Denver, CO: Love.

Soto, G. (1997). Special education teacher attitudes toward AAC: Preliminary survey. *Augmentative and Alternative Communication, 13,* 186–197.

Utley, B.L. (1993). Facilitating and measuring the team process within inclusive educational settings. *Clinics in Communication Disorders, 3*(2), 71–85.

Vandercook, T., York, J., & Forest, M. (1989). The McGill action planning system (MAPs): A strategy for building the vision. *Journal of The Association for Persons with Severe Handicaps, 14,* 205–215.

Villa, R.A., & Thousand, J.S. (1994). One divided by two or more: Redefining the role of a cooperative education team. In J.S. Thousand, R.A. Villa, & A.I. Nevin (Eds.), *Creativity and collaborative learning: A practical guide to empowering students and teachers* (pp. 79–101). Baltimore: Paul H. Brookes Publishing Co.

Warren, S.F., & Yoder, D.J. (1994). Communication and language intervention: Why a constructivist approach is insufficient. *Journal of Special Education, 28,* 248–258.

Wesley, P.W., Buysse, V., & Tyndall, S. (1997). Family and professional perspectives on early intervention: An exploration using focus groups. *Topics in Early Childhood Special Education, 17,* 435–456.

Wood, M. (1997). Whose job is it anyway? Educational roles in inclusion. *Exceptional Children, 64,* 181–195.

York, J., Giangreco, M.F., Vandercook, T., & Macdonald, C. (1992). Integrating support personnel in the inclusive classroom. In S. Stainback & W. Stainback (Eds.), *Curriculum considerations in inclusive classrooms: Facilitating learning for all students* (pp. 101–116). Baltimore: Paul H. Brookes Publishing Co.

Zangari, C., Kangas, K., & Lloyd, L. (1988). Augmentative and alternative communication: A field in transition. *Augmentative and Alternative Communication, 4,* 60–65.

9

Commonly Asked Questions

Challenges to Effective Communication Intervention

This chapter is designed to address certain difficulties that may arise when making use of alternative modes of communication. Specific situations are presented that have occurred in the author's experiences. Possible suggestions are provided with accompanying explanations that may prove to be helpful to the direct service provider in similar situations.

Every student with a severe disability is a unique individual who brings with him or her different experiences, skills, interests, needs, and desires. As a result, what works with one student may not work with another, even though they may share a diagnosis. The following suggestions, therefore, are just that—suggestions. If not exactly right for a given student, the information should at least help team members find an effective solution for their particular circumstances.

Question 1: Parents do not like the idea of their child using an augmentative communication device (ACD) for fear it will take the place of speech; however, their child is not using speech and really needs an alternative way to communicate. What should be done? (Chapter 1)

Family members (and some team members) may not fully understand the intent of ACDs. It is quite natural to assume that such a device could take the place of and, consequently, hinder the development of speech. As a result, not everyone on the team will be equally excited about using such devices. Furthermore, because people do not typically use ACDs, they may find them unnatural. Certain cultures and families may consider using something external to their child intolerable. They may perceive ACDs as difficult to learn, not really necessary, too expensive to maintain, and too disruptive of family routine (Hourcade, Parette, & Huer, 1997). A family's desire to fit in may be so great that it supersedes providing communication outlets for their child. A family's emphasis on their child using speech to communicate often indicates a strong desire for the child to be perceived as typical and to be accepted by others. Such expectations are hardly unrealistic and are certainly understandable. Team members can do a lot to support parents and other family members in their desire to have their child fit in and feel welcomed.

All team members need factual information that addresses their concerns. The fact that ACDs can actually support the development of speech and certainly do not suppress its development is critical information to share with family and team members (Beukelman, 1987; Clarke, Remington, & Light, 1986; Cregan, 1993; Romski & Sevcik, 1992). Individuals involved in teaching students with severe disabilities need to understand the value of ACDs in helping the individual communicate effectively when speech is not yet possible or not clearly understood. ACDs help these students interact with others while speech is developing. If parents or other team members prefer a concentration on speech development as a means of communication, this preference should be acknowledged and respected. Most individuals using ACDs would prefer to communicate more naturally (Murphy, Markova, Moodie, Scott, & Bon, 1995; Smith-Lewis & Ford, 1987); nonetheless, educators should try to highlight for parents the ways that ACDs can support the development of speech. Families may be more accepting of ACDs if they can view them as ways to *acquire* speech rather than supplant it. The direct services providers need to be clear that they are *not* giving up on speech but are instead helping the student communicate to avoid frustration. This goal should be a welcome one for all concerned.

Question 2: The pace of the general education class is very fast. As a teacher, I don't feel that I have the kind of time necessary to work on communication skills with the student. How can I meet the student's need for learning how to communicate and still keep her with the rest of the class? (Chapter 3)

The pace of the general education classroom is faster than most special education classrooms. The stimulation level also tends to be higher. These characteristics are not necessarily bad for the student who needs more time for processing information. Those supporting the student must realize that keeping up with all aspects of the activity occurring in the classroom should probably not be the primary goal for this student. Concentrating on certain aspects of an activity and letting others go may ease some of the difficulty. Identifying when communication typically occurs in the classroom (as discussed in Chapter 3) may help teachers plan instruction.

For example, in an eleventh-grade ceramics class, students produce many products over the course of the semester. Obviously, the goals of students with severe disabilities do not directly parallel those of their peers without disabilities. Teachers should concentrate on helping these students acquire skills that relate to specific activities but not at the expense of other important skills, such as communication. Emphasis should be less on the activity (in this case, making clay products) and more on assisting the student in asking for help (via facial expressions, manipulation of appropriate objects), commenting on classmate's work (via facial expressions, pointing to pictorial or written comments that say, "That's neat," or "Cool"), making design decisions (via pointing or looking at options), and asking classmates to look at what they are making (via vocalizations, pointing to products).

Following is another example in which a teacher focuses more on helping the student with disabilities with his or her specific goals rather than on keeping the student at the same pace as the rest of the class. In a preschool class, children quickly choose songs to sing and perform the movements that accompany them. For Emily, a child with severe and multiple disabilities, having one opportunity a day to choose a song and moving to this song may be more important than trying to keep up with everything that is occurring. While the other children are going through particular movements, Emily can make movements (bouncy movements or whatever she appears to enjoy) with the teacher's help. Frequently during the song, the teacher stops and asks her if she would like to continue. If Emily responds positively (smile, vocalization, or arm movement), the teacher can resume helping her move. This teacher's approach is a direct result of the team's decision that it is more important for Emily to be able to express preferences than to be passively manipulated through all of the songs' movements. Given Emily's visual and physical disabilities, imitation is a fairly unrealistic goal, and considering that performing specific movements to songs becomes increasingly less important as children get older, the team concluded that they should focus on helping Emily achieve communication skills that not only allow her some control over this particular situation but will also help her in other situations.

Question 3: I have one student who always seems much more interested in engaging in self-stimulating behavior (e.g., finger flicking, head tapping, hand flapping, pushing in on eyelids) than in interacting with a classmate. How do I stop the behavior long enough to get him interested in another person? (Chapter 4)

Teachers should first try to understand the reason for this kind of behavior. What seems to motivate the student to engage in self-stimulating behavior? All behavior is purposeful (Donnellan, Mirenda, Mesaros, & Fassbender, 1984; Reichle & Wacker, 1993), and understanding the student's motive for engaging in the behavior can help the team determine ways to replace the behavior with more conventional behavior that will meet the student's needs and not interfere with the acquisition of additional skills.

A common reason for individuals to engage in self-stimulating behavior is boredom. Engaging in this behavior may serve to entertain the student and, consequently, may be very motivating. Many people resort to similar behaviors, such as twirling hair, kicking legs, doodling, clicking pens, twirling paperclips, when bored. Usually, interacting with another person alleviates the need to engage in the behavior, but not always. As suggested previously, communicating with the student by suggesting what the student might be trying to say may help to highlight the communicative potential of such behavior and may help the teacher focus on ways to address the situation. For instance, if a teacher determines that a student is communicating boredom, then it is the teacher's responsibility to try to more actively engage the student's interest. Ignoring the student's needs may only increase the undesired behavior.

Often, the presence and active interaction with peers without disabilities can help to diminish this type of behavior. Lee and Odom (1996) found that elementary students with autism and other disabilities decreased their self-stimulating behavior when peers were taught to interact with them. Likewise, Lord and Hopkins (1986) investigated the relationship between the stereotypic behavior of children with autism and interactions with peers without disabilities. They found that when there was an increase in interactions between children with autism and children without disabilities, the stereotypic behavior decreased. Other researchers have found similar relationships (Brusca, Nieminen, Carter, & Repp, 1989; Donnellan, Anderson, & Mesaros, 1984; Durand & Carr, 1991; Wacker et al., 1990). Interactions with responsive communication partners were perhaps sufficiently stimulating to reduce the need for the self-stimulating behavior. Because peers without disabilities in a general education classroom and throughout the school greatly outnumber the adults, engaging their interaction with the student with disabilities can prove extremely advantageous to the student.

Self-stimulating behavior can also indicate a desire to escape an unpleasant or unrewarding task (Durand & Carr, 1987; Wacker et al., 1990). The student may also have discovered that engaging in self-stimulating behavior results in considerably more adult attention. If the behavior is reinforced, it will likely increase. As long as the student succeeds in escaping work by engaging in the self-stimulating behavior (e.g., hand flapping), the behavior will be further reinforced. Again, understanding the student's motive for wanting to escape a task can help solve the problem behavior. For instance, is the task too boring, too challenging, too easy, or irrelevant? Can the task be changed? Can aspects of the task be changed? Was the student given any choices concerning the task? Can the student be taught to discontinue a task in another way?

If the student seems to be requesting more attention (if engaging in the self-stimulating behavior results in adult attention and this behavior ceases once the attention is gained), then teachers should give the student attention more frequently when the student is *not* engaging in this behavior. At the same time, teachers should ensure that the student has an alternative (and more conventional/acceptable) way to request attention.

Question 4: A student in my third-grade class uses his limited speech to echo what I say. For instance, if I say, "Show me your book," he will repeat, "Show me your book" or just "your book." It is very frustrating. What should I do? (Chapter 4)

Echolalia (repeating another's speech) is considered a form of unconventional verbal behavior, but it does not necessarily mean that it serves no function. In fact, some researchers think that it serves several purposes (McEvoy, Loveland, & Landry, 1988; Prizant & Duchan, 1981; Schuler & Prizant, 1985). Echolalic verbal behavior may serve to maintain a conversation, to signal a lack of understanding of what was said, to reduce stress, or to obtain desired actions or objects. In addition to serving specific functions, some think that echolalia assists in the development of more conventional behavior (Prizant, 1983; Schuler, 1979). If so, the echolalia should not necessarily be discouraged.

The first step in addressing this behavior is to carefully document circumstances under which the student engages in it. A functional analysis of this behavior should clarify the student's purpose for using it (Donnellan et al., 1984; Durand & Crimmins, 1987). Once this is determined, an appropriate plan of action can be taken.

If the student engages in echolalia whenever he or she does not understand what the teacher is saying, then perhaps the teacher can clarify the message using pictures or photographs. The teacher can also use gestures and objects to help clarify the message and can encourage the student to express him- or herself using the same alternative modes.

If the student engages in echolalia to gain attention, then the teacher should help the student develop another way to do so that is equally as simple and successful, such as raising a hand or using a VOCA.

If the student engages in echolalia to relieve boredom, the teacher should analyze the student's activities to determine whether they are sufficiently interesting. Is there a way to offer the student increased control over the task (e.g., deciding what materials to use, what order to do the steps, how to participate, where to work)? Could this increased control heighten the student's interest in the task?

A student may actually use echolalia as a way to maintain an interaction (Reichle, 1991). Of course, while wanting the student to maintain an interaction is desirable, the teacher should help the student find other ways of doing this (e.g., with the aid of pictures or photographs). Clearly, the reasons for the student engaging in this behavior need to be understood before the teacher can successfully intervene to teach the student more conventional ways of communicating.

Question 5: A student refuses to use his or her ACD. How should educators respond? (Chapters 4 and 5)

If a student refuses to use an ACD, it may well be that the device is not meaningful or does not meet a communicative need or both. Teachers may need to reevaluate the student's opportunities to communicate. They may find that they need to create different communicative situations in order to stimulate the student to communicate or that they may need to manipulate the environment in such a way that necessitates the student to make use of the ACD (Reichle, 1997). For example, Tom, a student with severe disabilities, seemed reluctant to use his device (a board with black-and-white graphic symbols) to initiate interactions. Instead, he was provided with a pictorial symbol (a picture of a funny facial expression) taped on a voice output communication aid (VOCA) to say in a funny, teasing voice, THAT'S SILLY. Either Tom liked hearing the voice or he liked the response he got from others when he said this. Whatever the reason, Tom began using this symbol to initiate interactions. Also, classmates learned to ask Tom what he thought of different things in case he wanted to express this feeling.

When students are physically able to use their ACDs and clearly have a need to communicate, they sometimes may not use the devices simply because they do not know how to. Another reason that students may not use their ACDs may be because they find them too difficult to use in comparison with other communicative means. As noted previously, those using ACDs often prefer to use unaided means of communication, such as speech, facial expressions, and gestures (Schubert, 1997; Smith-Lewis & Ford, 1987). Teachers may need to reevaluate the strategies they employ to help their students use their ACDs. Data that team members collect will probably indicate whenever progress is not being made, and such lack of progress is a clear sign that intervention needs to be altered. Team members should reconvene to decide on more appropriate and effective methods of intervention. Some members of a team may be successful in having the student recognize the benefit of using the ACD, whereas others may not be. Team members may be assisting a student to such a degree that the student is not compelled to use the ACD or is not given sufficient time within which to respond. Of course, team members need to do their best to communicate among themselves to avoid potential inconsistencies.

Finally, the problem may be with the ACD itself. It may be too awkward to use, or it may require more physical ability than the student is capable of exerting. For example, the ACD may resemble a book that requires the student to turn pages, but the student may have limited use of his or her hands and may find the ACD extremely taxing and inefficient as a result. Other possibilities that may make an ACD ineffective are if the symbols are too difficult for the student to understand, are not large enough, or are too cluttered for the student to visually comprehend. Teachers may need to experiment with different symbols and their placement in order to make the device as easy to use as possible. Teachers should also let students, whenever feasible, have greater control over which symbols they use and how these symbols are presented.

Question 6: The student has learned to initiate a conversation or respond to another's initiation but has difficulty sustaining the interaction. How can I help the student maintain the conversation? (Chapter 5)

Helping students maintain conversation is very challenging, especially when students with very limited communication skills have only been taught to make requests (Reichle, 1991). After a student makes a request, he or she often sees little reason to continue an interaction. In order to facilitate a student's ability to engage in conversations, educators must first, at a very basic level, provide the student with opportunities to converse, for the student with disabilities needs considerable practice with different conversation partners in different situations. These partners need to be responsive to the student's efforts by asking questions, allowing sufficient time for responses, providing visual cues, and engaging in other behaviors to facilitate interactions.

Students with disabilities must understand that conversations involve turn-taking not just making requests (Light & Binger, 1998), and teachers must provide these students with specific techniques to achieve this understanding. For example, a teacher can have the student interact with one or two other students without disabilities, which then allows the teacher to focus on cueing the student's interactions with his or her classmates. The teacher can work toward fading his or her support as the student learns how to independently sustain the interaction.

In order to help students maintain interactions, teachers should remember that conversations evolve most easily around topics that interest the conversants. A science experiment that creates an unexpected reaction or an exciting video game can provide the necessary stimulation needed to spark conversation. A photo album of class or home activities can form the basis for a conversational interaction. Teachers have a responsibility to introduce students with severe disabilities to potentially stimulating topics in order to help them develop communication skills and to make their education as rich and fulfilling as possible. Shared experiences of conversation partners also provides essential support for conversation content (see Chapter 7).

When making requests, for example, fails to develop into conversation, team members should encourage students in a variety of other purposes of communication (as described in Chapter 5). Teaching peers not to respond to everything the student *says* as if it were a request will stimulate the student with disabilities to engage in other functions of communication. For example, if a student shows interest in a particular object, an individual close by could ask, "What are you looking at?" wait for a reply, and follow with additional questions, such as, "Is this what you are looking at?" or comments, such as, "I've got one of those. They're pretty neat, aren't they?" If the student really does want the item, the teacher can encourage the student to use more specific communicative behavior (e.g., a *want* symbol). In addition, the conversation partner can provide an opportunity for sustained dialogue if he or she responds to the student in a manner that supports continued interaction. For example, Hunt, Alwell, and Goetz (1991) taught second- to fourth-grade students to maintain conversations using conversational books. Both students with and without severe disabilities were taught to use the books to choose a topic, ask a question, or make a comment. The student responding would answer the first student and then follow the answer with another question. This structured turn-taking approach was taught using a variety of prompts, such as gestures, verbal suggestions, direct verbal commands, and physical assistance. The three students with disabilities in this study all showed substantial increases in their turn-taking skills. Generalization to partners outside the study was not observed, however, which highlighted the need to train conversation partners, not just the student with disabilities.

Question 7: A student I support uses facilitated communication (FC); however, no one is really sure whether the student or the facilitator is actually communicating. How should I address this concern? (Chapter 5)

When used appropriately, FC is a teaching technique that combines physical and emotional support, high expectations, and a systematic fading procedure to help individuals communicate more effectively. A considerable amount of information exists on FC (Biklen, 1990, 1993; Biklen, Saha, & Kliewer, 1995; Biklen & Schubert, 1991; Cardinal, Hanson, & Wakeham, 1996; Salomon Weiss, Wagner, & Bauman, 1996). Many individuals with autism and other disabilities have benefited from the carefully planned and effective application of this support procedure (Biklen & Duchan, 1994; Crossley, 1992; Janzen-Wilde, Duchan, & Higginbotham, 1995). When using FC, as with many ACDs, the student points to symbols (letters, words, pictures, or objects) to convey a message. A facilitator helps the student perform the movement as efficiently as possible. When necessary, the facilitator steadies the student's hand or arm, provides appropriate resistance, helps the student lift his or her finger off the symbols, and interrupts repetitive movements. This support can be provided at the hand, wrist, forearm, shoulder, or wherever works best for the individual. Providing support does not mean directing the individual's movement. The facilitator and the person being facilitated work together (sometimes for considerable periods of time) until they have both learned the process. When done appropriately, the facilitator is able to gradually fade support to allow the student to communicate independently (Biklen, 1993; Crossley & Remington-Gurney, 1992).

Of course, any intervention technique that is misunderstood or not learned thoroughly can be misapplied. Sometimes a facilitator may inadvertently direct the movement of the student's hand or overinfluence the student's message. When this happens, determining the extent to which the message is truly the student's may be difficult. Whether the student learns to be passively involved (e.g., allow his or her hand to be moved) or to control the movement and convey a message depends on how the FC training occurs. Those facilitating (whether teacher, paraeducator, speech-language pathologist [SLP], or other student) need to be careful not to become the person composing the message. They must be patient, model the use of the ACD, wait for the student to start to indicate a message, encourage, provide feedback and physical support, and engage in other recommended practices for communication skills intervention in general.

FC as an intervention technique is not considerably different than other effective means of shaping communicative behavior. Unfortunately, the controversy that has emerged around this technique has clouded the reality of what the procedure actually entails (Biklen & Duchan, 1994; Green & Shane, 1994; Kaiser, 1994). The characteristics or components of this intervention technique reflect recommended practices in the field, and expecting students with disabilities to communicate and encouraging them to do so are desired qualities of any effective interaction. If FC allows students to be treated as competent individuals by others, then that is certainly a valuable outcome (Downing, 1994; Schubert, 1997). Light (1997) thought that messages are co-constructed between an adult and a child using AAC, with the adult building on the few words or symbols that the student is able to use. The co-construction occurs because the child has a limited number of symbols to express thoughts and limited experience with creating unique messages. Detractors of FC claim that, consequently, the adult assumes excessive responsibility for creating the message. This criticism, however, would have to apply to most interactions between those with and without an effective mode of communication.

Ultimately, we all influence one another when we interact. Our knowledge of what we know the other person wants to hear influences what we say and how we say it. Brown, Gothelf, Guess, and Lehr (1998) questioned whether it is ever really possible not to influence people with profound disabilities when we provide support. Being aware of such influence and making every effort not to overly influence those with whom we interact may be a more realistic goal than striving not to have any influence whatsoever.

Question 8: I never have what I need on the student's ACD. What do I do when I do not have the necessary symbols for a given situation? (Chapter 6)

A major characteristic of a good teacher is flexibility. No matter how well a teacher plans, inevitably things go awry. In the event that a teacher does not have an alternative plan, doing something is better than nothing, and every effort should still be made to include the student in the class's activities. Usually there are pictures (either on walls or in books) or objects in the room that can serve as substitute communication symbols. In addition, classmates, paraeducators, SLPs, or anyone with the skill can quickly hand draw pictures or improvise devices that can be used when necessary. Certainly, having an extensive supply of pictures (gathered from magazines or catalogs) located conveniently in the room can be very useful in this kind of situation. A good computer graphic design program can also produce quality pictorial information that may be useful. Offering the student a variety of pictures to choose from (some that relate and some that do not) encourages the student to make decisions about what to include in a report, mural, collage, or letter. In addition, pictures that show different facial expressions can be used to help the student express his or her feelings about the activity.

Lacking sufficient symbols to meet all of the communicative demands of every situation is a common problem. Professionals in the field struggle with ways to provide all students with ways to understand others and be understood. Students who use AAC typically have limited access to necessary symbols as compared with their speaking peers (Light, 1997). Educators must do everything possible to actively include students in communicative exchanges by being creative and persistent in our efforts. For example, focusing on finding one device that attempts to meet all of the student's needs may actually prove less efficient and successful than creating a variety of quick, simple devices tailored for specific activities. The example of the student, Angel, and the bat cave in Chapter 6 represents immediate solutions to the problem of providing communication means for students when their devices were not available.

Question 9: A student with severe disabilities has been placed in my general education classroom, but I've never had training in augmentative and alternative communication (AAC), and the school's SLP has had training and experience primarily in speech articulation, fluency, and spoken language. How do I know what's available, and where do I go for help? (Chapter 8)

One of the benefits of a team approach is that individuals with different backgrounds, knowledge, and experiences bring their expertise to the table. Typically, the SLP or communication disorders specialist will have information pertaining to a variety of alternative communication approaches, including a wide array of ACDs, their advantages and disadvantages for various students, as well as a list of manufacturers and ordering information. Most manufacturers will allow students to try out different devices prior to purchasing. This is always desirable if at all possible in order to avoid purchasing expensive devices only to have them sit unused on a classroom shelf. Too often, an ACD that initially seems ideal for a student ends up not working well because the student finds it too difficult, or it is not efficient, or the student simply does not like it.

Fortunately, there are many resources available to help in selecting ACDs. Several organizations showcase various ACDs at their conferences (e.g., California State University–Northridge, Technology and Persons with Disabilities, Communication Aid Manufacturers Association, Closing the Gap, International Society for Augmentative and Alternative Communication [ISAAC]). Conference attendees can speak directly with manufacturers, watch demonstrations of different ACDs, and receive hands-on training. Although some are relatively expensive to attend, others are not. Information on upcoming conferences and other resources can be obtained from organizations and agencies that support the use of ACDs. Some of these organizations include the ISAAC and its U.S. partner (USSAAC) and the American Speech-Language-Hearing Association (ASHA). The Internet is another excellent resource because most organizations dealing with AAC have web sites that are easy to access and provide considerable information, including links to related web sites for even more information. Web sites often provide pictures and descriptions of various ACDs along with their prices. Finally, the Appendix at the end of this book provides a list of several organizations and companies that may be helpful to the reader.

Question 10: We have no time to meet as a team and our intervention is inconsistent. What can be done? (Chapter 8)

Obviously, the best thing to do is to make time to meet, but anyone in the field of education knows that this is easier said than done. Professionals must resort to talking with other members of the team whenever they can (e.g., in classrooms, in lunchrooms, in the staff lounge, in the library, on yard duty, in the halls) (Graham, 1998). Finding time to meet is difficult enough when all team members are working on one school campus, which is not often the case. SLPs, for example, usually carry heavy caseloads that require them to spend their time at several different schools.

Initial meetings of team members are needed to clarify for everyone critical guidelines, such as how the student will be expected to communicate expressively and receptively, the means by which the student will be taught communication skills, when specific communication instruction will occur, and specific responsibilities of each team member. Otherwise inconsistencies will occur. Initial meetings may take more time until everyone feels fairly comfortable with one another and with the approach to be taken (York, Giangreco, Vandercook, & Macdonald, 1992). Once a consensus has been established regarding an approach, meetings that follow can be very brief, with a focus on the student's progress. Because meetings are important to ensure holistic and efficient programming, administrators need to help create time for team members to collaborate (McLaughlin, 1993).

Some advanced planning and direction by at least one member of the team will go a long way to make meetings as efficient as possible. York et al. (1992) suggested some specific strategies for teams who struggle to find time to meet.

1.   Meetings should begin promptly and should always end on time.
2.   Team members should be designated to assume different roles, such as facilitator, time keeper, and recorder. (These roles should rotate for every meeting.)
3.   An agenda should be determined prior to the meeting.
4.   Items on the agenda should be prioritized for discussion. (p. 112)

When scheduling and time restraints make meeting difficult, using videotapes to share information can be very effective. Studies using videotaped examples of desired behavior have demonstrated changes in the behavior of those viewing the videotapes (Fox & Westling, 1991; Reamer, Brady, & Hawkins, 1998). For example, Fox and Westling (1991) improved the interactions between parents and their children with profound disabilities by having parents view targeted behaviors on videotaped recordings. For the school environment, individual team members who feel confident in a particular approach and are seeing a student make progress could videotape themselves working with the student. These videotapes could then be shared with other team members who have questions or who feel as if their intervention is not achieving the same kind of results. Videotapes are convenient because team members can view them during their free time and can write down questions for the person who made the tape to discuss at a time convenient for both parties. In addition, team members who do not feel comfortable or confident with recommended intervention strategies can be videotaped so that other team members can offer feedback. Constructive verbal feedback can be provided while viewing the videotape together or shared following individual viewing, and written feedback can be given to the individual to review in private or during a face-to-face meeting.

Although face-to-face meetings are recommended, finding alternative ways to exchange information, ask questions, receive feedback, and brainstorm ideas are needed. Conferencing via telephone or e-mail may be an efficient way to "meet" if all team members have access to these modes of communication. Some form of effective information sharing is critical to maintain a truly collaborative team.

Question 11: Given my training as an SLP, I can see that the slight body movements made by a student can be truly communicative. Unfortunately, I cannot convince the others working with him on a daily basis that these are intentional movements. They do not think he is ready or able to communicate. My influence is not that great because I'm only there for a short time twice a week. Do you have any ideas? (Chapter 8)

Perhaps the greatest support we can provide a student is to assume that all students are capable of communicating and, therefore, to expect them to do so. Without this basic level of support, students with the greatest difficulty conveying messages are caught in a catch-22, in which training is withheld. The "readiness" model simply delays (sometimes permanently) effective and needed intervention. When educators adhere to this "readiness" model and fail to respond to students' initial communicative efforts, students may show signs of learned helplessness (Seligman, 1975), passivity, withdrawal, frustration, or aggressiveness. The need to communicate is so basic that ignoring a student's communicative efforts can be detrimental to the student's overall development (Cook-Gumperz, 1986; Hanson, Gutierrez, Morgan, Brennan, & Zercher, 1997; Vygotsky, 1978).

Obviously, training direct services providers to recognize and respond to a student's subtle communicative behaviors is an important first step. Modeling for team members to help them recognize the student's behaviors, when to help the student demonstrate these behaviors, and how to shape the behaviors into more conventional forms is usually very productive. If modeling while the class is in session is disruptive or simply not possible, then videotaping the student is an alternative. With videotaped observation, team members can carefully watch and rewatch communicative interactions, making note of specific intervention strategies. Team members can ask questions and discuss strategies without having to worry about talking in front of the student or disturbing a class. Several different activities can be videotaped so that all team members can see how communication intervention occurs within different activities.

Even if some team members are having difficulty seeing the student's communicative behavior, perhaps everyone can agree to actively include the student in all activities and to engage in recommended intervention practices as shown on the videotape. A trial period can be set, more videotaping can be done, and ongoing support and feedback can be provided to all. At the end of the trial period (e.g., 1 month), team members can reevaluate concerns and questions regarding the student's communicative behavior. Team members, however, would need to make a commitment to the trial period to ensure as much consistency within the team as possible.

The student with very subtle and hard to perceive communicative behavior must have supportive and responsive communicative partners (Heller, Alberto, & Bowdin, 1995). If present team members cannot or refuse to assume this role, then assigning different team members to work with the student may be necessary. By law the student is entitled to an appropriate education, and responsive communicative partners are definitely part of an appropriate education for students with severe communicative challenges.

Question 12: A student's parents continue to express the desire for more and more direct speech-language therapy for their child. The rest of the team feels that the student receives almost continuous communication intervention from his second-grade classmates, general educator, special educator, paraeducator, and SLP. It seems doubtful that greater involvement by the SLP would make that much difference. Do you have any ideas for working with these parents? (Chapter 8)

This situation occurs frequently, and it reflects parents' fears that their children might receive less instruction when they are included in general education classrooms. Of course, quantity does not necessarily imply quality, although many people assume that it does. Parental demand for increased services has been documented despite the lack of evidence to support the effectiveness of this kind of increase (Giangreco, 1996; Giangreco, Edelman, MacFarland, & Luiselli, 1997).

York et al. (1992) cautioned that increasing support services does not necessarily equate with better services. They warn that increased support services may decrease time with peers, cause disruptions with typical class activities, and possibly interfere with the support needs of other children. Parents may need more information to better understand the role of support services (e.g., speech-language therapy) and efficient service delivery models, as well as the benefits of inclusion. In this way, team members can help parents understand some of the potential pitfalls of valuing one specialist's contributions at the expense of a more integrated and holistic intervention approach.

The SLP provides intervention services as one member of a team whose members are all working in a concerted and organized effort to provide a student with the best education possible (Downing & Bailey, 1990); consequently, all team members will address the student's communicative needs, not just the SLP. Such an approach provides the student with more direct communication intervention because the student is surrounded by individuals (teachers, classmates, paraeducators, and students from other classes) who are assisting in this goal. The SLP may take a particular interest in ensuring that the student has the ACDs that are needed in different environments and that everyone is interacting successfully with the student, but he or she cannot be expected to meet all of the student's communicative needs on a one-to-one basis during a few periods per week. Explaining the logic of this approach to parents, so that it is clear that services are not being denied their child but are actually being enhanced, may be helpful. As one parent remarked to the author when her daughter entered kindergarten, "I wasn't too worried about her not receiving a lot of speech-language therapy. I knew she'd have about 30 SLPs with her all the time—the other children." These 30 "SLPs" were so effective with this young student, who had entered kindergarten using a few manual signs, that by the end of the year, not only was she no longer signing but she was sounding a lot like her peers.

REFERENCES

Beukelman, D. (1987). When you have a hammer everything looks like a nail. *Augmentative and Alternative Communication, 3,* 94–96.

Biklen, D. (1990). Communication unbound: Autism and praxis. *Harvard Educational Review, 60,* 291–314.

Biklen, D. (1993). *Communication unbound: How facilitated communication is challenging traditional views of autism and ability/disability.* New York: Teachers College Press.

Biklen, D., & Duchan, J.F. (1994). "I am intelligent": The social construction of mental retardation. *Journal of The Association for Persons with Severe Handicaps, 19,* 173–184.

Biklen, D., Saha, N., & Kliewer, C. (1995). How teachers confirm the authorship of facilitated communication. *Journal of The Association for Persons with Severe Handicaps, 20,* 45–56.

Biklen, D., & Schubert, A. (1991). New words: The communication of students with autism. *Remedial and Special Education, 12*(6), 46–57.

Brown, F., Gothelf, C.R., Guess, D., & Lehr, D. (1998). Self-determination for individuals with the most severe disabilities: Moving beyond chimera. *Journal of The Association for Persons with Severe Handicaps, 23,* 17–26.

Brusca, R.M., Nieminen, G.S., Carter, R., & Repp, A.C. (1989). The relationship of staff contact and activity to the stereotypy of children with multiple disabilities. *Journal of The Association for Persons with Severe Handicaps, 14,* 127–138.

Cardinal, D.N., Hanson, D., & Wakeham, J. (1996). Investigation of authorship in facilitated communication. *Mental Retardation, 34,* 231–242.

Clarke, S., Remington, B., & Light, P. (1986). An evaluation of the relationship between receptive speech skills and expressive signing. *Journal of Applied Behavior Analysis, 19,* 231–239.

Cook-Gumperz, J. (1986). Caught in a web of words: Some considerations on language socialization and language acquisition. In J. Cook-Gumperz, W. Corsaro, & J. Streeck (Eds.), *Children's worlds and children's language* (pp. 37–64). Hawthorne, NY: Mouton de Gruyter.

Cregan, A. (1993). Sigsymbol system in a multimodal approach to speech elicitation: Classroom project involving an adolescent with severe mental retardation. *Augmentative and Alternative Communication, 9,* 146–160.

Crossley, R. (1992). Getting the words out: Case studies in facilitated communication training. *Topics in Language Disorders, 12*(4), 46–59.

Crossley, R., & Remington-Gurney, J. (1992). Getting the words out: Facilitated communication training. *Topics in Language Disorders, 12*(4), 29–45.

Donnellan, A., Mirenda, P., Mesaros, R., & Fassbender, L. (1984). Analyzing the communicative functions of aberrant behavior. *Journal of The Association for Persons with Severe Handicaps, 9,* 201–212.

Donnellan, A.M., Anderson, J.L., & Mesaros, R.A. (1984). An observational study of stereotypic behavior and proximity related to occurrence of autistic child–family member interactions. *Journal of Autism and Developmental Disabilities, 14,* 205–210.

Downing, J. (1994). Facilitated communication: The impact on expectations. *Network, 3*(4), 28–30.

Downing, J., & Bailey, B.R. (1990). Sharing the responsibility: Using a transdisciplinary team approach to enhance the learning of students with severe disabilities. *Journal of Educational and Psychological Consultation, 1,* 259–278.

Durand, V.M., & Carr, E.G. (1987). Social influences on "self-stimulatory" behavior: Analysis and treatment application. *Journal of Applied Behavior Analysis, 20,* 119–132.

Durand, V.M., & Carr, E.G. (1991). Functional communication training to reduce challenging behavior: Maintenance and application in new settings. *Journal of Applied Behavior Analysis, 24,* 251–264.

Durand, V.M., & Crimmins, D. (1987). Assessment and treatment of psychotic speech in an autistic child. *Journal of Autism and Developmental Disorders, 17,* 17–28.

Fox, L., & Westling, D. (1991). A preliminary evaluation of training parents to use facilitative strategies with their children with profound disabilities. *Journal of The Association for Persons with Severe Handicaps, 16,* 168–176.

Giangreco, M.F. (1996). *Vermont interdependent services team approach (VISTA): A guide to coordinating educational support services.* Baltimore: Paul H. Brookes Publishing Co.

Giangreco, M.F., Edelman, S.W., MacFarland, S., & Luiselli, T.E. (1997). Attitudes about educational and related service provision for students with deaf-blindness and multiple disabilities. *Exceptional Children, 63,* 329–342.

Graham, A.T. (1998). Finding time to teach. *Teaching Exceptional Children, 30*(4), 46–49.

Green, G., & Shane, H.C. (1994). Science, reason, and facilitated communication. *Journal of The Association for Persons with Severe Handicaps, 19,* 151–172.

Hanson, M.J., Gutierrez, S., Morgan, M., Brennan, E.L., & Zercher, C. (1997). Language, culture, and disability: Interacting influences on preschool inclusion. *Topics in Early Childhood Special Education, 17,* 307–336.

Heller, K.W., Alberto, P.A., & Bowdin, J. (1995). Interactions of communication partners and students who are deaf-blind: A model. *Journal of Visual Impairment and Blindness, 89,* 391–401.

Hourcade, J.J., Parette, Jr., H.P., & Huer, M.B. (1997). Family and cultural alert! Considerations in assistive technology assessment. *Teaching Exceptional Children, 30*(1), 4–44.

Hunt, P., Alwell, M., & Goetz, L. (1991). Interacting with peers through conversation turntaking with a communication book adaptation. *Augmentative and Alternative Communication, 7,* 117–126.

Janzen-Wilde, M.L., Duchan, J.F., & Higginbotham, D. J. (1995). Successful use of facilitated communication with an oral child. *Journal of Speech and Hearing Research, 38,* 658–676.

Kaiser, A.P. (1994). The controversy surrounding facilitated communication: Some alternative meanings. *Journal of The Association for Persons with Severe Handicaps, 19,* 187–190.

Lee, S., & Odom, S.L. (1996). The relationship between stereotypic behavior and peer social interaction for children with severe disabilities. *Journal of The Association for Persons with Severe Handicaps, 21,* 88–95.

Light, J. (1997). "Let's go star fishing:" Reflections on the contexts of language learning for children who use aided AAC. *Augmentative and Alternative Communication, 13,* 158–171.

Light, J.C., & Binger, C. (1998). *Building communicative competence with individuals who use augmentative and alternative communication.* Baltimore: Paul H. Brookes Publishing Co.

Lord, C., & Hopkins, J.M. (1986). The social behavior of autistic children with younger and same-age nonhandicapped peers. *Journal of Autism and Developmental Disabilities, 16,* 249–262.

McEvoy, R., Loveland, K., & Landry, S. (1988). The functions of immediate echolalia in autistic children: A developmental perspective. *Journal of Autism and Developmental Disorders, 18,* 657–668.

McLaughlin, M.W. (1993). What matters most in teachers' workplace context. In J.W. Little & M.W. McLaughlin (Eds.), *Teachers' work: Individuals, colleagues, and contexts* (pp. 79–103). New York: Teachers College Press.

Murphy, J., Markova, I., Moodie, E., Scott, J., & Bon, S. (1995). Augmentative and alternative communication systems used by people with cerebral palsy in Scotland: Demographic survey. *Augmentative and Alternative Communication, 11*(1), 26–36.

Prizant, B.M. (1983). Language and communication in autism: Toward an understanding of the "whole" of it. *Journal of Speech and Hearing Disorders, 48,* 296–307.

Prizant, B.M., & Duchan, J. (1981). The functions of immediate echolalia in autistic children. *Journal of Speech and Hearing Disorders, 46,* 241–249.

Reamer, R.B., Brady, M.P., & Hawkins, J. (1998). The effects of video self-modeling on parents' interactions with children with developmental disabilities. *Education and Training in Mental Retardation and Developmental Disabilities, 33,* 131–143.

Reichle, J. (1991). Developing communicative exchanges. In J. Reichle, J. York, & J. Sigafoos (Eds.), *Implementing augmentative and alternative communication: Strategies for learners with severe disabilities* (pp. 133–156). Baltimore: Paul H. Brookes Publishing Co.

Reichle, J. (1997). Communication interventions with persons who have severe disabilities. *Journal of Special Education, 31*(1), 110–134.

Reichle, J., & Wacker, D.P. (Vol. Eds.) (1993). In S.F. Warren & J. Reichle (Series Eds.), *Communication and language intervention series: Vol. 3. Communicative alternatives to challenging behavior: Integrating functional assessment and intervention strategies.* Baltimore: Paul H. Brookes Publishing Co.

Romski, M.A., & Sevcik, R.A. (1992). Developing augmented language in children with severe mental retardation. In S.F. Warren & J. Reichle (Series and Vol. Eds.), *Communication and language intervention series: Vol. 1. Causes and effects in communication and language intervention* (pp. 113–130). Baltimore: Paul H. Brookes Publishing Co.

Salomon Weiss, M.J., Wagner, S. H., & Bauman, M.L. (1996). A validated case study of facilitated communication. *Mental Retardation, 34,* 220–230.

Schubert, A. (1997). "I want to talk like everyone": On the use of multiple means of communication. *Mental Retardation, 35,* 347–354.

Schuler, A.L. (1979). Echolalia: Issues and clinical applications. *Journal of Speech and Hearing Disorders, 44,* 411–434.

Schuler, A.L., & Prizant, B.M. (1985). Echolalia. In E. Schopler & G. Mesibov (Eds.), *Communication problems in autism* (pp. 163–182). New York: Plenum.

Seligman, M. (1975). Helplessness: On depression, development, and death. San Francisco: W.H. Freeman.

Smith-Lewis, M.R., & Ford, A. (1987). A user's perspective in augmentative communication. *Augmentative and Alternative Communication, 3*(1), 12–17.

Vygotsky, L.S. (1978). *Mind in society: The development of higher psychological processes.* Cambridge, MA: Harvard University Press.

Wacker, D.P., Steege, M.W., Northrup, J., Sasso, G., Berg, W., Reimers, T., Cooper, L., Cigrand, K., & Donn, L. (1990). A component analysis of functional communication training across three topographics of severe behavior problems. *Journal of Applied Behavior Analysis, 23,* 417–431.

York, J., Giangreco, M.F., Vandercook, T., & Macdonald, C. (1992). Integrating support personnel in the inclusive classroom. In S. Stainback & W. Stainback (Eds.), *Curriculum considerations in inclusive classrooms: Facilitating learning for all students* (pp. 101–116). Baltimore: Paul H. Brookes Publishing Co.

Augmentative and Alternative Communication Resource List

AbleNet, Inc.
1081 10th Avenue, SE
Minneapolis, MN 55415-1312
612-379-0956
800-322-0956
customerservice@notes.ablenetinc.com

Adaptivation
Post Office Box 626
Ames, IA 50010-0626
800-723-2783

Adaptive Communication Systems, Inc.
Post Office Box 12440
Pittsburgh, PA 15231
412-264-2288

Attainment Company, Inc.
Post Office Box 930160
Verona, WI 53593-0160
800-327-4269
info@attainment-inc.com
www.attainment-inc.com

Augmentative Communication News
One Surf Way, Suite #215
Monterey, CA 93940
408-649-3050
sarahblack@aol.com

Box-Talk
Post Office Box 1180
Litchfield, CT 06759
860-567-0107
boxtalk@esslink.com

Linda Burkhart
8503 Rhode Island Avenue
College Park, MD 20740
lindaub13@aol.com

Communication Aid Manufacturers
    Association (CAMA)
Post Office Box 1039
Evanston, IL 60204-1039
847-869-5691
cama@northsore.net

Communication Devices, Inc.
421 Coeur D'Alene Avenue, Suite 5
Coeur D'Alene, ID 83814-2862
208-765-1259
hollycom@nidlink.com

Communication Skill Builders
555 Academic Court
San Antonio, TX 78204
800-228-0752
www.hbtpc.com

Creative Communicating
Post Office Box 3358
Park City, UT 84060
435-645-7737
phci@creative-comm.com

Crestwood Co.
6625 North Sidney Place
Milwaukee, WI 53209
414-352-5678
Crestcomm@aol.com
www.communicationaids.com

Don Johnston, Inc.
1000 North Rand Road
Building #115
Wauconda, IL 60084
800-999-4660
djde@aol.com

Dynavox Systems Inc.
5001 Baum Boulevard
Pittsburgh, PA 15213
800-344-1778
www.dynavoxsys.com

Imaginart
307 Arizona Street
Bisbee, AZ 85603
520-432-5741
imaginart@aol.com

Innocomp
26210 Emery Road, Suite 302
Warrensville Heights, OH 44128-5771
800-382-8622
jerihoff@aol.com

International Society for Augmentative
    and Alternative Communication
    (ISAAC)
49 The Donway West, Suite 308
Toronto, Ontario M3C 3M9
CANADA
416-385-0351
isaac_mail@mail.cepp.org

Mayer-Johnson Co.
Post Office Box 1579
Solano Beach, CA 92075-7579
619-550-0084
mayerj@mayer-johnson.com

Prentke Romich Co.
1022 Heyl Road
Wooster, OH 44691-9744
330-262-1984 x257
tlb@prentrom.com

Special Communications
916 West Castillo Drive
Litchfield Park, AZ 85340
602-935-4656
carmussel@inficad.com

TASH International, Inc.
Unit 1, 91 Station Street
Ajax, ON LIS 3H2
CANADA
800-463-5685
tashcan@aol.com

Trace Research and Development Center
Room S-151 Waisman Center
University of Wisconsin
Madison, WI 53705-2280
608-263-2237
http://trace.wisc.edu

Words+
40015 Sierra Highway, B-145
Palmdale, CA 93550-2117
800-869-8521
info@words-plus.com

Zygo Industries, Inc.
Post Office Box 1008
Portland, OR 97207-1008
503-684-6006
www.zygo-usa.com

Index

Page numbers followed by *f* indicate figures; those followed by *t* indicate tables.

191